FreM

DEC 1 8 1973

1

822.33   McFarland, Thomas
             Shakespeare's pastoral comedy.
         Chapel Hill, University of North
         Carolina Press [1972]
             x, 218 p.   24cm.

             Includes bibliographical references.

             1. Shakespeare, William, 1564-1616--
         Comedies.   I.   Title.
         PR2981.M33
cb

*Shakespeare's
Pastoral Comedy*

Shakespeare's Pastoral Comedy

by Thomas McFarland

The University of North Carolina Press
Chapel Hill

Copyright © 1972 by The University of North Carolina Press
All rights reserved

No part of this book may be reproduced or utilized
in any form or by any means, electronic or mechanical,
including photocopying and recording, or by any
information storage and retrieval system, without
permission in writing from the publisher. The Association
of American University Presses' Resolution on Permissions
constitutes the only exception to this prohibition.

Manufactured in the United States of America
Printed by Heritage Printers, Inc.
ISBN 0–8078–1199–8
Library of Congress Catalog Card Number 72–81325

For Norma

Contents

Preface

Critical interpretations of Shakespeare's plays are somewhat like pianistic interpretations of Beethoven's sonatas. If true to the art they elucidate, they will in each case seem much like other interpretations. The similarities will necessarily outweigh the differences; for the words and the notes are already there. The plays are Shakespeare's and the sonatas are Beethoven's, not the property of the interpreter. What is better or worse in interpretations will reside not in originalities or critical individualism, but in subtleties of tone and conception attendant upon a responsibility to attain as nearly as possible to the work of art as its author set it down.

In the discussions that now follow, accordingly, there has been no attempt at novelty. But these readings perhaps exhibit more of a variation in their likeness to received opinion—sometimes coinciding almost exactly with that opinion, at other times diverging considerably—than is usual within the pages of any one book on Shakespeare. This effect is dictated by the circumstances of their development; for they arose, quite without reference to the work of other critics and scholars, simply as the product of meditating on and teaching the plays over a number of years.

That there are drawbacks to such a form of development is obvious; but that there are advantages might also be true. If in the first instance the critic runs the risk of becoming attached to errors from which the labors of other scholars might have saved him, he also frees himself from the burden of misunderstandings that are sometimes passed from scholar to scholar. In any event, such a form of development is possible because those things that lastingly affect us in Shakespeare cannot be conceived as the preserve of antiquarian scholarship. Shakespeare commands us not as a writer bound by the conventions and local options of a bygone milieu, but because he penetrated beyond such ephemera to the larger realities of human nature and of recurring human experience. And those realities are open to everyone's understanding. "I would be willing to live," said Coleridge, "only as long as Shakespeare were the mirror to nature."

My friends, Albert Cook, William R. Elton, Arthur C. Kirsch,

Samuel Schoenbaum, and David L. Stevenson, all read versions of the typescript and gave me the benefit of their varied learning and wise counsel. I wish to thank each singly for his generous and helpful criticisms, as I do likewise the anonymous readers for The University of North Carolina Press. Francesca Langbaum graciously translated for me a long extract from Sansovino's *Del Governo et amministratione di diversi regni*. Finally, whatever felicity of style the book may possess is largely the result of the ministrations of Peter Sutcliffe, who went through the entire manuscript and gave it unstintingly of his uniquely valuable skills.

THOMAS MC FARLAND

The Graduate School and University Center
of The City University of New York

Shakespeare's
Pastoral Comedy

I. Comedy and Its Pastoral Extension

Comedy is at once the opposite and the complement of tragedy. When Socrates forces Agathon and Aristophanes to admit that the "same man might be capable of writing both comedy and tragedy," he appeals to our instinctive understanding that the two modes are aspects of a single value. That value is a repudiation of a fear. What is feared is the thought that life may have no meaning.

Every work of art, indeed, is a consolation for the nothingness of our lives. "A poet," says Shelley, "is a nightingale, who sits in darkness and sings to cheer its own solitude with sweet sounds." It is, says Byron, "to create, and in creating live / A being more intense, that we endow / With form our fancy, gaining as we give / The life we image, even as I do now. / What am I? Nothing: but not so art thou, / Soul of my thought!"

Comedy and tragedy are opposing techniques of poetic consolation. Each attempts to reassure us. Each recasts experience so that it seems meaningful, in contrast to the chaotic succession of events in daily life. Indeed, as Shelley realized, all poetry "makes us the inhabitants of a world to which the familiar world is a chaos." The world of art is "a mirror which makes beautiful that which is distorted."

The ways in which the two techniques recast experience are dictated by the earliest and most dimly remembered reactions of primitive life. Tragic meaning is a refraction of heroic meaning: the hero is the man who demands from himself more than our customary capacity for courage and steadfastness. Our admiration for the shadowy tribesman who drives away the beast is identical to our admiration for the valor of Beowulf, and is likewise, when abstraction begins, the same as our admiration for the moral valor of a Thomas More. In all cases, however, the hero not only commands our gratitude for defending us, actually or symbolically, from alien terrors, but emphasizes, by the very fact of his heroism, his disjunction from the group. The hero is precisely a man who is not like other men. Tragedy recasts experience in the perspective of the elevation, but also of the isolation, of the heroic man.

Comic meaning, on the other hand, is an exfoliation of the primitive sense that there is safety in numbers: it celebrates the herd instinct. By eschewing the heroic intensification of human possibility, it likewise avoids the frightening isolation of that possibility. Where tragedy refers to the heroism of the individual for its assurance of meaning in life, comedy refers to the anonymous security of the group. "The comic poet," says Meredith, "is in the narrow field, or enclosed square, of the society he depicts; and he addresses the still narrower enclosure of men's intellects, with reference to the operation of the social world upon their characters." "The comic," he says again, "is perpetually springing up in social life."

If we regard the two techniques from the standpoints of their justifications in formal thought, we find tragedy analogous to philosophies of a solipsistic or egotistic kind, comedy to those concerned with analyzing the phenomenon of community. As examples of the former we can consider Schelling's "Everything is in the I and for the I. In the I philosophy has found its one and all." Or Husserl's "The objective world, the world that exists for me . . . derives its whole sense and its existential status, which it has for me, from me myself, from me as the transcendental Ego." Or perhaps Pascal: "Each one is an all to himself; for when he is dead, everything is dead for him. Hence it is that each believes himself to be all to everybody." It is because of such attitudes that Guardini is justified in saying that "Pascal's basic instinct is tragic-heroic in nature."

For comedy, on the other hand, philosophical correlatives are found in the numerous and diverse recognitions that no man is an island, that every man is involved in mankind. "Unlike a million of tigers," says Coleridge, "a million of men is very different from a million times one man. Each man in a numerous society is not only coexistent with, but virtually organized into, the multitude of which he is an integral part." The philosophy of community as formulated in Feuerbach, or in Sartre's *Critique de la raison dialectique*, emphasizes this, as do all the proliferated sciences of social involvement: sociology, economics, political science. The egocentric philosophy can always be countered by such statements as Jacobi's, "Without Thou, the I is impossible"; or Buber's, "Spirit is not in the I, but between the I and Thou." "To understand man," says Carlyle, "we must look beyond the individual man and his actions or interests, and view him in combination with his fellows. It is in Society that man first feels what he is; first becomes what he can be . . . the solitary man were but a small portion of himself, and must continue forever folded in, stunted and only half alive." "L'homme isolé," confirms Lamartine, "n'est pas tout entier homme."

Because the tragic protagonist is man isolated and at the same time man intensified, the symbol of all the fears he copes with is that greatest fear: death. The fear of death is rendered still greater by the fact that we must all face it alone: "on mourra seul." The meaningful conduct of life in the face of death must always be recognized as the innermost kernel of tragedy.

On the other hand, because comic man is man diminished in his individual strength and man as member of a group, the symbolic extension of all the fears he faces is isolation—the very condition of the tragic hero as he faces alone the approach of death. And symbolizing all the securities that comic man opposes to his fears is that security in which isolation is formally translated into togetherness, that is, marriage. "All tragedies," says Byron, "are finish'd by a death, / All comedies are ended by a marriage." Although we can easily think of tragedies that do not end in death, and comedies that do not end in marriage, Byron is for the most part right: death and marriage are the most appropriate, and by far the most commonly encountered, tragic and comic conclusions.

Tragedy faces death, and comedy looks to the perpetuity of the group; this is the Janus head of the comic-tragic complex. Not only can the individual die, but the chief reality of his life is that he *must* die. The group, however, remains as a group even though its members are in constant process of coming to be and passing away. England is England, even though the man Shakespeare is dead; the church is the church even though its martyrs have fallen. To look to the individual is to face death; to look to the group is both to deny the individual and to assuage the fear of death. But to deny death is in a fundamental sense to deny our existence in the world; hence it is that comedy, as has often been noted, tends to be less realistic, more artificial, than tragedy. "It is altogether a speculative scene of things," writes Lamb of the comedy of manners, "which has no reference whatever to the world that is."

Comedy, indeed, not only accepts artificiality, but revels in it. To cite a single instance, disguise, as we all know, almost never succeeds in our daily experience; certainly it could never mislead one who knew us well. But comedy not only constantly employs disguise; it frolics in its permutations. A man can successfully pass as a woman (as, say, the fair bride in *Epicoene*), a woman can be successfully passed off as a young man (as, say, Viola in *Twelfth Night*). Rosalind, in *As You Like It*, disguises herself as a boy, and is also able to deceive her lover with the impersonation; and then, in affirmation of the artificiality of the whole situation, can teasingly play, through her disguised identity, at being Rosalind again. When the lovers in *Così fan tutte* enter disguised as Albanians, or the lovers in *Love's Labour's Lost* enter disguised as Muscovites, the playful grotesquerie of the disguises are, in the artifice of the comic situation, accepted as proof against penetration. That the plot ensures their penetration is in no way an invalidation of their success as disguise.

Along with its tendency to artificiality, comedy tends to deal in typical rather than in individual characterizations. The uniqueness of the individual ego has no value in comedy; indeed, it is precisely this uniqueness, with its isolating anxiety as it faces death, that comedy seeks to repudiate. Thus it is the recurrence of the type, not the fragility of the individual, that is central to comedy. This truth is repeatedly attested in the names attached to comic figures: Malvolio, Sir Amorous La Foole, Lady Wishfort, Sir Benjamin Backbite, Mrs. Malaprop, Win-the-Fight Littlewit. We find the social type of the braggart warrior in a high incarnation such as Jonson's Captain Bobadill, and equally in the lowly world of the strip cartoon as Sergeant Schnorkel. We find the social type of the miser in a high incarnation as Molière's Harpagon, or in the twentieth-century world of television and radio as Jack Benny. The type of the ebulliently vital and independent Father Christmas can be Dekker's Simon Eyre, on one level, W. C. Fields on another.

Even when comic figures seem to assume individual contour, this depends on a particular blending of comic types, rather than on true individuality. Sir Toby Belch represents a compound of the Vice and the glutton. Sir Epicure Mammon blends three types of social excess—gluttony, lechery, and avarice—as does, on another level, Oliver Hardy. Falstaff involves a compound of at least three major types: the braggart warrior, the Vice, and the glutton ("he is not," notes Dryden, "properly one humour, but a miscellany of humours or images").

From such and similar examples two other features of the comic strategy are revealed. It becomes clear, first of all, that the comic essence remains intact all the way from the most skillfully articulated dramas of great masters down to the most intuitive jokings of popular culture. There is no diminution of the comic spirit from Jonson's Mosca, part Vice and part parasite, down to the cinematic roles of Jack Lemmon and, still lower, to the wily schemings of Bugs Bunny. The Wife of Bath participates in the comic archetype of the domineering female, but so, in the world of the "Peanuts" comic strip, does Lucy. Ralph Roister-Doister is a braggart warrior, as, in the beast fables of cinematic cartoon, is the mouse-oppressing cat named Tom.

Comedy, in short, as W. K. Wimsatt emphasizes, "is the metaphor of a more universal human condition than tragedy." Such aesthetic homogeneity does not characterize tragedy. There is a distinct cleavage between the catastrophic happenings of ordinary experience, which are usually merely dismal or depressing, and the special exhilaration of tragic events. The failure of almost all attempts at a "domestic tragedy," from *Arden of Feversham* to *Death of a Salesman,* can be cited as evidence. For tragedy is rarely attained, comedy abundantly attained, in the expressions of world culture. Indeed, as Albert Cook maintains, in *The Dark Voyage and the Golden Mean,* tragedy is precisely the "wonderful," comedy the "probable" perspective on human affairs.*

A second feature indicated by these examples is that comedy not only depends on types rather than individuals, but also finds these types adequate in themselves, or at the very least, not dependent upon any particular comic plot. "His plots were generally modelled, and his characters ready drawn to his hand," says Congreve of Terence—"He copied Menander, and Menander had no less light in the formation of his characters, from the observations of Theophrastus." Don Quixote exists as a comic entity outside the pages of his novel, as the drawing of Picasso or the philosophizing of Unamuno attests. Falstaff can be taken out of his context in the chronicle plots of the three Prince Hal plays and, even though diminished by the change, be reinvested with a different kind of plot in *The Merry Wives of Windsor.* The peculiar amalgam of cowardice, avarice, and lubricity that informs the comic

* This work was seminal for me when I first began to think about the nature of comedy; at this point in time, however, I find it difficult to distinguish what may first have been suggested to me there, what may have been suggested by later reading, and what may have developed from my own meditation.

persona of Bob Hope is unchanged though it appears in countless cinematic plots. A figure like Zero Mostel can move from a night club
monologue to a cinematic potpourri of Plautus without altering his
comic base. Or, to summon another kind of example, the skits of com-
media dell' arte were, in regard to plot, usually extempore, because
stability resided in the unchangingness of the comic types assembled
in the acting company: Pantalone was always himself, Harlequin always himself, regardless of plot.

This freedom of the comic character type from plot results in a playful, gamelike organization of the plot itself. Tragic plot or mythos is
burdened with the large task of revealing tragic character. Comic plot,
questions of character settled beforehand in the comic typology, becomes frolicsome and restive, complex and mazelike. Such plot veers
toward the nature of dance, and has as its hallmark the repetitions,
formalities, and artificialities of dance. Indeed, much of comic suspense resides in our expectation of the inevitable completion of a
repetitive series. When, in *Le Nozze di Figaro*, Cherubino hides behind an armchair so as not to be found in Susanna's room by the
Count, comic suspense demands, and the plot provides, that the Count
himself must also hide so as not to be found by Don Basilio. When, in
The School for Scandal, Lady Teazle hides behind a screen so as not to
be found in Joseph Surface's room by Sir Peter, comic suspense demands, and the plot provides, that Sir Peter must hide in the closet so
as not to be found by Charles. An action that in real life would seem
an expression of individuality becomes, by its repetition in a comic
series, a humbling of individuality in the assertion of "thus do they
all." In *Love's Labour's Lost*, when Berowne enters, with a paper in
his hand, and reveals that he has fallen in love, it inevitably follows
that the King of Navarre then enters, also with a paper, also in love, to
be overheard by the now-hidden Berowne, both of them to be overheard by the omnisciently secure audience. And it still further follows,
in a kind of saraband, that Longaville enters, also with a paper, also in
love, and the King of Navarre hides. And then Dumain enters, also
with a paper, also in love, and Longaville hides. When Berowne then
gloats, " 'All hid, all hid'—an old infant play" (4.3.74),* we understand that the play, the game, the dance, must then complete itself in

* All quotations from Shakespeare are taken from *William Shakespeare: The
Complete Works*, ed. Peter Alexander (New York, 1952). References are to act,
scene, and line.

an equally formal reversal: Longaville advances from hiding to confront and chide Dumain; the King advances to confront and chide Longaville; Berowne advances to confront and chide the King. And then, in a concluding figure, Berowne himself is confronted and chided when Jaquenetta and Costard enter and present the King with the letter revealing his own participation in the "sweet fellowship in shame"—a perfect expression for the humbling of individual pretension in exchange for the security of being in a group.

Again, when in *The Comedy of Errors* we are provided with the extravagant hypothesis of a pair of accidentally separated identical twin brothers, the dancelike pattern of comic plot demands, and the tendency of comedy toward artificiality serenely accepts, that these identical twin brothers have a pair of identical twin servants. And when Dromio of Ephesus is thought by Antipholus of Syracuse to be Dromio of Syracuse, the completion of the dance motif demands that Dromio of Syracuse be thought by Antipholus of Ephesus to be Dromio of Ephesus, and the errors proceed in all possible configurations. When, in *Le Misanthrope*, Arsinoé, under cover of friendship, launches a spiteful attack on Célimène ("Je viens, par un avis qui touche votre honneur / Témoigner l'amitié que pour vous a mon coeur"), we anticipate happily the repetition of the same kind of attack, in the same tone, on Arsinoé by Célimène ("Madame, j'ai beaucoup de grâces à vous rendre. / . . . J'en prétends reconnaître, à l'instant, la faveur / Par un avis aussi qui touche votre honneur"). In *Much Ado*, Don Pedro, Claudio, and Leonato trick the hidden Benedick into thinking Beatrice loves him, and comic suspense demands the repetition of the figure on the other side: Hero, Margaret, and Ursula trick the hidden Beatrice into thinking Benedick loves her. And the comic fact that both movements succeed by appealing to the vanity of the hidden observer involves not only those observers but the audience itself in "a sweet fellowship in shame": a diminished, but by that very fact more socially probable and secure, conception of the individual.

And so it goes in a comic plot, complication following complication, in symmetrical pairings, partings, and repetitions, as though some minuet-like dance were being performed. The men and women separate, come together, intermingle, come close, move apart, go around again. The motif of the dance, indeed, frequently saturates the very language of high comedy. "Play, music," commands the Duke at the conclusion of *As You Like It*, "and you brides and bridegrooms all, /

With measure heap'd in joy, to th' measures fall." "Come, come, we are friends. Let's have a dance ere we are married," says Benedick at the conclusion of *Much Ado*. "Their purpose is to parley, court, and dance," says Boyet as the suitors approach in *Love's Labour's Lost*; and then the four noblemen, disguised, actually prepare to dance with the four ladies, masked, as the motif of disguise mingles with the motif of dance to form a happy game that resolves all the fears of individual existence in the real world. Dance, which is a social form, is as a motion artificial; contrasted to the work-a-day walkings of reality, it emphasizes comedy's artificiality. And disguise, also artificial, hides a person under a persona and thereby emphasizes comedy's turning from the individual.

Comic plots are more artificial, complex, and gamelike than tragic or novelistic plots for still another reason. They have no obligation to unfold character, but they also have no problems about either their point of departure or their destination. Almost all comic plots terminate in a coming together of separate individuals into a group, usually focused by the microcosmic coming together in marriage. "Ay, ay, that's as it should be," says Sir Oliver, at the end of *The School for Scandal*, "and, egad, we'll have the wedding to-morrow morning." To conclude a comedy, disguises are laid aside and true identities restored; lovers cease to pine in isolation or misunderstanding and join in marriage; falsity or antisocial behavior is exposed to the healthy scrutiny of the group; more serious defects are simply forgiven. At the end of *The Two Gentlemen of Verona*, for instance, Valentine forgives Proteus, Julia sheds her disguise and claims Proteus for marriage, the Duke forgives Valentine and gives Silvia for marriage, and the Duke, at Valentine's request, forgives the outlaws. In a true paradigm of the comic conclusion, the Duke says "I here forget all former griefs, / Cancel all grudge," and Valentine seals the happy occasion by saying to Proteus, "our day of marriage shall be yours; / One feast, one house, one mutual happiness."

If the "mutual happiness," with the word "mutual" no less essential than the word "happiness," provides the classic state of repose toward which comedy tends, it also indicates that state from which comedy departs: that is, an atomized social state, in which some are tricked or manipulated, or are mistaken or unaware of reality, while others trick or manipulate, or perpetrate mistakes and misunderstandings. The state of repose toward which comedy moves is, in other words, preceded by a state of chaos. "Prima turbulenta, tranquilla ultima"—

thus Donatus, a late-classical commentator on Terence, summarizes the movement of comic plot. Jonson's *Bartholomew Fair*, with its multiplication of human types milling around in amiable hubbub, is the very model of the comic world before its resolution. To be sure, few comedies attain the marvelous richness of *Bartholomew Fair*, but all comedies in at least some degree present a world of knaves and fools, of gulls and cony-catchers. The plot of a typical comedy begins in social divisiveness and ends in unity, begins in misunderstanding and ends in knowledge, begins in arrogance and ends in humiliation of that arrogance, or begins in trickery and ends in trust.

Traditional comedy, in short, tends toward the affirmation of society's primacy, unity, and rightness (I am not sure I accept so-called "black comedy" as in fact comedy). It finds the norm of society to be the moral norm, and regards deviation from society's standard as the source of all error. "Society, the vital articulation of many individuals into a new collective individual" is, declares Carlyle, "greatly the most important of man's attainments on this earth; that in which, and by virtue of which, all his other attainments and attempts find their arena, and have their value. Considered well, Society is the standing wonder of our existence; a true region of the Supernatural; as it were, a second all-embracing Life, wherein our first individual Life becomes doubly and trebly alive."

This is why comic character types, rather than comic plots, generate the primary meaning of comedy (although, once established as types, the greatest comic figures—witness Falstaff and the Wife of Bath—take on individuality also). For comic character types are precisely deviants from the social norm. And comic plot is designed to remove the threat of such deviance. All social unity is, as unity, a single norm: "Come, come," says the Duke at the conclusion of Part One of *The Honest Whore*, "we'll have you friends; join hearts, join hands"—such concord could conclude one of Shakespeare's comedies quite as fittingly as it does this one of Dekker's. Variation resides only in the kinds·of deviation permitted by the character types. Katherina, in *The Taming of the Shrew*, deviates from the social norm of submissive wife as set up in the play, is rebuked and humbled, and the play concludes with a reaffirmation of the norm she has flouted. The Wife of Bath, however, needs no plot in which to function. She too is a social deviant in that she flouts the norm of submissive wife, but the norm she flouts is set up by social wisdom in itself. In a play, the deviance of a character type thrusts against the standard as set in the play, but the standard as set in the play must always be an analogue of the standard as set in social wisdom outside the play. The fatness of Falstaff, for instance, is identified in the language of *The Merry Wives of Windsor* as a mark of his deviance from the social norm of the play. The fatness of a comic entertainer such as Jackie Gleason, however, is risible without a play, because society itself provides the norm that identifies corpulence as a deviation.

The comic figure outside a literary context is ephemeral, in the sense that Jackie Gleason is ephemeral by comparison to Falstaff, who, in virtue of his literary context alone, is gathered into an "artifice of eternity." It is noteworthy, nonetheless, that though Falstaff is Shakespeare's greatest comic creation, and perhaps the deepest ever achieved, none of the plays in which he appears can be called Shakespeare's best comedy (two, indeed, are not comedies at all). For a comedy, like any other work of art, depends upon its form as a whole, as well as upon the breath of the comic spirit it incorporates. The comic spirit as such, in its appearance in Chaucer, in Rabelais, in Cervantes, is as rich as any presented by our culture. But comedy, as an achieved art form, reaches its apex not in these writers, but in the plays of Shakespeare, Aristophanes, Molière, and Ben Jonson. For it is in these dramas that the most significant of social deviations are interwoven into the most intricate patterns of plot to achieve the most satisfying affirmations of a unified society: "One feast, one house, one mutual happiness."

The ways in which comic character types deviate from the norm are various. They may stand above it (as judges, lawyers, kings, saints, intellectuals, physicians) and thereby criticize it by implication. They may threaten it with destruction (as soldiers), or censure it (as policemen). They may stand beneath it (as servants, the aged, the adolescent). Or they may stand outside it (as bachelors, spinsters, the excessively proud). In each case the tactic of comedy is to isolate the deviant type by portraying it as false or ridiculous. Thus it is that the miles gloriosus—the soldier, who might destroy the members of a society, but who in fact is a coward and therefore will not do so—is perhaps the largest and most durable of comic types. Schoolmasters, philosophers, priests, and other such "medicine men" of society are likewise depicted as hollow, and hence ridiculous in their pretensions to special status: think of Thwackum and Square, of Holofernes and Sir Nathaniel. The saint becomes Canon Chasuble, or Casper Milquetoast. The judge becomes Adam Overdo, or Sammy Davis, Jr. The comic lawyer is a shyster; the professor is an absent-minded fool; the physician is a quack—or a Sganarelle; the scientist is a madman—or a Subtle. The comic policeman is Dogberry, or a Keystone Cop. The servant is Face, or one of countless other upstarts. The aged man becomes Senex, or Pantalone, or one of the numberless types representing futile endeavor from a man too old to try: Jonson's Morose, for instance.

Most such symbols of social threat repelled, however, are part of the gallery of chaos in which comedy begins. The formal protagonists are usually neither those who stand above, nor those who stand below society, nor again those who threaten it directly, but those who stand outside it, most notably those who will not get married. For bachelorhood and spinsterhood are the ultimate social deviations in the world of comedy, and also the most easily cured. "A young man married is a man that's marr'd," says Parolles to Bertram in *All's Well* (2.3.291), but Parolles, as the miles gloriosus, speaks as an enemy of society; and the comic resolution of the play is achieved, on the one hand, by exposing Parolles as a coward, and on the other, by forcing Bertram to accept the full social responsibility of marriage. In *Much Ado* there is "a kind of merry war betwixt Signior Benedick" and Beatrice (1.1.52), so that Don Pedro says of Benedick, "Thou wast ever an obstinate heretic in the despite of beauty," and Benedick affirms that "I will live a bachelor" (1.1.202–3, 213). Beatrice, for her part, "cannot endure to hear tell of a husband" (2.1.314), and hopes that in heaven Saint Peter will show her "where the bachelors sit, and there live we as merry as the day is long" (2.1.40–41). But Don Pedro early observes that she would be "an excellent wife for Benedick" (2.1.316), and the burden of the main plot thus becomes to "bring Signior Benedick and the Lady Beatrice into a mountain of affection th' one with th' other" (2.1.330–31).

The affections of the sexes, indeed, are probably the single deepest theme of comic drama. For not only is sex the glue that binds society together, the attraction that makes it impossible for man to live alone, but it is the means by which society maintains its immortality. Accordingly, one of the most central of all comic situations is that of the *Lysistrata*, where war, which tears society apart, is nullified by sex, which holds it together. The Athenian men are forced to leave their disruptive half-society of men—for war is equivalent to the state of bachelorhood—and return to the women, and the social order of peace and marriage, in order to regain the sexual satisfaction that has been denied them.

Bachelorhood is the most formal and frequently encountered comic deviance, for it fits most naturally into the formal resolution of marriage. Comedy, in fact, is not only deeply concerned with sex, but more specifically with the social control of sex. The sexual impulse is a dynamism of such power that it holds society together, but also, in certain forms, it can tear it apart. Romantic love, for instance, is opposed to the norm of society. The romantic lover tends to reject, rather than accept, the rules and conventions, and even the pertinence, of society; he feels that "She is all kingdoms, all princes I / Nothing else is." It is scarcely fortuitous that the most moving conceptions of romantic love (Tristan and Isolde, Antony and Cleopatra, Juan and Haidee) not only turn toward the tragic, but also bring together lovers outside the social convention of marriage. Thus it is that romantic love is regarded by comedy as a natural enemy, and as a fit target for comic repudiation and ridicule. "I leave myself, my friends, and all, for love," laments the socially unacceptable Proteus at the beginning of *The Two Gentlemen of Verona*; love has made him "neglect my studies, lose my time, / War with good counsel, set the world at nought; / Made wit with musing weak, heart sick with thought" (1.1.67–69).

Romantic love, however, is not the only form in which the sexual situation can appear as a comic deviation. Within marriage itself numerous possibilities occur. Any mismatched marriage, most frequently that of a young girl with an old man, is seen by comedy as a threat to the social order, and hence a subject of ridicule. "When an old bachelor marries a young wife," says Sir Peter Teazle in *The School for Scandal*, "what is he to expect? 'Tis now six months since Lady Teazle made me the happiest of men—and I have been the most miserable dog ever since!" "For she was wilde and yong, and he was old, / And demed himself been lyk a cokewold," says Chaucer in *The Miller's Tale*: "Men sholde wedden after hir estaat, / For youth and elde is often at debaat." Of all improper marriages perhaps the most intrinsically comic is that in which the woman assumes the dominant role, and the man recedes from his manhood. A very large part of the enormous comic power of the Wife of Bath derives from this deviation. But it appears everywhere: in Noah's wife in the Wakefield *Noah* or Chester *Deluge*; in Tyb, the shrewish wife of John Heywood's timid Johan Johan; in Maggie, in the comic strip *Bringing up Father*. There are also endless variations on the character type of the insubordinate or reluctant bride: Beatrice in *Much Ado*, Rosaline in *Love's Labour's Lost*, Elizabeth in *Pride and Prejudice*. And of course, all spinsters and mothers-in-law are regarded by comedy as threats to marriage and therefore humorous—Lady Bracknell perhaps most marvelously in the latter instance.

Almost as central as the theme of the struggle of the sexes is the theme of the abuse of money, and for much the same reason. Money is a prime symbol of society's trust in itself. Devaluations of money historically occur in war-ridden, sick, or decomposed societies, as in the collapse of Confederate currency in the American Civil War, or of German currency after the First World War. Money, like sex, is essential to society. But the abuse of money, like the abuse of sex, is an ominous threat to society's well-being, and so it too looms large as a comic theme. Jonson's *Volpone* is as firmly founded on this motif as is Molière's *L'Avare*. And the plot of *Volpone*, which is a variation of the *captatio*, or treasure hunt, is an inverted form of the same fundamental plot as that of *The School for Scandal*.

The two major comic themes of sex and money do not exclude one another. Volpone has designs not only upon the money of Corbaccio but upon the wife of Corvino. In *The Comedy of Errors*, Antipholus of Ephesus's trouble with his wife—("My wife is shrewish when I keep not hours"—3.1.2) interlocks and permutes with Antipholus of Syracuse's trouble with his money—("Where is the thousand marks thou hadst of me?"—1.2.81). "I come to wive it wealthily in Padua;" says Petruchio in *The Taming of the Shrew*, "If wealthily, then happily in Padua" (1.2.73–74). Morose, in Jonson's *Epicoene*, is gulled into a hilariously improper supposed marriage so that his nephew will not be disinherited, and he is then relieved of the supposed marriage in exchange for his money. And perhaps the most unequivocal of all comic beginnings is the opening sentence of *Pride and Prejudice*: "It is a truth universally acknowledged, that a single man in possession of a good fortune, must be in want of a wife."

These two themes, although they are the most central for comedy, do not of course exhaust comic possibilities. Any kind of deviation from the norm of the group is a potential comic theme. "Whether a character is good or bad is of little moment," says Bergson, "granted he is unsociable, he is capable of becoming comic." As deviations become more absolute, however, they begin to move toward the boundary line that separates comedy from tragedy. For comedy cures only minor deviation: "comedy," as Sir Philip Sidney says, "is an imitation of the common errors of our life." "In comedy," asserts Donatus, "the onsets of dangers are slight, and the terminations of actions are happy" ("... in comoedia ... parvi impetus periculorum, laetique sunt exitus actionum. . .") . We have all experienced situations where a joke goes too far, where laughter fails to kindle and instead is replaced by tense, white-faced rage. Indeed, the greatest comic figures, Falstaff, Don Quixote, the Wife of Bath, all skirt the boundary line of tragedy. A figure such as, say, Heathcliff, cannot be brought into the comic domain, and Darcy, who in his fierce pride is somewhat like Heathcliff, can barely be kept inside it. "I cannot forget the follies and vices of others so soon as I ought," confesses Darcy—"My good opinion once lost is lost for ever." "*That* is a failing indeed!" replies Elizabeth; "But you have chosen your fault well.—I really cannot *laugh* at it." The whole movement of comedy is a process that makes unimportant "the follies and vices of others," and Darcy's inability to do so pushes him, in this instance, beyond the comic pale.

The test is the test of laughter. There are times when people laugh when a more appropriate response would be an exclamation of dismay: that is to say, certain events are properly laughable, and certain are not. Rape is not laughable, although seduction can be; murder is not laughable, although a beating can be. Comedy, as Ben Jonson says, tries to show us an "image of the times / And sport with human follies, not with crimes." For comedy is precisely a strategy of obtaining security from the threats of life. It does not stand up to death or catastrophic event as tragedy does, but rather eliminates them as a possibility. In the world of the animated cartoon, the cat is blown up by a bomb, only to emerge unhurt. Charlie Chaplin is devoured by a giant machine and survives. Falls, collisions, beatings, none of these hazards of actual life damages the miraculously invulnerable participants of comic reality. Although Gammer Gurton and Dame Chat lock in truly murderous combat, their comic world guarantees their freedom from pain and destruction. "The comic mask," notes Aristotle, "is ugly and distorted, but does not imply pain"; in comedy "the deadliest enemies— like Orestes and Aegisthus—quit the stage as friends at the close, and no one kills or is killed."

On those occasions when comedy does attempt to deal with death, the result is a precarious tour de force such as *Arsenic and Old Lace* (which toys with the verbiage of death rather than confronting the actuality), or, more likely, a tasteless cinematic failure such as *The Trouble with Harry.*

Despite the theoretical objection to its presence, however, it was not uncommon in medieval and Renaissance comedy for death or dangerous situation to occur, or for death to appear in Arcadia (in as early a prototype as *Daphnis and Chloe* Dorcon is killed by pirates); and the rise of the genre of 'tragi-comedy," as we may see both from actual plays and from Fletcher's observations, deliberately encouraged the introduction of motifs of threat into comic plots. Accordingly, one whole aspect of Shakespeare's comic practice, both before and after the impact of Beaumont and Fletcher (who were amply prefigured by Guarini), approaches genuine confrontation with death. In *Cymbeline,* Cloten is beheaded by Guiderius. In *Troilus and Cressida,* Hector is treacherously slain by Achilles and his henchmen. In *Measure for Measure,* Claudio faces death from the beginning, and the play dwells insistently on death's meaning. In each case the comic rule of the avoidance of death or catastrophe is tested by the exception. But the rule holds firm; or the genre itself gives way. In fact, as Madeleine Doran points out, even "tragi-comedy gets some of its special effect by keeping the danger of death without death itself" (*Endeavors of Art: A Study of Form in Elizabethan Drama* [Madison, 1972], p. 205).

So in *Cymbeline,* where death does occur, the function of comedy is distorted and pushed beyond its limits, and comic symmetries dissolve into asymmetrical grotesqueries of locale, characterization, and time scheme. For example, a consul from antique Rome joins a Renaissance Italian Machiavel in leading an army at Milford Haven in Wales. In this play, indeed, it is as though the harmonies of *Cosi fan tutte* are threatened by the tormented strainings of *Wozzeck.* Likewise, in *Troilus and Cressida* a state of unending warfare is substituted for the normal state of a healthy society, and the famous speech of Ulysses reveals how forlornly lost is all hope of restored health; the play is such a study in sickness, corruption, and disillusioned idealism that many (the editors of the First Folio, for example) have thought it a tragedy. *Measure for Measure* manages, just barely, to remain within the legitimate boundaries of comedy, and in doing so becomes one of Shakespeare's greatest and most tormented achievements. The comic abuse of sex is here transformed into fornication, defined by the law as criminal, and its punishment is not social censure but death. And yet the play develops a kind of calculus in its mensuration of death, as though the tangents of comedy infinitesimally approach, but never quite coincide with the curve of tragedy. Claudio is threatened with death, but after an agonizing approach to that reality, the threat is removed from him and transferred to the brutish Barnardine, but just in time Barnardine too is spared, and the head of the pirate Ragozine substituted. But Ragozine does not die within the confines of the play, and hence, despite its persistent flirtation with the possibility of death, *Measure for Measure* never crosses the comic boundary.

These plays, with more or less success, and more or less variation, all participate in the comic function. It is true that they contain little that excites laughter. But it is important to realize that laughter is merely a comic tool; it has no necessary relationship to the comic essence, which is the criticism of individuality by the standard of the group. "Nor is the moving of laughter alwaies the end of *Comedy*," notes Ben Jonson in his *Discoveries*; and L. C. Knights observes that "once an invariable connexion between comedy and laughter is assumed we are not likely to make any observations that will be useful as criticism." The comic resolution ideally places us in a happy world, but not a ridiculous world. So despite John Dennis's insistence that "Laughter is the Life, and the very soul of Comedy," the ridiculous, that which excites to laughter, must be understood as a part of the comic process rather than a part of the comic goal. "Laughter," Bergson emphasizes, "aims at correcting"; likewise, "the function of comedy," as Molière says in his preface to *Tartuffe*, "is to correct men's vices." Yet laughter, as Freud stressed, is a human activity with its own psychological foundation; comedy comes upon it, and because of its fittingness for the comic purpose, uses it.

We laugh at that which is out of place, or is unexpected in a context of expectation. "Laughter," says Kant, "is an affection arising from the sudden transformation of a strained expectation into nothing." "The cause of laughter," says Schopenhauer, is "the sudden perception of the incongruity between a concept and the real objects which have been thought through it in some relation."

But the context of expectation is supplied by the group, and all real laughter is an appeal to the group. Laugh and the world laughs with you, weep and you weep alone. Laughter is the group's way of identifying, and rejecting, a deviance from its standards. "Society," says Freud, is a "third and dispassionate person in the combat" of wit—"By belittling and humbling our enemy, by scorning and ridiculing him, we directly obtain the pleasure of his defeat by the laughter of the third person, the inactive spectator." Laughter both devalues the object that excites it (we know how cruel is laughter's potential), and reaffirms the superiority of all those who join in; laughter, as Hobbes realized, is a "sudden Glory arising from some sudden Conception of some Eminency in our selves, by Comparison with the Infirmity of others." What we can laugh at does not threaten us.

Of the four great comic dramatists, Shakespeare probably evokes the least laughter. Certainly, though laughter is often elicited in his work, it appears more sparsely than in the crowded action of Ben Jonson's greatest plays. The so-called bitter comedies—to number the problem comedies (*All's Well, Measure for Measure,* and *Troilus and Cressida*) with the four comedies of the last phase (*Pericles, Cymbeline, The Winter's Tale,* and *The Tempest*)—contain only sporadic incitements to laughter, and amount to almost half of Shakespeare's comic production. In the rest, the happy comedies (to use Dover Wilson's designation) or the romantic comedies (to use that favored by Phialas), laughter tends to be restricted to individual characters or motifs of the subplot. Nor, with Shakespeare, does laughter necessarily coincide with comic quality. *The Comedy of Errors* arouses generous amounts of laughter, but *All's Well,* a much more profound comedy, arouses virtually none.

It might be said that the bitter comedies represent a failing of Shakespeare's comic vision, except that this view, while it might account in some degree for *Cymbeline* or *Pericles,* is palpably inadequate to explain *All's Well* or *Measure for Measure.* It might be urged that they participate in the "Jacobean melancholy" of the early seventeenth century, but this view, even granting the existence of such a special melancholy strain, merely transfers the explanation from Shakespeare's art to the culture of his time, and then still leaves unanswered questions (see, e.g., Anne Righter, *Shakespeare and the Idea of the Play* [London, 1962], pp. 172 ff.). Or one might think—many have in fact argued it, and I myself incline to this view—that the bitter comedies mirror a continuing crisis in Shakespeare's personal life, one that involved him in a revulsion against human society and all its ideals. Although such a matter must, in the absence of precise information, remain largely inferential, it seems clear that the same fury that informs *Timon of Athens* in the tragic realm informs *Troilus and Cressida* in the comic, that the disillusionment in *Hamlet* is reflected in *Measure for Measure*. In any event, I cannot agree with those who do not sense such fury and disillusionment in the plays, or who recognize those qualities merely as artistic stratagems or conventions. When, to cite a single example, C. J. Sisson finds the "sorrows of Shakespeare," taken as an explanation of dramatic emphases, to be a "mythical" conception, he seems to be testifying less to an awareness of the meanings and correlations of Shakespeare's representations than to a blandness in his own experience of life.

Among the plays that do not participate in the fury and disillusionment of the bitter comedies, four display a preoccupation with pastoral themes and landscape. They are *The Two Gentlemen of Verona*, *Love's Labour's Lost*, *A Midsummer-Night's Dream*, and *As You Like It*. And among those that do participate in the problems of the bitter comedies, two, *The Winter's Tale* and *The Tempest*, also substantially involve themselves in pastoral motifs. A considerable amount, therefore, of Shakespeare's comic writing makes use of the machinery of pastoral. An investigation of this use of pastoral should lead to a deeper understanding both of Shakespeare's achievement and of the high seriousness of the comic ideal.

Much here is unexciting. Shakespeare's involvement with pastoral, as a historical phenomenon, reflects a pervasive Elizabethan preoccupation with shepherds and shepherdesses, and with a highly benign and highly artificial environment in which such characters might move. Accordingly, on one level at least, he doubtless employed pastoral simply to exploit a taste that was current in his day. In doing so, however, he came upon a device that gave to comedy a profoundly meaningful symbolic extension.

Inasmuch as a large and ever-increasing number of recent books and articles have dealt with pastoral—in antiquity as well as in the Renaissance, in the form of specialized studies as well as in the form of generalized surveys, critically as well as historically—it seems necessary at this point to describe only briefly the characteristics and history of the mode, and thenceforth to devote argument to the more urgent and less fully treated questions of pastoral's semiological basis and of its relationship to comedy. To be sure, these matters, or at least the former one, have themselves not been overlooked by modern commentators: the studies of Petriconi, Empson, Poggioli, Harry Berger, and more recently, Donald Friedman and Harold Toliver (to name only six) all shed light on the meaning of pastoral. Nonetheless, I feel that the semiological inquiry can be extended further and complicated more richly.

"*Pastorals*," says Drayton, in a rather rough-and-ready definition," "*as they are a Species of Poesie, signifie fained Dialogues, or other speeches in Verse, fathered upon Heardsmen.*" A fuller definition urges that pastoral is "a representation of shepherds and shepherdesses with their actions and passions, which must be such as may agree with their natures, at least not exceeding former fictions . . . ; they are not to be adorned with any art but . . . singing and poetry, or such as experience may teach them. . . . But you are ever to remember shepherds to be such as all the ancient poets, and modern of understanding, have received them; that is, the owners of flocks, and not hirelings." So says John Fletcher, in the Preface to his *The Faithful Shepherdess*. But an adjustment must be made in the definition: the figures in a pastoral setting were, for the Englishman of Shakespeare's time, as well as for ancient poets, less important than the setting itself; or rather, they provided an index to the setting. For the pastoral was above all an ideal landscape. Sidney's description of Arcadia may serve as a paradigm for the usual features of such an imaginary place:

There were hills which garnished their proud heights with stately trees; humble valleys whose base estate seemed comforted with refreshing of silver rivers; meadows enamel'd with all sorts of eye-pleasing flowers; . . . here a shepherd's boy piping, as though he should never be old; there a young shepherdess knitting, and withal singing, and it seemed that her voice comforted her hands to work. . . . As for the houses of the country . . . , they were all scattered, no two being one by th' other, and yet not so far off as that it barred mutual succor: a shew, at it were, of an accompanable solitariness and of a civil wildness.

Some such landscape underlies all evocations of the pastoral. In the world of pastoral, the gliding brook is limpid, the stream is silvery, the pastures are green, the breeze is soft. " 'Twas alwaies Spring; warme *Zephyrus* sweetly blew / On smiling flowres, which without setting grew"—these lines, translating Ovid's pastoral vision of a golden age, go to the very heart of the matter. "Even now every field, every tree is budding; now the woods are green, and the year is at its fairest" ("et nunc omnis ager, nunc omnis parturit arbos, / nunc frondent silvae, nunc formosissimus annus")—thus writes Virgil, in his third eclogue. "It was the beginning of spring and all the flowers were in bloom, in the woods, in the meadows, and on the mountains. Already there was a buzzing of bees, there was a sound of singing birds, there were gambollings of new-born lambs"—so says Longus, in *Daphnis and Chloe*. The pastoral is a landscape that retains the features of ordinary landscape—trees, flowers, hills, valleys, streams—and is therefore not completely fanciful. But it abstracts the harmful aspects of nature and leaves only the benign. "We must therefore use some illusion to render a Pastoral delightful;" says Pope in his *Discourse on Pastoral Poetry*, "and this consists in exposing the best side only of a shepherd's life and in concealing its miseries." There are flowers, but no poison ivy; breezes, but no hurricanes; streams, but no tidal waves; honeybees but no centipedes: "non serpens; nec cauda scorpius unca" (no snake; nor hook-tailed scorpion), as Mantuan says.

Historically, the pastoral vision was first clearly projected by Theocritus, and was eventually transferred into the Latin imagination by Virgil. Bruno Snell describes how Virgil, chancing upon a passage in Polybius that described the musical contests in the historian's native Arcadia, forthwith exchanged the too-familiar Sicilian setting of Theocritus for this more exotic locale in Greece, even though the actual Arcadia, as opposed to the spiritual landscape, was a bare and ordinary place (*The Discovery of the Mind: The Greek Origins of European Thought*, trans. T. G. Rosenmeyer [New York, 1960], pp. 281 f.). And Virgil made other changes. Theocritus had shown "some interest in realistic detail." But Virgil ceased "to see anything but what is important to him: tenderness and warmth and delicacy of feeling. Arcadia knows no reckoning in numbers, no precise reasoning of any kind. There is only feeling, which suffuses everything with its glow; not a fierce or passionate feeling: even love is but a delicate desire, gentle and sad" (p. 288). The pastoral world increasingly became a region where landscape and feeling intermingled in a sweet and lovely nostalgia. The God Pan, who lived in Arcadia, was, even in the pastorals of Theocritus, incessantly hailed as the pastoral deity; for Pan is the symbol of the interfusion of men and their surroundings.

We need not linger over a history accessible in many other places. The pastoral vision was current not only in post-Virgilian antiquity; it also disseminated itself into the culture of Europe during the Middle Ages and the Renaissance. By the time it surfaced in England in the early and middle sixteenth century, it had been, or was being, powerfully enhanced by continental recapitulations and variations, mainly in Latin, Italian, French, and Spanish, by Petrarch, Mantuan, Tasso, Guarini, Sannazaro, Ronsard, and Montemayor, to name only the most prominent participants in this intercultural system of poetic reference. In all its forms it flourished mightily. W. W. Greg notes with regard to one form, pastoral drama, in one country, Italy, that "in 1614 Clementi Bartoli of Urbino possessed no less than eighty pastoral plays; while by 1700 . . . Giannantonio Moraldi is said to have brought together in Rome a collection of over two hundred" (*Pastoral Poetry and Pastoral Drama* [Oxford, 1906], p. 212). Hallett Smith notes with regard to another form, pastoral poetry, in another country, England, that "The Elizabethan poet usually began, as Virgil had done, by writing pastoral poetry. And, since many poets begin and not all of them continue, the proportion of pastoral to the whole literary production of the Elizabethan period is fairly high" ("Pastoral Poetry; the Vitality and Versatility of a Convention," in *Elizabethan Poetry* [Cambridge, Mass., 1952], p. 1).

In England the sense that pastoral evocation participated in a tradition, and subsisted by means of the aesthetic category of imitation, was always clear. Thus Alexander Barclay, probably writing in the second decade of the sixteenth century, said that

> . . . the famous Theocrite
> First in Syracuse attempted for to write
> Certain egloges or speeches pastoral,
> Introducing shepherds, men homely and rural,
> Which in plain language, according to their name,
> Had sundry talking—sometime of mirth and game,
> Sometime of things more like to gravity
> And not exceeding their small capacity.
> Most noble Virgil after him long while
> Wrote also egloges after like manner style,
> His wits proving in matters pastoral
> Or he durst venture to style heroical.
> And in like manner now lately in our days
> Hath other poets attempted the same ways,
> As the most famous Baptist Mantuan,
> The best of that sort since poets first began;
> And Francis Petrark also in Italy
> In like manner style wrote plain and merrily. . . .

Though the pastoral tradition of "plain language" to which Barclay alludes (which stemmed from Theocritus's own deliberate use of Doric dialect to render bucolic speech) perhaps encouraged such poetasters as Barnabe Googe and George Turbervile to try their talentless hands at this kind of poetry, it should not be forgotten that a very substantial portion of the greatest achievement of both Spenser and Milton, to say nothing of Shakespeare, came to fruition in pastoral language and the landscape to which it referred. Indeed, the tradition remained strong until the advent of Romanticism. Even then, if one adopts the view of Empson, one can see the pastoral continuing in various versions, although divorced from the formal tradition of classical imitation. Wordsworth, for instance, approaches nature with a directness that in a sense is a repudiation of pastoral, certainly of pastoral artifice, but in another sense, particularly with his emphasis upon "low and rustic life" and the "language really used by men," is pastoral in a new avatar (there are places, moreover, such as in the eighth book of *The Prelude* or the fourth book of *The Excursion*, where he directly participates in the Theocritan tradition). And for Pope, of course, the pastoral was a natural and considerable poetic form. Indeed, as his own practice, taken together with such theoretical disquisitions as those of Rapin and Fontenelle, demonstrates, the pastoral was peculiarly fitted to the so-called neoclassic sensibility (see further J. E. Congleton, *Theories of Pastoral Poetry in England, 1684–1798* [Gainesville, Fla., 1952]).

Shakespeare, therefore, was able to draw on a singularly powerful and vital tradition. "Of all the antique poetical genres," says Curtius, pastoral poetry "has had, after the epic, the greatest influence. . . . Arcadia was forever being rediscovered. This was possible because the stock of pastoral motifs was bound to no genre and to no poetic form" (*European Literature and the Latin Middle Ages*, trans. W. R. Trask [New York, 1953], p. 187). There was the rich legacy of the pastoral romance, from Longus in antiquity to the flowering of Sidney's *Arcadia* in Shakespeare's own time. There was the equally rich tradition of the pastoral eclogue: Virgil was always present in a cultivated man's consciousness, and there had recently appeared Spenser's brilliant *Shepheardes Calendar* (as Dryden said, "the Sheapherd's Kalendar of *Spencer*, is not to be match'd in any Modern Language"). There was the pastoral lyric, beautifully exemplified by the collection in *En-*

gland's Helicon. And there was, from Tasso and Guarini, a new tradition of pastoral in drama. "Tasso in his Aminta," said Pope, "has as far excell'd all the Pastoral writers, as in his *Gierusalemme* he has outdone the Epic Poets of his country. But as this piece seems to have been the original of a new sort of poem, the Pastoral Comedy, in *Italy*, it cannot so well be consider'd as a copy of the ancients." Actually, there were pastoral comedies preceding the *Aminta*—Ferrarese Beccari's *Il Sacrificio*, Alberto Lollio's *L'Aretusa*, Agostino Argenti's *Lo Sfortunato*— but Tasso's work so far outshone its models that, with respect to its influence in world literature, it justifies Pope's assertion. The *Aminta*, and a dozen years later, Guarini's *Il Pastor Fido*, were, however, not the sole influences in European culture. In England itself, works like Lyly's *Gallathea* and Peele's *Arraignment of Paris* had presented the artificiality of pastoral romance in dramatic form.

But Shakespeare's superimposition of pastoral motifs upon the world of comedy is not merely a further step in the tradition of Lyly and Peele, nor is the tone of his pastoral comedy identical with theirs. In his work pastoral is not just a fanciful game of veiled references to the court of Elizabeth, but a strengthening and deepening of comedy itself. And this process was possible because of a fundamental affinity between the realm of comedy and the realm of pastoral. Jonson, indeed, repudiated the "heresy" that "mirth by no means fits a pastoral," and asserted instead that "there's no scene more properly assumes / The sock" (*The Sad Shepherd*, Prologue, 32–35).

The compatibility of comedy and pastoral resides first of all in a common tendency toward artificiality. Frank Kermode, in his *English Pastoral Poetry from the Beginnings to Marvell* (London, 1952), emphasizes at the outset that pastoral "probably suggests the word 'artificial' rather than the word 'natural' " (p. 11). And Johan Huizinga repeatedly points out the artificiality of the pastoral vision: comparing it to the historical imitation of the ideal of poverty, he says that "the imitation of the shepherd's life, on the other hand, was rarely more than a sort of party game"; and comparing it to the decay of the chivalric ideal, he says that "the bucolic ideal was safeguarded from such constant decay much more than the chivalric ideal because it had fewer points of contact with reality" ("Historical Ideals of Life," in *Men and Ideas: History, the Middle Ages, the Renaissance*, trans. J. S. Holmes and H. van Marle [Cleveland, 1966], pp. 83, 89). For its part, comedy, as has been noted earlier in this chapter, accepts and revels in the artificial. "Comedy," as Bergson says, "lies midway between art and life."

Comedy and pastoral are compatible, secondly, because they both function as social microcosms. "The comical," as Freud says, "appears primarily as an unintentional discovery in the social relations of human beings." And pastoral too always asserts a social vision: "a shew, as it were, of an accompanable solitariness and of a civil wildness." Indeed, it is here that Wordsworth's "egotistical sublime," as in *Resolution and Independence*, tends to remove his own pastoral version from the classical tradition; even though many poems, from *Peter Bell* to *Michael*, from *The Old Cumberland Begger* to *The Ruined Cottage*, tend to reaffirm the strong social emphasis of that tradition. Curtius, after noting that the Greeks rarely evoked the image of an empty landscape, preferring rather a peopled environment, says of the pastoral that it "demands a sociological framework," that it "has a personnel of its own, which has its own social structure and thus constitutes a social microcosm: neatherds (whence the name bucolic), goatherds, shepherdesses, etc." (p. 187).

Still another connection between comedy and pastoral is the common stress upon the affections of the sexes. This greatest of comic themes is related to, although not precisely congruent with, a persistent erotic strain in pastoral. "The shepherd's world," says Curtius, "is linked to nature and to love. One can say that for two millenniums it draws to itself the majority of erotic motifs." "In Theocritus, as in Virgil," says Snell, "the shepherds are less concerned with their flocks than they are interested in poetry and love." Speaking of "the amazing vitality of the pastoral form," Huizinga finds that "The reason for the great vitality of the form is undoubtedly to be found in its basically erotic character." *Daphnis and Chloe* provides an outstanding example from antiquity. And Pleusidippus, in Greene's *Menaphon*, indicates a warm appreciation of the truth: "O Arcady, Arcady, storehouse of nymphs and nursery of beauty!" More openly salacious is Cloe, in Fletcher's *The Faithful Shepherdess*: ". . . from one cause of fear I am most free: / It is impossible to ravish me, / I am so willing." Likewise, the themes of comedy, as the late-classical grammarian Diomedes emphasizes, are "love affairs and seductions" ("amores, virginum raptus").

To be sure, the world of the eclogue is, to an almost extreme degree, the very world of romantic love that comedy views with distrust, and that moves in the direction of tragedy. Longing, and the sadness of separation, rather than the sturdy pleasures of married life, are the dominant emotions in the world of the eclogue: the homosexual strain in the pastoral realm, notably as represented by Virgil's Corydon, is an index to the prevailing condition of love as sweet pain rather than happy fulfillment. This pain is even more explicitly present in the tenth eclogue, where Gallus's rejection by his mistress involves even the Gods in despair. Pan himself arrives ("Pan deus Arcadiae venit") to lament the cruelty of love; but love and its pain conquer all ("omnia vincit Amor").

But as a recent commentator has stressed, "unrequited love" is subtly inimical to the bucolic. Corydon's fair Alexis "is a divisive influence. . . . All is turned upside down. Corydon, when he should be searching for beauty which would remain as timeless as the countryside, is actually in pursuit of love as temporary as it might prove fickle." The second eclogue "is a study in realignment, in the reintegration of the shepherd with his surroundings"; it records "the challenge that hostile forces present for the pastoral myth." And Gallus, conquered by love, is seen as ultimately the "partisan of an anti-pastoral art" (Michael C. J. Putnam, *Virgil's Pastoral Art* [Princeton, 1970], pp. 13, 114–15, 394).

In this context, the meaning of the pastoral preoccupation with romantic love is not very different from comedy's rebuke to that love. And in any event, both the raptures and disappointments of that preoccupation are, in comedy, viewed as deviations from the norm, and can be resolved by the comic termination of marriage. Thus Aminta, after experiencing the exquisitely extended sorrow of pastoral rejection at the hands of Silvia, is finally accepted by her, at which point her father Montano is summoned to give the lovers his consent for marriage. The chief comic process in *As You Like It* is a rebuking of Orlando's pastorally extravagant love. "The worst fault you have is to be in love," says Jaques drily (3.2.265), and this fault is ameliorated not by further excesses of romantic emotion but by the marriage of Orlando and Rosalind.

These similarities between comic and pastoral provide Shakespeare with a basis for using the pastoral functionally rather than as mere ornament. From a tactical standpoint, the pastoral serves him as does laughter; that is, it identifies disharmonies as faults rather than as catastrophes, and points the way to the possibility of their disappearance. Poetic statements that "attempt to reconcile some conflict between the parts of a society," says Empson, "usually bring in, or leave room for the reader to bring in, the whole set of pastoral ideas" (*Some Versions of Pastoral*, p. 19). For troubles are muffled in the world of the pastoral. "Arcadia," as Snell notes, "was a land of symbols, far distant from the quarrels and acrimony of the present." In *The Two Gentlemen of Verona*, for instance, the machinations of "false perjur'd Proteus" threaten to go beyond the realm of the comic; but the action shifts into the forest, where the pressure of conflicting interests is simplified. The "pastoral process," as Empson has stressed, is one "of putting the complex into the simple" (p. 23). Thus Valentine says:

> This shadowy desert, unfrequented woods,
> I better brook than flourishing peopled towns.
> Here can I sit alone, unseen of any,
> And to the nightingale's complaining notes
> Tune my distresses and record my woes.
>
> [5.4.2–6]

In the forest, indeed, even Proteus's attempted rape of Silvia is transformed into a readily forgivable misdemeanor.

The pastoral invocation in *As You Like It* follows the same pattern as that in *The Two Gentlemen*. The faithlessness, dishonesty, and attempted murder at the beginning of the play are actually the stuff of tragedy rather than comedy; but when the action is transferred to the forest of Arden, its reverberations are muffled by the sylvan imagery, and crimes are softened to deviances and thence resolved by the balm of marriage.

So, too, the situation in *The Tempest*. The newcomers to the island are guilty of grave crimes, and some of them even plot murder there; while Caliban, already on the island, is ready for both rape and murder. But in the serene ambiance of the enchanted locale, no crime is more than the fault of a willfull child, which, after reprimand and immediate but tempered punishment, can be forgiven. In general, the pastoral, whenever Shakespeare superimposes it upon the comic, provides a benign and favored environment for the healing of the social stresses and strains of comic deviation, even when those stresses go beyond what comedy ordinarily attempts to resolve.

In transferring action to this ideal realm, Shakespeare does not violate the nature of comedy. It is true that comedy, because of its intensely social focus, is more usually set in the city; indeed, under the impact of the revival of Terence and Plautus, and with hints from Vitruvius and, more explicitly, Serlio, stage scenery of the English Renaissance began to represent a town as the normal background for comic action. "The Comic scene," said Serlio, "has houses appropriate to private persons, as citizens, lawyers, merchants, parasites, and other similar persons. Above all, the scene should have its house of the procuress (*ruffiana*), its tavern, and its church" (*The Renaissance Stage: Documents of Serlio, Sabbattini and Furttenbach*, ed. B. Hewitt [Coral Gables, Fla., 1958], p. 27). But the abandonment of this spiritual comic center for the open country actually involves no dislocation of tone, even though, as Kermode says, the "simplest kind of pastoral poetry assumes that the quiet wildness of the country is better than the cultivated and complex life of the hurrying city and court" (p. 17). There is no dislocation of tone simply because the pastoral, as an artificial realm, is actually a projection from the life of the city or court— is the other side, as it were, of social need—rather than a true imitation of country life (for an early exemplar of this truth, see Virgil's *Georgics*, 2.458–74). Statements drawn from a diverse trio of authorities perhaps serve to establish the point beyond dispute. In pastoral, as Kermode emphasizes, "the cultivated, in their artificial way, reflect upon and describe, for their own ends, the natural life" (p. 12). "The bucolic was never really naïve and natural," says Huizinga—"In Theocritus himself it was a product of urban lassitude: a flight from culture" (p. 84). And as Chambers points out, "Renaissance comedy, like the classical comedy upon which it was based, was essentially an affair of continuous action, in an open place, before a background of houses"; but he also notes that pastoral scenes were common, "for the urban preoccupation has its regular reaction in the direction of pastoral" (*The Elizabethan Stage* [Oxford, 1923], 3:27, 107).

In *The Importance of Being Earnest*, accordingly, it is a fulfillment rather than a dislocation when the action moves from the sophistications of London to the supposed naïvetés of Hertfordshire. "I had no idea there were any flowers in the country," drawls the city-bred Gwendolen. "Oh, flowers are as common here, Miss Fairfax, as people are in London." Cecily's riposte reveals that the language of the country, in this version of pastoral, both shares and heightens the sophistication of the city. *Le Hameau* is the just complement of *le petit Trianon*.

If pastoral, by assuming much of the burden of the comic reclamation, tends to decrease comedy's reliance on laughter to achieve its healing aim, the relatively smaller function of laughter in Shakespeare's comedy, as compared to the whirling humor of Ben Jonson (excepting, of course, both the bitter comedy of *Volpone* and such pastoral experiment as *The Sad Shepherd*) is thereby made understandable. The reciprocal comic function of pastoral and laughter, indeed, is assured by another thing they have in common. By abstracting from the cares and troubles of life, pastoral tends toward a state of childlike security. As Huizinga says, in the "bucolic fantasy the ideal of happiness predominated over the ideal of virtue—virtue was there negative, primarily innocence, the lack of a stimulus to sin in the state of simplicity, equality, freedom, and abundance." In short, the bucolic fantasy corresponds to childhood's happiness. "Were art to redeem man," says Ortega y Gasset, speaking of a certain revolt against ponderous conceptions of artistic functions, "it could do so only by saving him from the seriousness of life and restoring him to an unexpected boyishness. The symbol of art is seen again in the magic flute of the Great God Pan which makes the young goats frisk at the edge of the grove" (*The Dehumanization of Art*, trans. Helene Weyl [Princeton, 1968], p. 50). Again, as Empson insists, "child-cult" is a "version of pastoral" (p. 15). Still again, as S. K. Heninger emphasizes, "from its inception, pure pastoral has described some half-remembered place in archaic terms, a nostalgic reminiscence of an idealized child-scape" ("The Renaissance Perversion of Pastoral," *JHI* 22 [1961]: 255). Such, largely, is for Freud also the psychological truth of comic wit. "The specific character of the comic" is "the awakening of the infantile." Wit and comic pleasure reach for euphoria, and "the euphoria which we are thus striving to obtain is nothing but the state of a bygone time.... It is the state of our childhood in which we did not know the comic, were incapable of wit, and did not need humor to make us happy."

In their common turning toward the security of childhood, the alliance between the pastoral and the comic leads us further, toward a consideration of the phenomenon of play, for the defining activity of childhood is play.

Play involves deliberate artifice, and in its social form as game, relies almost wholly on artifice. At the same time it is in its spontaneity one of humankind's most cherished activities. For the act of play is always an icon of security. We play as children not only because we are children, but because we are secure from care. And we play in a yard or a park as the pastorally comic society plays in its Arcadia. Play, indeed, requires not only a locale, but in its social forms, requires the concept of "in bounds" for its validation as game.

Thus, although tragedy can claim, by facing the human fact of death, to be less artificial than comedy, comedy finds in its combination of artifice and laughter the equally human fact of play. Indeed, by its discovery of this fact comedy authenticates a better claim, as drama, to the art form called "a play" than does tragedy.

Though it is an activity that belongs to childhood, play, paradoxically, underlies the most adult dignity of man. "The child's best-loved and most intense occupation is with his play or games," says Freud—"As people grow up . . . they cease to play, and they seem to give up the yield of pleasure which they gained from playing. But whoever understands the human mind knows that hardly anything is harder for a man than to give up a pleasure which he has once experienced. Actually, we can never give anything up; we can only exchange one thing for another. What appears to be a renunciation is really the formation of a substitution or surrogate." This surrogate, in Schiller's analysis, is art: "We shall never be wrong in seeking a man's ideal of Beauty along the selfsame path in which he satisfies his play impulse." "But surely, you must long have been tempted to object, surely the Beautiful is degraded by being turned into mere play?" "But why call it a *mere* game, when we consider that in every condition of humanity it is precisely play, and play alone, that makes man complete." "What sort of phenomenon is it that proclaims the approach of the savage to humanity: so far as we consult history, it is the same in all races who have escaped the slavery of the animal state: a delight in appearance, a disposition towards ornament and play." Thus Schiller's most climactic statement complements Freud: "To declare it once and for all, man plays only when he is in the full sense of the word a man, and *he is only wholly man when he is playing.*"

This collage of quotations from the *Briefe über die ästhetische Erziehung des Menschen* emphasizes the dignity of play and its centrality for art. And it emphasizes by implication the dignity of comedy as well. For of all art forms, comedy, as reinforced by the motifs of pastoral, affirms and explores most satisfyingly the play element in literary activity.

In doing so it discovers other attitudes equally universal and even more profound. As Huizinga has pointed out, in his *Homo Ludens*, there is an element of play in human culture as such. And the analogy can be taken still deeper, to account for all human activity. Hence the sombre apprehension of Sir William Temple: "When all is done, Human Life is, at the greatest and the best, but like a froward Child, that must be Play'd with and Humor'd a little to keep it quiet till it falls asleep, and then the Care is over." In the moment of truth uncovered by Temple's Epicurean testament, even the tragic vision of woe and catastrophe is subsumed. Plotinus supplies a perspective that makes tragedy's subsumption by play even more explicit:

Man-made weapons directed against fellow mortals in quaintly set out battles, like Pyrrhic dances, show what children's games are all our human affairs; and they show us, too, that death is nothing very serious. . . . Murders, death in all its shapes, the capture and sacking of towns, all must be considered as so much stage show, so many shiftings of scenes, the horror and outcry of a play. . . . Who could be troubled by such griefs, except that he understands only the lower and outer life, never dreaming that all the tears and mighty business are but a sport?
[*Enneads*, 3.2.15]

Even Plato himself, in what I. M. Crombie calls "a remarkable and haunting passage," urges the same seemingly radical opinion:

Man's life is a business which does not deserve to be taken too seriously. . . . What I mean is that man ought to be serious about serious things, and not about trifles, and that while God is the real object of all serious effort, man is constructed . . . as a plaything of God, and that is really the best thing about him. We all, both men and women, should accept this role and spend life in making our play as perfect as possible. . . . What, then, is our right course? We should pass our lives in the playing of certain games—sacrificing, singing, and dancing. . . .
[*Laws*, 803B–D]

From these two perspectives supplied by the Platonic tradition—the view of Plotinus in which even the tragic confrontation of death and catastrophe is annulled by play, and the view of Plato in which play assumes a sacramental character—the final meanings of comedy may be sighted.

Plotinus emphasizes that death loses its sting when subsumed under the human reality of play. He thereby provides a key to the significance of the intrusion of sadness and death into the world of the eclogue. For where comedy turns its back on death, the pastoral, though it represents a state of youth and happiness, has from its earliest beginnings recognized the fact of death. In the very first idyll of Theocritus one of the happy shepherds, Thyrsis, sings a lament for the death of Daphnis; and in Virgil's fifth eclogue Mopsus sings of the death of Daphnis and of the inscription of Daphnis's tomb, while Menalcas sings also of Daphnis: "These rites shall be thine forever." Indeed, as Panofsky has emphasized in a famous article ("*Et in Arcadia Ego:* Poussin and the Elegiac Tradition," in *Meaning in the Visual Arts* [New York, 1955], pp. 295–320), the representation of a death's head in a pastoral landscape, with the inscription *Et in Arcadia ego*—signifying that even in Arcadia there is death—has had a long and varied history in both literature and the visual arts.

Still more than in the eclogue, it is in the tradition of the pastoral elegy that death involves itself with the Arcadian vision. Stemming from Theocritus's successors in the Greek bucolic mode, Bion and Moschus, more strongly than from Theocritus himself, this tradition employs the full panoply of the pastoral landscape to achieve a funeral poem. Two laments, or epitaphs, set the genre: the first, Bion's lush *Adonidos Epitaphios*, which developed the form of Thyrsis's song, has had countless epigones, including Shakespeare's *Venus and Adonis*; and the second, the *Epitaphios Bionos*—once attributed to Moschus— sings that "The Dorian Orpheus is dead" (ἀπώλετο Δώριος Ὀρφεύς). In Milton's *Lycidas*, Shelley's *Adonais*, and Arnold's *Thyrsis*, this variant of pastoral attained major rank in the English poetic tradition.

And yet the recognition of death, even in the pastoral elegy, is very different from a tragic recognition. The tragic method is one by which the disharmonies and ruptures of existence are faced in their full reality, while meaning is nonetheless claimed for life. In the pastoral environment, on the other hand, the fact of death is muffled. "Virgil does not exclude frustrated love and death," says Panofsky, "but he deprives them, as it were, of their factuality" (p. 301). The muffling agent is the languid opulence of the pastoral evocation: the smell of honeysuckle and the droning of bees. Indeed, in such an environment, nothing but youth and happiness seems truly real. A passage from the seventh idyll of Theocritus can perhaps convey how overpowering is this sense of environmental well-being:

Many an aspen, many an elm bowed and rustled overhead, and near by, the hallowed water gushed purling forth from a cave of the nymphs, while the brown cricket chirped busily amid the shady leafage, and the tree-frog murmured aloof in the dense thornbrake. Lark and goldfinch sang and turtledove moaned, and about the spring the bees hummed and hovered to and fro. All nature smelled of the opulent summertime, smelled of the season of fruit. Pears lay at our feet, apples on either side, rolling abundantly, and the young branches lay splayed upon the ground because of the weight of their plums.

In such a realm, death has no terror. When Keats says that "I have been half in love with easeful Death," that "Now more than ever seems it rich to die," the statements occur in the poetic context of just such a pastoral evocation:

> I cannot see what flowers are at my feet,
>   Nor what soft incense hangs upon the boughs,
> But, in embalmed darkness, guess each sweet
>   Wherewith the seasonable month endows
> The grass, the thicket, and the fruit-tree wild;
>   White hawthorn, and the pastoral eglantine;
>   Fast fading violets cover'd up in leaves;
>   And mid-May's eldest child,
>   The coming musk-rose, full of dewy wine,
>   The murmurous haunt of flies on summer eves.

Thus, although the pastoral elegy is a funeral poem, it denies, rather than affirms, the reality of death. Funerals themselves, as a matter of fact, are attempts, with their flowers and mourning friends, to pastoralize and socialize the fact of death. Funerals are for the living, not for the dead, and in America at least, are commonly concluded by a feast scarcely distinguishable, in resolute surface gaiety, from a wedding feast. And Spenser, in his *Astrophel*, not only pastoralizes the death of Sidney, but socializes it as well, by calling in a group of pastoral remembrances by various hands, beginning with an effort by Sidney's sister, the Countess of Pembroke. "Hearken, ye gentle shepheards, to my song, / And place my dolefull plaint your plaints emong," says Spenser at the outset, and then begins on his own contribution:

> A gentle shepheard borne in Arcady,
> Of gentlest race that ever shepheard bore,
> About the grassie bancks of Haemony
> Did keepe his sheep, his little stock and store.
> Full carefully he kept them day and night,
> In fairest fields; and Astrophel he hight.

Such artificiality diminishes the fact of death, and the reassuring environment of pastoral renders the fact more bearable.

Milton makes explicit the pastoral alleviation of death. Although *Lycidas*, like the Greek bucolic elegies that were its models, pastorally softens the meaning of death, it then proceeds, unlike those models, to an overt denial of death's reality:

> Weep no more, woeful Shepherds weep no more,
> For *Lycidas* your sorrow is not dead,
> Sunk though he be beneath the wat'ry floor,
> So sinks the day-star in the Ocean bed,
> And yet anon repairs his drooping head,
> And tricks his beams, and with new spangled Ore,
> Flames in the forehead of the morning sky:
> So *Lycidas*, sunk low, but mounted high,
> Through the dear might of him that walk'd the waves,
> Where other groves, and other streams along,
> With *Nectar* pure his oozy Locks he laves,
> And hears the unexpressive nuptial Song,
> In the blest Kingdoms meek of joy and love.
> There entertain him all the Saints above,
> In solemn troops, and sweet Societies
> That sing, and singing in their glory move,
> And wipe the tears for ever from his eyes.

In this version, the pastoral elegy becomes not only a lament for death, but the herald of a new life in paradise. This vision was always implicit in pastoral. Virgil, in his ninth eclogue, conceives Julius Caesar as deified among the stars, and Sannazaro, in the first of his piscatorial eclogues, conceives the drowned Phyllis as either in the high aether or in Elysium. But outside the genre of the pastoral elegy, we can see that this vision was inherent in pastoral evocation generally. Marvell, for instance, whose poetic imagination was so deeply stirred by the pastoral tradition, seems, in *The Garden*, to think of the pastoral environment as a way-station to paradise:

> Here at the Fountains sliding foot,
> Or at some Fruit-trees mossy root,
> Casting the Bodies Vest aside,
> My Soul into the boughs does glide:

> There like a Bird it sits, and sings,
> Then whets, and combs its silver Wings;
> And, till prepar'd for longer flight,
> Waves in its Plumes the various Light.

And this holy waiting—to use Heidegger's term—takes place in the context of a pastoral evocation that in its opulence is much like the vision of Theocritus:

> Ripe Apples drop about my head;
> The Luscious Clusters of the Vine
> Upon my Mouth do crush their Wine;
> The Nectaren, and curious Peach,
> Into my hands themselves do reach;
> Stumbling on Melons, as I pass,
> Insnar'd with Flow'rs, I fall on Grass.

We see in such a description, indeed, that not only is the pastoral realm a way-station to paradise, but that it also prefigures and symbolizes paradise itself. As Marvell makes clear, the difference between his garden, and that "happy Garden-state" of Eden, is only a slight shift of imagination—or none at all.

If the pastoral vision is, in its potentiality and inner logic, a vision of paradise in which death is repudiated, it does not thereby leave behind the concerns of comedy. We realize that the "one feast, one house, one mutual happiness" with which *The Two Gentlemen of Verona* concludes, and which is the typical comic resolution, can serve equally well for the social state of heaven: not only can, but does, in the whole direction of its meaning. For the state of heaven, and the resolution of a comedy, are in all phenomenological aspects interchangeable. Both the general social bearings of comedy and its particular emphasis on marriage are reflected in the paradise Milton depicts in *Lycidas*; the "unexpressive nuptial Song" is heard in "the blest Kingdoms meek of joy and love," which are inhabited by "solemn troops, and sweet Societies." Indeed, because we cannot imagine a state of existence in which we could live without a world around us, heaven is a place. But heaven is also a society, and its state as society takes precedence over its state as place. Simply by consulting our own hopes we realize that what primarily marks the idea of heaven is the anticipation of happy reunion with those we love. "I trust we shall," said Sir Thomas More

on his way to the scaffold, "once in heaven, see each other full merrily, where we shall be sure to live and love together in joyful bliss
eternally."

The alliance of comedy and pastoral realizes what neither mode
could adequately achieve by itself: the representation of paradise. An
alliance is necessary, for such a representation must be conceived simultaneously as happy society and blessed place. All comic and pastoral
meanings converge upon this truth. The coming together of comic
laughter and pastoral in the reclamation of childhood, and the union
of all three in the happiness of play, pass in the words of Plotinus into
a depreciation of the importance of death, and in the words of Plato
into a sacramental activity.

These two opinions, originating outside the Christian tradition, find
confirmation within the Christian tradition. No single idea in Christianity is so important as the conquest of death, and the achievement
of new life in paradise. "If there be no resurrection of the dead," Paul
declared with the most unequivocal seriousness, "then is Christ not
risen: And if Christ be not risen, then is our preaching vain, and your
faith is also vain" (1 Cor. 15:13–14). But the positive content of
Christianity is that Christ has in fact risen, and that heaven and its
joy do exist, to the final discomfiture of death: "Behold, I shew you a
mystery; We shall not all sleep, but we shall all be changed, In a moment, in the twinkling of an eye, at the last trumpet: for the trumpet
shall sound, and the dead shall be raised incorruptible, and we shall be
changed. . . . O death, where is thy sting? O grave, where is thy victory?"

Likewise, Plato's opinion as to the sacramental nature of play, which
is the activity of childhood, finds analogous emphasis within the Christian belief: "But Jesus said, Suffer little children, and forbid them not,
to come unto me: for of such is the kingdom of heaven." (Matt. 19:14).
"Suffer little children to come unto me, and forbid them not: for of
such is the kingdom of God" (Luke 18:16). There seems, indeed, to
be a very deep human connection between play and religion. Lévi-
Strauss, in his study of savage thought, accentuates the connection
even in the most primitive societies:

All games are defined by a set of rules which in practice allow the playing of any number of matches. Ritual, which is also 'played', is, on the
other hand, like a favoured instance of a game. . . . The formal structure
of what might at first sight be taken for a competitive game is in fact
identical with that of a typical ritual . . . in which the initiates get

symbolically killed by the dead whose part is *played* by the initiated; they feign death in order to obtain a further lease of life. In both cases death is brought in only to be duped (*The Savage Mind* [Chicago, 1968], pp. 30, 32).

The analogy of savage play and ritual, with the aim of duping death, is paralleled by the avoidance of death in comedy and the muffling of death in pastoral. In a further statement, Lévi-Strauss describes the relationship between game and ritual in a way that is almost identical with the relationship that obtains between comic plot and comic resolution:

> Games thus appear to have a *disjunctive* effect: they end in the estab-lishment of a difference between individual players or teams where originally there was no indication of inequality. . . . Ritual, on the other hand, is the exact inverse; it *conjoins*, for it brings about a union (one might even say communion in this context) . . . between two initially separate groups . . . (p. 32).

The affinity of play and religion, however, does not indicate that the alliance of pastoral and comedy serves as propaganda for Christianity, or as an explicit theological witness to Christian truth. Nor does it follow that Shakespeare, in projecting his elevated vision of a har-moniously happy society, is thereby a Christian proselyte. His work is assuredly not inimical to Christianity; he may or may not have been a decided Christian in his personal faith. But R. M. Frye, in his *Shakespeare and Christian Doctrine*, has argued at length that al-though Shakespeare demonstrates an educated man's knowledge of Christianity—which in his day was considerably more extensive than it would be now—his plays cannot be considered as vehicles for the conveyance of Christian beliefs. Even if they were such vehicles, the question would still remain as to why they speak to those without such beliefs, in different lands and different times.

To supply an answer, it is necessary to consider both the comic-pastoral alliance and the Christian message as representatives of an-other structure: the structure of hope. To say this is not to say that the Christian message is less important than the structure of hope; or that Paul's anxiety about whether there was or was not in fact a resurrection poses a trivial question. On the contrary, it is a question the answer to which, positive or negative, can fairly be said to make all other possi-bilities insignificant. But because of the conditions of our existence, the positive answer must remain in the area of personal faith, whereas the analysis of the structure of hope reveals that structure phenomeno-logically as a human universal, as something that depends in no way on personal belief or historical accident.

Christian faith is itself a structure of hope, is, as defined by the author of Hebrews, "the substance of things hoped for" (11:1). And modern theology, under the influence of Jürgen Moltmann, is increas-ingly disposed to view the whole of Christianity in the perspective of hope. "Das Christentum," says Moltmann, "ist ganz und gar und nicht nur im Anhang Eschatologie, ist Hoffnung."—Christianity is com-pletely, and not merely as an afterthought, a doctrine of final things; it is hope (*Theologie der Hoffnung* [München, 1964], p. 12).

The structure of hope, however, is best indicated by the phenomeno-logical analysis of futurity in the work of Heidegger, Sartre, and most of all, Jaspers. In these philosophers the question is taken up without reference to Christian belief, and the existential universality and neces-sity of horizons of anticipation, and their corollaries, structures of hope, become impressively apparent. By their analyses we come to see more clearly what in some ways we always knew, that the future exists only as a disposition of the present, as a horizon of the now. When we arrive in time at the future, it has disappeared and become another fleeting now. "So we beat on," writes Scott Fitzgerald, "boats against the cur-rent, borne back ceaselessly into the past." Paradoxically, however, what we expect to be is the largest constituent of what we now are: existence is futurity.

It is one of those truths so profound as to become almost common-place, although for all that attended to only in passing by the demi-urges of our cultural history. But its witness does appear, and in the most diverse contexts of the most dissimilar writers. Dr. Johnson, for instance, insists that "*the present* was never a happy state to any human being; but that, as every part of life, of which we are conscious, was at some point of time a period yet to come, in which felicity was expected, there was some happiness produced by hope." Carlyle states the fact even more inclusively: "It has been well said," he writes in *The French Revolution*, " 'Man is based on Hope; he has properly no other posses-sion but Hope; this habitation of his is named the Place of Hope.' " "Our being's heart and home," declares Wordsworth in an exalted passage, is "With hope . . . hope that can never die, / Effort, and expectation, and desire, / And something evermore about to be." Or, still again, we may note the words of Pascal:

We are never content with the present moment. We anticipate the future, which is so slow in coming, as though to hasten its advance; or we call back the past to check its too rapid flight; so careless that we wander about in times that do not belong to us, and neglect the only time that is ours. . . . The fact is that the present, as a rule, causes us pain. . . . We try to keep it alive by means of the future, and think to order things which are not within our control, against an hour which we have no certainty of ever reaching (*Pensées*, ed. H. F. Stewart [New York, 1950], p. 457).

Human existence thus involves paradoxes of this sort: we are not now, because we live in what is to come, but we are not what is to come, because it is not yet. So Coleridge, looking back over the whole course of his life, feels that "Youth and Hope" are the "twin realities of this phantom world!" (*Table Talk*, 10 July 1834). "Hope alone," urges Moltmann, "is to be called 'realistic,' because it alone takes seriously the possibilities with which all reality is fraught" (*Theologie der Hoffnung*, p. 20).

Accordingly, not only have some theologians found despair—the abandonment of hope—to be the unforgivable sin against the Holy Spirit (Matt. 12:32), but modern psychiatric practice is increasingly aware that mental disease can be described as the destruction, distortion, or repression of an individual's structure of hope. As Erikson says:

You see, hope is a very basic human strength without which we couldn't stay alive, and not something invented by theologians or philosophers. You may remember Spitz's studies in which he shows that children who give up hope because they do not get enough loving and not enough stimulation may literally die. . . . Religions only sanctify what they recognize as given if they concern themselves with hope as a basic human attitude which must be transmitted from parent to child and be restored by prayer. By this I do not mean to imply that the highest Hope is "only" a facsimile of the earliest, but that the whole plan of man's concerns develops in ontogenetic stages. And in this context, hope is the basic ingredient of all strength (Richard I. Evans, *Dialogue with Erik Erikson* [New York, 1969], p. 17).

It is by the light of such human truths that Philip Wheelwright concludes, quite independently of the continental tradition of phenomenological analysis, that "man lives always on the verge, always on the borderland of a something more," and arrives thereby at an absolute formula: "the threshold character of human existence" (*The Burning Fountain* [Bloomington, 1959], pp. 8, 17). Bloch asserts the same truth in the language of phenomenology: "longing, expectation, hope need their own hermeneutic; the glimmer of the before us (*Vor-uns*) demands its specific concept." "The world is a disposition toward something, a tendency to something, a latency of something"—and to retain the wordplay of the original, "*Das Sein das das Bewusstsein bedingt, wie das Bewusstsein, das das Sein bearbeitet, versteht sich letzhin nur aus dem und in dem woher und wonach es tendiert.* Wesen ist nicht Ge-wesenheit; konträr: das Wesen der Welt liegt selber an der Front" (*Das Prinzip Hoffnung* [Frankfurt-am-Main, 1959], I, 5, 17, 18).

The matter is one of profoundest importance, in its own right no less than in its bearing on the semiotics of pastoral comedy. For phenomenological analysis reveals only what all humanity has at some time felt. We live in hope and anticipation. The unattainability of the future makes all turning toward it a turning toward a fiction. But we cannot choose, unless we terminate existence, not to have a future; therefore that fiction is more important than what we carelessly call reality, which is sloughed off and left behind us with each passing moment of life. The representation of the fictive reality for which we hope is a task near the heart of all literary concerns (and pastoral, by the same fact, is seen as one of the most legitimate of the forms such concern can take). As Santayana says,

We can have no pleasure or pain, nor any preference whatsoever, without implicitly setting up a standard of excellence, an ideal of what would satisfy us there. To make these implicit ideals explicit, to catch their hint, to work out their theme, and express clearly to ourselves and to the world what they are demanding in the place of the actual— that is the labour of reason and the task of genius.

The theological idea of paradise, and its fictional co-ordinate, the world of pastoral comedy, are in this apprehension in no way diminished by their artificiality. Indeed, their artificiality is their authentication, for they thereby escape the taint of existence and its disappearance in time. Life in the condition of existence is shot through with the longing of Blake's sunflower:

> Ah Sun-flower! weary of time,
> Who countest the steps of the Sun:
> Seeking after that sweet golden clime
> Where the travellers journey is done.

> Where the Youth pined away with desire,
> And the pale Virgin shrouded in snow:
> Arise from their graves and aspire,
> Where my Sun-flower wishes to go.

The search for a pastoral "sweet golden clime" is not, therefore, restricted to literature; it permeates the activity of men in actual life. The lure of Florida, of California, of the Riviera is a form of pastoral longing. The magnetic attraction of Italy for German intellectuals from Winckelmann to Thomas Mann reflects the power and vitality of the Arcadian vision. Goethe, indeed, who in his *Wilhelm Meister* hails so sweetly "das Land, wo die Zitronen blühn," appends as epigraph to his autobiographical *Italienische Reise* the words, "Auch ich in Arkadien!"

And when, incidentally, T. S. Eliot, in *The Rock*, speaks sadly of "decent godless people," whose "only monument" is "the asphalt road / And a thousand lost golf balls," he uncovers, perhaps unintentionally, another pastoral preoccupation in daily life. In fact, the habit of playing golf on Sunday complements, rather than rejects, the meaning of church on Sunday. The modern golf course is a miniature Arcadia, a land of green grass and gentle streams; a land, moreover, where one plays rather than works. The fanatical devotion to the game of golf, from presidents to paupers, testifies to how much these green plots are cherished. And although nothing else—great buildings, venerable monuments, nature itself—seems proof against real estate developers, road builders, and other eroders of modern life, the golf course often seems miraculously inviolate against the inroads of urban blight. Roads detour around it; buildings do not choke it.

Yet the structure of hope can never really be transformed into an attained present; and its future, however we may wish it otherwise, must remain always a fiction. We may share Wordsworth's plaint:

> Paradise, and groves
> Elysian, Fortunate Fields—like those of old
> Sought in the Atlantic Main—why should they be
> A history only of departed things,
> Or a mere fiction of what never was?

Nonetheless, paradisal hopes, when turned to the real world, demonstrate the strongest kind of resistance to actuality. Indeed, the whole vast literature of utopian projection, which is one of Bloch's chief examples of the structure of hope, confirms what we know—that such hope must be a fiction. The very word Utopia, with its prefix ringing changes upon the Greek *eu* and the Greek *ou*, represents itself simultaneously as "good place" and "no place." Thus it is no accident that the most famous of all utopian projections, Plato's *Republic*, was the production of a man who, by his conception of ὀρέγεσθαι, or longing, fixed his eye more raptly than anyone else upon that which is not but ought to be. And Sir Thomas More, the man who coined the name Utopia, and whose representation of that realm is the most influential in English literature, was a man with gaze unswervingly fixed on the hope of heaven. "I mervail that you, that have been always hitherto taken for so wise a man, will now so play the fool to lie here in this close, filthy prison. . . . And seeing you have at Chelsea a right fair house, your library, your books, your gallery, your garden, your orchard . . . I muse what, a God's name, you mean here still thus fondly to tarry." But More responds: " 'I pray thee, good Mistress Alice, tell me one thing.' 'What is that?' quoth she. 'Is not this house,' quoth he, 'as nigh heaven as my own?' "

It is, accordingly, not surprising that Shakespeare's most explicit utopian projection occurs within the context of one of his most perfectly pastoral projections: the enchanted island of *The Tempest*. There Gonzalo, echoing the words of Montaigne, plans a perfect commonwealth:

> I' th' commonwealth I would by contraries
> Execute all things; for no kind of traffic
> Would I admit; no name of magistrate;
> Letters should not be known; riches, poverty,
> And use of service, none; contract, succession,
> Bourn, bound of land, tilth, vineyard, none;
> No use of metal, corn, or wine, or oil;
> No occupation; all men idle, all;
> And women too, but innocent and pure;
> No sovereignty;— . . .
> All things in common nature should produce
> Without sweat or endeavour. Treason, felony,
> Sword, pike, knife, gun, or need of any engine,
> Would I not have; but nature should bring forth,

> Of its own kind, all foison, all abundance,
> To feed my innocent people. . . .
> I would with such perfection govern, sir,
> T' excel the golden age.
>
> [2.1.141–62]

With the phrase, "the golden age," the hope of Christian heaven and the ultimate pastoral ideal become virtually the same; for the Golden Age, though not associated with Theocritus, is entwined with his tradition. Indeed, Harry Levin's recent *The Myth of the Golden Age in the Renaissance* demonstrates that the fiction of the Golden Age was hardly less current in the Renaissance than was pastoral itself. For the way the matter really stands, as Pope says very simply, is that "Pastoral is an image of what they call the Golden age." Even traditions not strictly pastoral—those of Ovid's *Metamorphoses* and Virgil's *Georgics*—are joined together in a larger conception of pastoral meaning by a common concern for the Golden Age. The *Georgics*, for instance, though like pastoral in their nostalgic evocation of rural landscape, are radically unlike pastoral in their emphasis on the necessity of toil ("labor omnia vicit"—1.145). In the first book, however, Virgil refers to the time before Jove when no tillers subdued the land ("ante Iovem nulli subigebant arva coloni"—1.125) and then, without naming it, proceeds to a description of the Golden Age. And when at the end of the fourth book he summarizes his poem and praises Augustus Caesar as bringing a great future, his translator, Dryden—"entirely in the spirit of Virgil," as a commentator says—added to the strict sense by making the next line read "On the glad earth the golden age renews." For, says the commentator, there "is indeed a prevailing sense in the *Georgics* that the Roman state is moving towards a new Golden Age" (John Chalker, *The English Georgic* [Baltimore, 1969], p. 10).

It is therefore in the largest ramification of pastoral meaning that Charles, in *As You Like It*, describes the forest in these words:

> They say he is already in the Forest of Arden, and a many merry men with him; and there they live like the old Robin Hood of England. They say many young gentlemen flock to him every day, and fleet the time carelessly, as they did in the golden world.
>
> [1.1.105–9]

Now the ideal of the golden world is an avatar of an anthropological phenomenon that Mircea Eliade elucidates as the longing for a past that is thought of as "that great time" ("in illo tempore"). It seems reasonable to ascribe the origin of such a social belief to idealized memories of the absolute security and contentment of earliest childhood. These memories, which exist in the timelessness of the unconscious mind, are, because of their dimness, mistaken as referring to historical time, become socialized by virtue of the fact that almost everyone shares them, and are on that account projected into an ideal of a lost golden age. In any event, the sense of "in illo tempore" emerged into Western literature with Hesiod's postulation of "a golden race" of men. The ideal disseminated itself throughout antiquity until, in Virgil's fourth eclogue, it was shifted from a nostalgia for a happy past to a hope of the future. There the poet speaks of the birth of a child, and forecasts that "a golden race" will spring up throughout the world ("ac toto surget gens aurea mundo").

This so-called "messianic" eclogue was, understandably, taken by later writers to be a prophecy of the birth of Christ. And if they were no doubt wrong from an historical standpoint, they were right from a phenomenological standpoint; for pagan and Christian hopes here come together in their most essential aspects. Moreover Virgil, in transferring the "gens aurea" from the past to the future, brings the conception into specific congruence with the subsequent hope of Christianity, which thinks of heaven as futurity. Actually both conceptions of the golden time, either as in the past, or as in the future, accord with Christian belief, because paradise is a word that Christianity uses not only for heaven but also for the perfection of a past: for the garden of Eden.

Indeed, an ideal world, which is a world of eternal youth, really has no before or after. Only from the standpoint of actual life do before and after have meaning; and actual life is dissipated by time and riddled by paradox. It is this disjunction between the unsatisfactoriness of actual life and the euphoria of an ideal vision that is central to the meaning of pastoral. There is no inconsistency between Blake when he feels that "The Whole Creation Groans to be deliverd" and Blake when he affirms that "The Nature of my Work is Visionary or Imaginative it is an Endeavour to Restore what the Ancients calld the Golden Age." And when Sannazaro turns the pastoral vision inside out, as it were, in the epilogue to his *Arcadia*, he reveals the existential condition of man; it was the need to rectify just such a condition that originally provided the impetus for the vision:

Our Muses are perished; withered are our laurels; ruined is our Parnassus: the woods are all become mute; the valleys and the mountains for sorrow are grown deaf; Nymphs or Satyrs are found no more among the woods: the shepherds have lost their song; the flocks and the herds scarcely find pasture among the meadows and with muddying feet for scorn they roil the crystal springs; nor do they deign any more, seeing themselves to lack milk, to nourish their own offspring. Likewise the beasts abandon their wonted dens; the birds take flight from their sweet nests; the hard and insensate trees cast down their fruits upon the earth before their due maturity; and the tender flowers all together wither away throughout the saddened country-side. The piteous bees within their hives leave to perish unperfected the honey that they had begun. Everything is lost; all hope is vanished; every consolation is dead (*Arcadia & Piscatorial Eclogues*, trans. Ralph Nash [Detroit, 1966], pp. 152–53).

If the rejection of the pastoral vision is equivalent to the vanishing of hope and the death of consolation, the converse is likewise true. In the pastoral ideal of a golden age, hope and consolation find their most benign lodging. As Huizinga says,

No other single illusion has charmed humanity for so long and with such an ever fresh splendor as the illusion of the pining shepherd's pipe and surprised nymphs in rustling woods and murmuring brooks. The concept is very closely akin to that of the golden age, and constantly overlaps it: it is the golden age brought to life (*Men and Ideas*, p. 84).

So, outside the specific confines of the pastoral, Ovid invokes the Golden Age: "Aurea prima sata est aetas. . . . ver erat aeternum . . ." (*Metamorphoses*, 1.89, 107). The Ovidian invocation, however, with its "eternal spring," and flowers that grew without planting, is wholly congruent with the implications of pastoral. The Golden Age is translated ("ver aeternum" becomes "primavera eterna") into explicitly pastoral contexts in Tasso's *Aminta*:

> O bella età de l'oro,
> non già perché di latte
> sen' corse il fiume e stillò mele il bosco;

> O happy Age of Gould; happy houres;
> Not for with milke the rivers ranne
> And hunny dropt from ev'ry tree;
> Nor that the Earth bore fruits, and flowres, . . .

Also by Guarini, in the fourth act of his *Il Pastor Fido*:

> Fair Golden Age! when milk was th' only food, . . .
> Let's hope: our ills have truce till we are hurld
> From that [base present age]

And again in Samuel Daniel's *A Pastoral*:

> O happy golden age,
>   Not for that rivers ran
>   With streams of milk, and honey dropp'd from trees . . .
>   Not for no cold did freeze
>   Nor any cloud beguile
>   Th' eternal-flow'ring spring . . .
> But only for that name . . .
>   Call'd Honor . . .
>   Was not yet vainly found . . .
>   Nor were his hard laws known . . .
>   But golden laws like these
>   Which Nature wrote, "That's lawful which
>   doth please."

In thus spurning the "hard laws" of reality for the "golden laws" of pleasure, the poem chooses Freud's "pleasure principle" as opposed to his "reality principle." But the "pleasure principle" is the instinct of children, and in espousing it rather than the "reality principle" of adult life, the golden age identifies itself as the reconstitution of childhood's happiness. There, interfused with pastoral, it joins with comedy and play to symbolize the hope of that perfect society: paradise.

By weaving together these strands of hope and longing, Shakespeare's pastoral comedy asserts a seriousness as profound, and lays claim to meanings as dear, as any that are achieved by tragedy or indiacted by religion. "The religious life," says Durkheim at the conclusion of his great work, *Les formes élémentaires de la vie religieuse*, is "the eminent form and, as it were, the concentrated expression of the whole collective life. If religion has given birth to all that is essential in society, it is because the idea of society is the soul of religion." This truth, metamorphosed into the playful happiness of dramatic art, encloses the final meanings of Shakespeare's preoccupation with the mixture of comic and pastoral motifs.

Accordingly, in the five readings that now follow, the reciprocity of social and religious concern, though variously realized by the individual requirements of Shakespeare's differing efforts of pastoral-comic representation, reveals itself as the common denominator of the plays' significance.

But the theory of comedy, in its pastoral extension, should not be fitted or harshly imposed upon recalcitrant materials. The following discussions of incident and character and setting strive not toward the illustration of a theory, but simply toward clarification of the plays as unique works of art. The meaning that emerges from the discussions should be nothing other than the understanding of the plays themselves. Yet, stirring through all such understanding—like a solar wind, omnipresent even if undetected except by means of special preparation—are the ideas of hope, joy, and sacred community that constitute the perennial vitality of Shakespeare's pastoral comedy.

II. Full of Dear Guiltiness

The Playfulness of *Love's Labour's Lost*

*T*he setting of *Love's Labour's Lost* is not that of Arcadia. The action occurs in the King of Navarre's park. Such a variation of the pastoral environment is significant for the special kind of playfulness in which the plot revels.

The park, though not Arcadia, is nonetheless truly a pastoral environment. There is no hint of city life within its confines; its inhabitants, particularly those of the subplot, where we might anticipate a world of tradesmen, carpenters, blacksmiths, and other cogs in the economic machine of urban actuality, are singularly free from the necessity of providing for the maintenance of life. Instead, the denizens of the subplot constitute a wonderful array of playful irrelevances, a veritable rout of Comus. There are a braggart warrior (with nothing to fight), a curate (with no souls that require his care), a constable (but no crime), a schoolmaster (but no school), a clown, a page, a forester. At the other end of the social spectrum, there are a king, a princess, and noble lords and ladies: figures exempt from the necessity of work and predisposed toward the happiness of play.

The park, indeed, circumscribes the full range of pastoral hope. "The word 'paradise,'" says Giamatti in *The Earthly Paradise and the Renaissance Epic*, "derives from the Old Persian word *pairidaēza* —formed on *pairi* (around) and *diz* (to mould, to form) which meant the royal park, enclosure, or orchard of the Persian king." Giamatti continues:

The subsequent history of the word has two branches: it becomes the Hebrew *pardēs*. ... The Hebrew word, *pardēs*, meant a park or garden ... [it] referred only to those gardens, forests, or parks in the Old Testament, and maintained the original meaning of *pairidaēza*.

The earliest link between the simple word and the specific place, between garden and the garden of Eden, paradise and the earthly paradise, occurs through the Greek adaptation of *pairidaēza* into *para-*

deisos. The word first occurs in Xenophon and means a royal park. . . . ([Princeton, 1966], pp. 11–12).

Paradeisos thus originally meant "a royal park," and the setting of *Love's Labour's Lost* in the King of Navarre's park can be seen as by-passing the Arcadian mediation in favor of a direct attainment of paradise at the outset.

Such an environment permits the comic action to proceed along unusual lines. First of all, it assures that there will be no serious deviations from the norm, and consequently no heavy burden of comic criticism and social redemption. There can be no real trouble in paradise. An action such as that of *Measure for Measure*, not to speak of *Troilus and Cressida*, would have no integrity in this environment. Here we are far removed from their world of transgression and wrong; and even folly, in this happy place, is a merely nominal conception. Relieved of the burden of using laughter as a form of what Freud called "veiled aggression," the play frolics in an easy merriment matched, in Shakespeare's art, only by that of *A Midsummer-Night's Dream*.

Secondly, as the play is able to present us at its outset with the ideal of happy playfulness that most comedy achieves only at its conclusion, this ideal setting tends, in order to counteract the possibility of mere formlessness, to mold the play. That is, from its paradisal perspective, in the fullness of its frolic, it gives itself rules: it transforms its play into game. By becoming a game, with rules and goals, it guarantees itself as action rather than merely as celebration. And because game is at once an intensely free, and an intensely artificial, human action, the specifically gamelike character of *Love's Labour's Lost* accentuates both its carefreeness and its deliberate artificiality. Since comedy itself tends to be artificial, and even more so does the idea of paradise, this emphasis in no way contradicts the decorum of the comic mode.

The rules of the game are laid down at the beginning:

> That is, to live and study here three years.
> But there are other strict observances,
> As: not to see a woman in that term . . .
> And one day in a week to touch no food.

> [1.1.35–39]

By deciding to see no woman, the men deliberately allow themselves to fall from comic grace, and thereby deliberately fabricate the comic task of the play: the reclamation from deviant bachelorhood to socially acceptable marriage—or the hope of marriage. That this fault, however, is both an artificial fault and a merry one, and one that furthermore will certainly be eradicated, is indicated early on. "O, these are barren tasks, too hard to keep, / Not to see ladies, study, fast, not sleep!" / says Berowne in immediate response to the King's conditions for the game (1.1.47–48). When the King counters that "Your oath is pass'd," Berowne says:

> Let me say no, my liege, an if you please:
> I only swore to study with your Grace,
> And stay here in your court for three years' space.
>
> [1.1.50–52]

Such a statement isolates the central condition—that the men see no women—from the others, and focuses attention upon it as the motive fault of the comedy. And that it is, in its artifice, a playful and insignificant fault is indicated by the words that follow: "You swore to that, Berowne, and to the rest," says Longaville. "By yea and nay, sir, then I swore in jest," replies Berowne, establishing the world of merriment (1.1.54).

That the play not only sports with folly, but with artificial folly, and therefore will sport very lightheartedly, is further indicated by a breaking of the rules simultaneously with their institution. The King, in just the words that would be used by the leader of a game, rebukes Berowne's protests: "Well, sit you out; go home, Berowne; adieu." Berowne, however, affirms his willingness to play: "No, my good lord; I have sworn to stay with you" (1.1.110–11). He then reads the "strictest decrees" set up to enforce the rules:

> "Item. If any man be seen to talk with a woman within the term of three years, he shall endure such public shame as the rest of the court can possibly devise."

> This article, my liege, yourself must break;
> For well you know here comes in embassy
> The French king's daughter, with yourself to speak—
> A maid of grace and complete majesty—
>
> [1.1.128–34]

And to the King's flustered "Why, this was quite forgot. . . . We must of force dispense with this decree; / She must lie here on mere necessity" (1.1.139, 145–46), Berowne provides the reassurance of comic health:

> Necessity will make us all forsworn
> Three thousand times within this three years' space
>
> [1.1.47–48]

And again:

> I'll lay my head to any good man's hat
> These oaths and laws will prove an idle scorn.
>
> [1.1.287–88]

There are thus no real problems, only a game of mock problems. In cheerful symmetry, the action then demands playfulness within playfulness. "But is there no quick recreation granted?" asks Berowne. The King's reply—"Ay, that there is"—introduces the braggart warrior, Don Adriano de Armado, as an object of the laughter of the game's participants:

> How you delight, my lords, I know not, I;
> But I protest I love to hear him lie,
> And I will use him for my minstrelsy.
>
> [1.1.172–74]

And Longaville appends happily:

> Costard the swain and he shall be our sport;
> And so to study three years is but short.
>
> [1.1.177–78]

In so identifying the members of the subplot as objects of recreation for the gaming members of the main plot, the play sets up a relationship between the symmetrically repetitive world of the noblemen (where every action tends to be multiplied by four) and the straggling disarray of the clowns and bumpkins; and at the same time it institutes a kind of Chinese-box motif of happiness within happiness, game within game, pastime within pastime. The rustics' play-within-a-play, the pageant of the Nine Worthies, is the fulfillment of this motif. Likewise, the masked conversation-dance of the noblemen and the ladies reflects the motif of symmetrical play into, as it were, a mirrored infinity of carefreeness. The erstwhile students, now forsworn, resolve "to woo these girls of France," and the King says, "let us devise

/ Some entertainment for them in their tents" (4.3.368–69). Berowne, in an especially sweet evocation of comedy's happiness as filtered through pastoral, then adds:

> In the afternoon
> We will with some strange pastime solace them,
> Such as the shortness of time can shape;
> For revels, dances, masks, and merry hours,
> Forerun fair Love, strewing her way with flowers.
>
> [4.3.372–76]

The Princess, forewarned, says to her ladies, in explicit acceptance of a new game within the game,

> There's no such sport as sport by sport o'erthrown,
> To make theirs ours, and ours none but our own;
> So shall we stay, mocking intended game,
> And they well mock'd depart away with shame.
>
> [5.2.153–56]

The structure of that game within a game unfolds in symmetrical repetitions of language:

> BOYET. What would you with the Princess?
> BEROWNE. Nothing but peace and gentle visitation.
> ROSALINE. What would they, say they?
> BOYET. Nothing but peace and gentle visitation.
> ROSALINE. Why, that they have; and bid them so be gone.
> BOYET. She says you have it, and you may be gone.
> KING. Say to her we have measur'd many miles
> To tread a measure with her on this grass.
> BOYET. They say that they have measur'd many a mile
> To tread a measure with you on this grass.
>
> [5.2.178–87]

Even the intended symmetrical dance of the courtiers is a repetition and playfully distorted reflection of an intended clownish dance of the bumpkins:

> DULL. I'll make one in a dance, or so; or I will play
> On the tabor to the Worthies, and let them dance the hay.
> HOLOFERNES. Most dull, honest Dull! To our sport, away.
>
> [5.1.133–35]

The repetitive symmetries of the language are everywhere inter-twined with similar symmetries of plot. The King's language in broach-ing the nature of the oath taken by the courtiers and himself is expan-sive, lays claim to virtue:

> Navarre shall be the wonder of the world;
> Our court shall be a little Academe,
> Still and comtemplative in living art.
> You three, Berowne, Dumain, and Longaville,
> Have sworn for three years' term to live with me
> My fellow-scholars, and to keep those statutes
> That are recorded in this schedule here.
> Your oaths are pass'd; and now subscribe your names,
> That his own hand may strike his honour down
> That violates the smallest branch herein.
>
> [1.1.12–21]

Such language, and the confidence of virtue that accompanies it, finds a humorously distorted reflection in the pomposity of Don Adriano de Armado: "that unlettered small-knowing soul"; "which, as I remem-ber, hight Costard"; "sorted and consorted, contrary to thy established proclaimed edict and continent canon"; "with a child of our grand-mother Eve, a female; or, for thy more sweet understanding, a woman" (1.1.239–51). The fact that Costard "sorted and consorted" with Jaquenetta and thus broke the rules of the King's game ("It was pro-claimed a year's imprisonment, to be taken with a wench"—1.1.268–69), reiterates the fact that the king has just been forced to break the edict himself by admitting the embassy of the French king's daughter. And just as Don Adriano's hilarious pretense to virtue is deflated by finding that he himself is in love ("Boy, I do love that country girl that I took in the park with the rational hind Costard"—1.2.112–13), so is the King's, by the sight of the Princess of France:

> BOYET. . . . Navarre is infected.
> PRINCESS. With what?
> BOYET. With that which we lovers entitle "affected."
>
> [2.1.229–31]

The occasion of the King's formal revelation of his love is a signal for the play to move into its most elegant sequence of symmetrical repetitions. Berowne enters, with a paper in his hand:

By heaven, I do love; and it hath taught me to rhyme and to be melancholy; and here is part of my rhyme, and here my melancholy. Well, she hath one o' my sonnets already; the clown bore it, the fool sent it, and the lady hath it: sweet clown, sweeter fool, sweetest lady! By the world, I would not care a pin if the other three were in. Here comes one with a paper; God give him grace to groan!

Berowne then stands aside; the King enters, obligingly groans: "Ay me!" Berowne, hiding, says to the audience:

Shot, by heaven! Proceed, sweet Cupid; thou hast thump'd him with thy bird-bolt under the left pap. In faith, secrets!

The King then reads a love poem from the paper; next he drops the paper, hears someone coming, and also hides himself: "What Longaville, and reading! Listen, ear." Still hidden, Berowne says:

Now, in thy likeness, one more fool appear!
LONGAVILLE. Ay me, I am forsworn! . . .
KING. In love, I hope; sweet fellowship in shame!
BEROWNE. One drunkard loves another of the name.
LONGAVILLE. Am I the first that have been perjur'd so?

Then Longaville, after reading his own poem, also steps aside as Dumain enters, and amid a barrage of asides from the hidden commentators, reads his own poetic confession of love. At its conclusion he signals the reversal of the fourfold figure of confession and concealment:

O, would the King, Berowne, and Longaville,
Were lovers too! Ill, to example ill,
Would from my forehead wipe a perjur'd note;
For none offend where all alike do dote.

[4.3.10–20, 40–47, 119–22]

So each lover emerges in reverse order, assumes a chiding air of virtue, is discomfited by the next lover, until Berowne, the first to hide, is at last exposed also, and admits his participation in the "sweet fellowship in shame":

BEROWNE. Guilty, my lord, guilty! I confess, I confess.
KING. What?

> BEROWNE. That you three fools lack'd me fool to
> make up the mess;
> He, he, and you—and you, my liege!—and I
> Are pick-purses in love, and we deserve to die.
>
> [4.3.201–5]

In such a series of symmetrical figures, we realize the similarity of this playful action to the formality of dance, and likewise to the formality of game. Bergson, speaking not of this drama but of comedy as such, supplies pertinent commentary:

Life presents itself to us as evolution in time and complexity in space. . . . A continual change of aspect, the irreversibility of the order of phenomena, the perfect individuality of a perfectly self-contained series: such, then, are the outward characteristics . . . which distinguish the living from the merely mechanical. Let us take the counterpart of each of these: we shall obtain three processes which might be called *repetition, inversion,* and *reciprocal interference of series.* Now, it is easy to see that these are also the methods of light comedy, and that no others are possible.

As a matter of fact, we could discover them . . . *a fortiori* in the children's games, the mechanism of which they reproduce.

Thus Berowne says, when the King and Longaville also hide themselves, " 'All hid, all hid'—an old infant play" (4.3.74).

This elegant process of repetition serves, however, not only to emphasize the gamelike nature of the action, but also to substitute society for the individual. As Dumain says, "none offend where all alike do dote." Indeed, one of the play's frolicsome sorties is to identify what is in fact healthy from a social standpoint (the affections of the sexes) as, in the artificial rules of the King's game, socially reprehensible or deviant ("... your Grace is perjur'd much, / Full of dear guiltiness"— 5.2.778–79). But the absurdity of the bookish vow is highlighted from the first. As Berowne says,

> Study is like the heaven's glorious sun,
> That will not be deep-search'd with saucy looks;
> Small have continual plodders ever won,
> Save base authority from others' books.
>
> [1.1.84–87]

And the King, by his reply to such reasoning, validates the adequacy of the courtiers' learning as it stands: "How well he's read, to reason against reading!" (1.1.94). "Navarre and his book-men," "the Prince and his book-mates"—such humorously contemptuous phrases by the Princess (2.1.226, 4.1.93) indicate the ludicrousness of the role initially assumed by the courtiers, who must be transformed by the action of the play into "affection's men-at-arms" (4.3.286).

The process of socialization is simultaneously a process of humiliation: the courtiers are drawn into a "sweet fellowship in shame." Indeed, the humbling of the pretense to individuality, and its potentially tragic ramifications, is an especially labyrinthine course of the play's action. Two possibilities of tragic individuality threaten the comic paradise: heroic action that might lead to death; romantic love that might become tragic. Both are laughingly disarmed.

The possibility that the dance of courtship might lead to a tragic love is nullified by both the language and the action of the play. The "civil war of wits" between the women and the men, especially between Berowne and Rosaline, which prefigures the wit combats of Beatrice and Benedick in *Much Ado*, serves like them to undercut the plausibility of romantic love, to dry up, as it were, the moisture of emotion. Romantic love is constantly mocked:

> PRINCESS. But, Katharine, what was sent to you
> from fair Dumain?
> KATHARINE. Madam, this glove.
> PRINCESS. Did he not send you twain?
> KATHARINE. Yes, madam; and, moreover,
> Some thousand verses of a faithful lover;
> A huge translation of hypocrisy,
> Vilely compil'd, profound simplicity.
> MARIA. This, and these pearl, to me sent Longaville;
> The letter is too long by half a mile. . . .
> PRINCESS. We are wise girls to mock our lovers so.
> ROSALINE. They are worse fools to purchase mocking so.
> That same Berowne I'll torture ere I go.
> O that I knew he were but in by th' week!
> How I would make him fawn, and beg, and seek,
> And wait the season, and observe the times,
> And spend his prodigal wits in bootless rhymes. . . .
> PRINCESS. None are so surely caught, when they
> are catch'd,
> As wit turn'd fool. . . .
>
> [5.2.47–70]

Such verbal rebukes to romantic love's ideal of the unworldly special-
ness of lovers are teasingly augmented in the action of the play:

> PRINCESS.   The gallants shall be task'd,
> For, ladies, we will every one be mask'd;
> And not a man of them shall have the grace,
> Despite of suit, to see a lady's face.
> Hold, Rosaline, this favour thou shalt wear,
> And then the King will court thee for his dear;
> Hold, take thou this, my sweet, and give me thine,
> So shall Berowne take me for Rosaline.
> And change your favours too; so shall your loves
> Woo contrary, deceiv'd by these removes.
>
> [5.2.126–35]

As the courtiers attempt the language of romantic love, therefore, their
attempts are made ridiculous by the falseness of their objects. The
audience, meanwhile, knowing that they "woo contrary, deceiv'd by
these removes," basks in the superiority of true knowledge: romantic
love is an illusion; marriage alone is real, and marriage is a social, not an
individual, affirmation. The effect of the deception is acknowledged
by Berowne: "By heaven, all dry-beaten with pure scoff!" (5.2.263),
and the ladies, after the humiliated courtiers have departed, merrily
emphasize the meaning of the rebuke:

> ROSALINE.   The King is my love sworn.
> PRINCESS. And quick Berowne hath plighted faith to me.
> KATHARINE. And Longaville was for my service born.
> MARIA. Dumain is mine, as sure as bark on tree.
> BOYET. Madam, and pretty mistresses, give ear:
> Immediately they will again be here
> In their own shapes; for it can never be
> They will digest this harsh indignity.
>
> [5.2.282–89]

But indignity, if not harsh at least playfully thorough, is what the
courtiers must indeed digest; and their indignity is at once a lowering
of their individual self-esteem and a denigration of the meaning of
tragic love. Berowne exchanges the heroic expansion of the King's
play-opening language for a language of rueful diminution:

And I, forsooth, in love; I, that have been
  love's whip;
A very beadle to a humorous sigh;
A critic, nay, a night-watch constable;
A domineering pedant o'er the boy, . . .
This senior-junior, giant-dwarf, Dan Cupid; . . .
Dread prince of plackets, king of codpieces, . . .
And I to be a corporal of his field,
And wear his colours like a tumbler's hoop!
What! I love, I sue, I seek a wife—
A woman, that is like a German clock,
Still a-repairing, ever out of frame,
And never going aright. . . .
Nay, to be perjur'd, which is worst of all;
And, among three, to love the worst of all,
A whitely wanton with a velvet brow,
With two pitch balls stuck in her face for eyes;
Ay, and, by heaven, one that will do the deed,
Though Argus were her eunuch and her guard. . . .
Well, I will love, write, sigh, pray, sue, and groan:
Some men must love my lady, and some Joan.

[3.1.164–95]

As romantic love's claim to a transcending dignity is thus lowered into the rueful commonplace of general human affections, so too the elevation of the courtiers as possible heroes is lowered into a children's game of mock warfare. At the beginning of the play the King activates the heroic potential:

Therefore, brave conquerors—for so you are
That war against your own affections
And the huge army of the world's desires—

[1.1.8–10]

The antisocial stand, presented in the image of heroic warfare, is deflected into a "civil war of wits" whereby the courtiers become "affection's men-at-arms." The language of warfare is derisively applied to the situation of courtship, and accordingly denatured:

KING. Saint Cupid, then! and, soldiers, to the field!
BEROWNE. Advance your standards, and upon them, lords;

> Pell-mell, down with them! But be first advis'd,
> In conflict, that you get the sun of them.

[4.3.362–65]

Such a transformation of warfare's threat into the encounters of the sexes (including the change of the military "get the sun" to its punning sexual meaning, and also Berowne's earlier punning change from tragedy to sexuality in "we deserve to die") echoes a persistent comic tradition. Thus, for example, Ralph Roister-Doister's courtship of Dame Custance erupts not only into the language of warfare, but actually into a wild and hilarious melee, in which, predictably, the females rout the males, and the miles gloriosus is humiliated. The situation in this play is too sophisticated for the crudeness of such physical combat, but the language frolics as warfare's terror is made harmless by sex:

> BOYET. Prepare, madam, prepare!
> Arm, wenches, arm! Encounters mounted are
> Against your peace. Love doth approach disguis'd,
> Armed in arguments; you'll be surpris'd.
> Muster your wits; stand in your own defence;
> Or hide your heads like cowards, and fly hence.

[5.2.81–86]

One of the most persistent motifs in *Love's Labour's Lost* is, indeed, the ridicule of all heroism. Heroism implies the existence of danger; in paradise there can be no real threat of danger, and consequently no need for heroism. As Ovid says of the golden age, "sine militis usu / mollia securae peragebant otia gentes"—"nations, secure, without need for armed men, passed their time in gentle ease" (*Metamorphoses*, 1.99–100). If heroism does exist in such a place, a disquieting possibility also exists. So not only is the language of heroism disarmed by the situation of courtship, but it is also discharged into the world of rustics and fools. Such is a major significance of the bumpkins' pageant of the Nine Worthies. The discrepancy between the invocation of heroic figures of history and legend, and the clownish figures who act the roles, displaces heroism into the artificiality, and the ludicrousness, of the play-within-a-play. The bumpkins' parody of the heroic pointedly reflects the humiliation of the courtiers. As Costard departs to bid the rustics prepare, the King says, "Berowne, they will shame us; let them not approach." But Berowne replies, "We are shame-proof, my lord and 'tis some policy / To have one show worse than the King's and his company" (5.2.509–11). And the bungling of the skit, together with the comments of its noble audience, dissolves the threat of tragic heroism in communal laughter:

> DUMAIN. Most rare Pompey!
> BOYET. Renowned Pompey!
> BEROWNE. Greater than Great! Great, great,
> great Pompey! Pompey the Huge!
> DUMAIN. Hector trembles.
> BEROWNE. Pompey is moved. . . .
> DUMAIN. Hector will challenge him. . . .
> ARMADO. By the North Pole, I do challenge thee.
> COSTARD. I will not fight with a pole, like a
> Northren man; I'll slash. . . .
> DUMAIN. Room for the incensed Worthies!
>
> [5.2.671–85]

Costard's threat to "slash" makes him share in the ritualistic harmlessness of the "Bold Slasher" who appears in English folk play variants. In a situation where Judas Maccabaeus, Hector of Troy, Alexander the Great, Pompey the Great, and Hercules are represented by "the pedant, the braggart, the hedge-priest, the fool, and the boy" (5.2.538–39), the realm of isolation and death in which a true hero moves is transformed into the paradoxical security of the happy group.

Even when, at the end of the play, death does appear, it serves, again paradoxically, to emphasize the ease of the paradisal enclosure.* When the messenger enters, his woeful news is juxtaposed against the lightness of the action within the park:

> PRINCESS. Welcome Marcade;
> But that thou interruptest our merriment.
> MARCADE. I am sorry, madam; for the news I bring
> Is heavy in my tongue. The King your father—

* I maintain this opinion despite the established acting tradition by which Marcade's entrance is given spectacular emphasis (see, e.g., Granville-Barker, *Prefaces to Shakespeare* [Princeton, 1959], 2:426), and despite the equally established critical tradition that sees it as altering the whole tone of the play (e.g., Cyrus Hoy, "*Love's Labour's Lost* and the Nature of Comedy," *Shakespeare Quarterly* 13 [1962]: 38–39).

PRINCESS. Dead, for my life!
MARCADE. Even so; my tale is told.

[5.2.704–9]

Only in the world outside the park does death hold sway; we cannot mourn the King of France, for within the world of the park and the confines of the play he has never existed. His reported death, indeed, serves within the play merely to justify the teasing title, *Love's Labour's Lost*. For the lovers have broken their oaths—however injudiciously given—and must be punished for their "dear guiltiness." Just as the guiltiness is only formal, however, so too is the punishment. To the King's impassioned suit to "Grant us your loves," the Princess responds with a conditional acceptance:

> . . . go with speed
> To some forlorn and naked hermitage,
> Remote from all the pleasures of the world;
> There stay until the twelve celestial signs
> Have brought about the annual reckoning.
> If this austere insociable life
> Change not your offer made in heat of blood . . .
> Then, at the expiration of the year. . . .
> I will be thine. . . .

[5.2.782–95]

The year's delay (which punishes in the same coin as that of the original vows) is, however, only apparently the result of the lovers' perjury; it is really necessary as mourning time for the death of the Princess's father. Until the instant of the lovers' return from their year of exile, the Princess will shut

> My woeful self up in a mournful house,
> Raining the tears of lamentation
> For the remembrance of my father's death.

[5.2.796–98]

Thus even death is made part of the game. And the delay in a sense makes the victory of happiness yet sweeter:

> BEROWNE. Our wooing doth not end like an old play:
> Jack hath not Jill. These ladies' courtesy
> Might well have made our sport a comedy.

KING. Come, sir, it wants a twelvemonth and a day,
And then 'twill end.
BEROWNE. That's too long for a play.

[5.2.862–66]

So the world of the park is proof against death and in no need of heroism. The dissolution of the heroic standard melts all figures into the
same common pot, and the bumpkins' parody of the heroism of the
Nine Worthies is prefigured in the words of Berowne, as he surveys
the perjur'd bookmen and confessed lovers:

O me, with what strict patience have I sat,
To see a king transformed to a gnat!
To see great Hercules whipping a gig,
And profound Solomon to tune a jig,
And Nestor play at push-pin with the boys,
And critic Timon laugh at idle toys!

[4.3.161–66]

The repudiation of the heroic not only accords with the task of
Love's Labour's Lost as comedy; it also accords with a larger meaning
of the pastoral vision. The King opens the play with an invocation, in
the heroic-romantic language of Spenser, of "fame" and "honour":

Let fame, that all hunt after in their lives
Live regist'red upon our brazen tombs,
And then grace us in the disgrace of death;
When, spite of cormorant devouring Time,
Th' endeavour of this present breath may buy
That honour which shall bate his scythe's keen edge,
And make us heirs of all eternity.

[1.1.1–7]

It is the style achieved by Spenser, but also, and particularly in its apprehension of the threat of time, a style that recalls the sweetness of
Shakespeare's tragic sonnets in celebration of love; and it is therefore
a style that implies events alien to the pastoral paradise. The idea of
"fame" is alien to the concept of happy play for its own sake. As Milton
says, the spur of fame tends to counteract the reality of pastoral play:

Were it not better done as others use,
To sport with *Amaryllis* in the shade,
Or with the tangles of *Neaera's* hair?

> *Fame* is the spur that the clear spirit doth raise
> (That last infirmity of Noble mind)
> To scorn delights, and live laborious days, . . .

Still more specifically, the word "honour" represents the chief of all
threats to pastoral bliss. It is the absence of "honour," even more than
the presence of honeyed breezes and green fields, that defines the
golden age as sung by Daniel; or by Tasso, where honor ("onor") is
"quel vano / nome senza soggetto"—that empty name without a substance (*Aminta*, 1.2.669–73). "Honour," indeed, despite C. B. Wat-
son's unsatisfactory awareness of the fact, is a word often used equivocally in Shakespeare, as in its Machiavellian meanings in *Antony and
Cleopatra*, or its sardonic rejection in Falstaff's catechism. In *Love's Labour's Lost*, however, it becomes the sign of the absolutely alien; to
restore the golden age the play must evict honor. And the play does so.
It is specifically the courtiers' "honour" that is taken upon their oaths:

> Your oaths are pass'd; and now subscribe your names,
> That his own hand may strike his honour down
> That violates the smallest branch herein.
>
> $\qquad\qquad\qquad\qquad\qquad$ [1.1.19–21]

But as Berowne later sums up the matter, the oath and the "honour"
for which it stands are alien:

> Let us once lose our oaths to find ourselves,
> Or else we lose ourselves to keep our oaths.
>
> $\qquad\qquad\qquad\qquad\qquad$ [4.3.357–58]

And to find themselves is also to find paradise. "What fool is not so
wise," writes Longaville, "To lose an oath to win a paradise?" (4.3.68–
69). The King, mocking him, thereby emphasizes the exchange: "You
would for paradise break faith and troth" (4.3.139).

The eviction of honor, and the rejection of the heroic, represent the
main function of the chief figure of the subplot, Don Adriano de
Armado. Don Adriano is ostensibly the butt of the courtiers' humor:

> Costard the swain and he shall be our sport;
> And so to study three years is but short.
>
> $\qquad\qquad\qquad\qquad\qquad$ [1.1.177–78]

He is also specifically indicated as a figure ludicrously compatible with the motifs of nobility (with its implication of "honour") and the game:

> MOTH. You are a gentleman and a gamester, sir.
> ARMADO. I confess both; they are both the varnish
> of a complete man.
>
> [1.2.42–43]

His name indicates his character type: the braggart warrior. With the actual threat of the Spanish armada so recent in Elizabethan minds, a "traveller of Spain" (1.1.161) named Armado provided associations of the utmost reality, associations too of extreme foreboding. Don Adriano, however, as a miles gloriosus should, focuses not only emotions of apprehension, but emotions of security and superiority as well. Indeed, because the fearsome threat of the Spanish armada could be recalled in the secure knowledge of English superiority and of God's special favor, Don Adriano participates in the consequent wave of well-being as fully as he does in the previous threat. As Boyet says, "This Armado is a Spaniard, that keeps here in court; / A phantasime, a Monarcho, and one that makes sport / To the Prince and his book-mates" (4.1.91–93).

In any event, a miles gloriosus in a pastoral environment, when compared to, say, a real warrior such as Marlowe's Tamburlaine, is a house cat to a tiger. Don Adriano's pastoral progenitor, Lyly's Sir Tophas, shows how completely nominal the braggart's threat must be to a society fully protected by the pastoral environment:

> SAMIAS. Sir Tophas, spare us.
> TOPHAS. You shall live: you, Samias, because you are little; you, Dares, because you are no bigger; and both of you, because you are but two; for commonly I kill by the dozen, and have for every particular adversary a peculiar weapon.
> SAMIAS. May we know the use, for our better skill in war?
> TOPHAS. You shall. Here is a bird-bolt for the ugly beast the blackbird.
> DARES. A cruel sight.
> TOPHAS. Here is the musket for the untamed or, as the vulgar sort term it, the wild mallard.

SAMIAS. O desperate attempt! . . .

TOPHAS. Here is a spear and shield, and both necessary, the one to conquer, the other to subdue or overcome the terrible trout. . . .

SAMIAS. O wonderful war! [*aside*] Dares, didst thou ever hear such a dolt?

[*Endymion*, 1.3.78–104]

Don Adriano's threat, however, is ridiculed not so much in ludicrous physical encounters, as in pointless verbal expenditures. As the King says, he is

A man in all the world's new fashion planted,
That hath a mint of phrases in his brain;
One who the music of his own vain tongue
Doth ravish like enchanting harmony;

[1.1.162–65]

And Berowne concurs:

Armado is a most illustrious wight,
A man of fire-new words, fashion's own knight.

[1.1.175–76]

Inasmuch as a threat of action usually precedes action, the *miles gloriosus* was traditionally represented as a man who verbally vaunted, but then did not act. This intrinsic implication of his character is, in Don Adriano, heightened, both by removing entirely the object of expected action, and by making the boasting ever more prolix and fanciful. Don Adriano becomes not a threat but "a plume of feathers," "a vane," "a weathercock" (4.1.87–88). The rush of verbosity is, wickedly, both a testimonial within the play to Don Adriano's harmless but ludicrous inflation and at the same time a parody of Lyly's euphuism: "So it is," writes Armado,

besieged with sable-coloured melancholy, I did commend the black oppressing humour to the most wholesome physic of thy health-giving air; and, as I am a gentleman, betook myself to walk. The time When? About the sixth hour; when beasts most graze, birds best peck, and men sit down to that nourishment which is called supper. So much for the time When. Now for the ground Which? which, I mean, I walk'd upon; it is ycleped thy park. Then for the place Where? where, I mean, I did encounter that obscene and most prepost'rous event that draweth from my snow-white pen the ebon-coloured ink which here thou viewest, beholdest, surveyest, or seest. But to the place Where? It standeth north-north-east and by east from the west corner of thy curious-knotted garden.

[1.1.225–36]

Armado's inane precision mocks that "logicality" that Jonas Barish has elucidated as "the basic principle of Lyly's style" ("The Prose Style of John Lyly," *ELH* 23 [1956]: 27). A random sample of Lyly's style reveals how cleverly Shakespeare has caught its tone in other respects:

> For as the bee that gathereth honey out of the weed, when she espieth the fair flower flieth to the sweetest; or as the kind span-iel, though he hunt after birds, yet forsakes them to retrieve the partridge; or as we commonly feed on beef hungerly at the first, yet, seeing the quail more dainty, change our diet: so I, although I love Philautus for his good properties, yet, seeing Euphues to excel him, I ought by nature to like him better. By so much the more therefore my change is to be excused, by how much the more my choice is excellent; and by so much the less I am to be condemned, by how much the more Euphues is to be commended. Is not the diamond of more valew than the ruby bicause he is of more virtue? Is not the emerald preferred before the sapphire for his wonderful property? Is not Euphues more praiseworthy than Philautus, being more witty?

In Armado we sense the exaggeration that gives point to the caricature, while recognizing that the balanced clauses, repeated phrase patterns, invidious comparisons, and festooned rhetorical questions are a parody of Lyly (for a survey of the "restricted number of figures"—eight of them—that are the characteristic elements of euphuism, see G. K. Hunter, *John Lyly: The Humanist as Courtier* [Cambridge, Mass., 1962], p. 265):

> By heaven, that thou art fair is most infallible; true that thou art beauteous; truth itself that thou art lovely. More fairer than fair, beautiful than beauteous, truer than truth itself, have commiseration on thy heroical vassal. The magnanimous and

most illustrate king Cophetua set eye upon the pernicious and indubitate beggar Zenelophon; and he it was that might rightly say, "Veni, vidi, vici"; which to annothanize in the vulgar,—O base and obscure vulgar!—videlicet, He came, saw, and overcame. He came, one; saw, two; overcame, three. Who came?—the king. Why did he come?—to see. Why did he see?—to overcome. To whom came he?—to the beggar. What saw he?—the beggar. Who overcame he?—the beggar. . . .

[4.1.60–71]

The character of Armado, in thus reaching out of the play to parody the style of Lyly (and sometimes perhaps that of others), and to parody the threat of the Spanish armada, represents what is an undoubted, although not always clearly identifiable, tendency of *Love's Labour's Lost* to engage in topical allusions. The awareness of the existence of these references has resulted in numerous attempts, some convincing, others less so, to isolate them. For instance, it seems not improbable that *"if the latter half of 1592"* is the date of Shakespeare's first draft of the play, then "he may have wished to incorporate in it certain aspects of the Harvey-Nashe controversy" (W. Schrickx, *Shakespeare's Early Contemporaries; the Background of the Harvey-Nashe Polemic and* Love's Labour's Lost [Antwerp, 1956], p. 246). As David Bevington says, "*Love's Labor's Lost* has exercised the ingenuity of investigators more than any other of Shakespeare's early plays, partly because its names of Navarre (Henry IV), Berowne (Biron, Henry IV's general), Dumaine (Du Mayenne, brother of the Guise), Longaville (Longueville, Governor of Normandy), and perhaps Armado (Armada) and Moth (Marquis de la Mothe, Henry's amiable diplomat) were unquestionably names in the news during the early 1590's" (*Tudor Drama and Politics; A Critical Approach to Topical Meaning* [Cambridge, Mass., 1968], p. 15).

In this connection, three points should be made. First of all, topical references are not alien to the comic spirit. On the contrary, they occur frequently, as in all the monologues by nightclub entertainers that depend upon the audience's knowledge of ephemeral, usually political, events. It is easy to call to mind popular comic entertainers who build entire careers upon this one device. Secondly, topical reference is not alien to pastoral either. In fact, one use of the pastoral, from Theocritus and Virgil through Spenser and Milton, was the deliberate masked presentation of people or events from actual life, sometimes, especially in the *Shepheardes Calendar* and *Lycidas*, with the object of satirizing abuses. As Spenser's E. K. says, the pastoral eclogue can "be mixed with some Satyrical bitternesse." Puttenham, indeed, believed that the form was originated so as "under the vaile of homely persons and in rude speeches to insinuate and glaunce at greater matters, and such as perchaunce had not bene safe to have beene disclosed in any other sort."

These two points having been noted, however, it remains to modify them by a third. Except for the incorporation of the threat of the Spanish armada into the name Armado, probably no single one of these topical references need be identified today. The critic is not obliged to become, in Ben Jonson's words, a "state decipherer, or politic picklock of the scene, so solemnly ridiculous as to search out who was meant" by the various characters of this or other plays. Moreover, as has recently been urged in another context, "the trouble with political allegory is that it soon loses its effectiveness. The hidden secret of 1590 may need no concealment and may have become irrelevant by 1620 and certainly by 1960. The more contemporary a poet makes his political allegory, the less interesting it becomes for succeeding generations" (Michael Murrin, *The Veil of Allegory* [Chicago, 1969], p. 118). We can be content with knowing that the comedy's playfulness appealed to the social consciousness of its original audience—or of certain privileged members of that audience. But each society has its own ephemera; and the true meaning of *Love's Labour's Lost* is intrinsic, not extrinsic. The extrinsic references constitute a kind of corona of mask and game. Their function was, by an immediate appeal to the existing social sense of the audience of the 1590s, to reinforce the social sense set up in the play. All comedy is able to avail itself of such extrinsic assistance; no comedy that aspires to more than an ephemeral summoning of social awareness can thereby rest content.

Accordingly, it really makes little difference whether, as Bradbrook and others contend, *Love's Labour's Lost* is an account of the School of Night, with Armado as Sir Walter Raleigh. Nor does it make much difference, even if it were true, whether, as Frances Yates would have it, Berowne's "name and some of his characteristics . . . were deliberately meant to recall [Giordano] Bruno to the audience" (*A Study of Love's Labour's Lost* [Cambridge, 1936], p. 127). The fictional pedant Holofernes may well have mocked the actual pedant Gabriel

Harvey (or Florio, or Harriot); but the humor resides in the type, not in the man: we all know our own pedants.

What does make a difference is that we should not miss the forest in our zeal to identify the trees. It is important to see this comedy in all its vernal wonder, to experience it as a curious-knotted frolic at heaven's gate. The Holofernes-like pursuit of topical meaning largely accounts for the fact that, until recently, *Love's Labour's Lost* has been spectacularly misunderstood, and by critics who in other moments rendered happier judgments. For Dryden, it was one of those plays "so *meanly* written that the comedy neither caused your mirth, nor the serious part your concernment." Dr. Johnson, who, as both *Rambler* 36–37 and his insensitivity to *Lycidas* show, was not sympathetic to the meanings enclosed in pastoral, said that "in this play, which all the editors have concurred to censure, and some have rejected as unworthy of our poet, it must be confessed that there are many passages mean, childish and vulgar. . . ." And Hazlitt achieved the nadir of stultification with his opinion that "If we were to part with any of the author's comedies, it should be this."

It is, however, neither to acquiesce in such dismal misconceptions, nor to become involved in the vain pursuit of receding topicalities, to be aware that a large function of the play's language is to parody literary modes of the day. The modes thus parodied have become, on their own terms, a part of our heritage, and they thereby accompany those intrinsic meanings of the play that exist not as social ephemera but as artistic permanence.

The recognition of this element of parody in Don Adriano's language therefore gives an added dimension to the comedy's playfulness. For Don Adriano is the chief link between the subplot and the main plot. His consummate foolishness warrants him an honored place in the rout of bumpkins, whilst the fact that he is not only a "gentleman and gamester," but a grandee of Spain, provides him a place in the society of noblemen. His euphuistic flow, accordingly, mediates between the linguistic foolishness of the bumpkins, and the linguistic games of the noblemen.

The play, indeed, constitutes on one level "a great feast of languages," to use Moth's description of Holofernes, Sir Nathaniel, and Armado (5.1.33). As Dover Wilson says, "of all the games played with the English tongue in the theatre of the age, *Love's Labour's Lost* was the most zestful, and must have seemed to contemporaries the most fascinating" (*Shakespeare's Happy Comedies* [London, 1962], p. 61). Without any certainty that all modes are identifiable, it is possible to experience at least two besides Don Adriano's "mint of phrases." There is an almost perfect imitation (achieved also, in a more serious context, in Shakespeare's Sonnet 106) of the Spenserian reverberation of *The Faery Queene*:

> This child of fancy, that Armado hight,
> For interim to our studies shall relate,
> In high-born words, the worth of many a knight
> From tawny Spain lost in the world's debate.
>
> [1.1.168–71]

And there is an equally exact parody of the Marlovian sensuality of *Dido* and the Marlovian exuberance of *Tamburlaine*:

> Love's feeling is more soft and sensible
> Than are the tender horns of cockled snails;
> Love's tongue proves dainty Bacchus gross in taste.
> For valour, is not Love a Hercules,
> Still climbing trees in the Hesperides?
>
> [4.3.333–37]

The echo of Marlowe's "Still climbing after knowledge infinite" in the subtly distorted "Still climbing trees in the Hesperides" achieves the elegance proper to the linguistic games of the noblemen.

Such elegance would not be proper with the characters of the subplot, and their linguistic foolery is accordingly bumpkin-broad. The malapropistic delights of Dogberry are prefigured in the Stygian opaqueness of Dull: "I myself reprehend his own person" (1.1.181); "the collusion holds in the exchange" (4.2.40–41). The macaronic nonlanguage of Holofernes teasingly complements the Lyly-parody of Armado by a parody of Lyly's grandfather, the author of the famous Latin grammar used by schoolboys:

> The deer was, as you know, sanguis, in blood; ripe as the pomewater, who now hangeth like a jewel in the ear of caelo, the sky, the welkin, the heaven; and anon falleth like a crab on the face of terra, the soil, the land, the earth.
>
> [4.2.3–6]

The Latinate pedantry of Holofernes interweaves itself with the malapropistic stupidity of Dull:

> NATHANIEL. Truly, Master Holofernes, the epithets are sweetly
> varied, like a scholar at the least; but, sir, I assure ye it was a
> buck of the first head.
> HOLOFERNES. Sir Nathaniel, *haud credo* [I don't believe it].
> DULL. 'Twas not a *haud credo*; 'twas a pricket [buck of the sec-
> ond year].
>
> [4.2.7–11]

And at the opening of the Fifth Act, members of the subplot come
together in a linguistic Babel that must be relished in all its voices:

> HOLOFERNES. *Satis quod sufficit.*
> NATHANIEL. I praise God for you, sir. Your reasons at dinner
> have been sharp and sententious; pleasant without scurrility,
> witty without affection, audacious without impudency, learned
> without opinion, and strange without heresy. I did converse
> this *quondam* day with a companion of the King's, who is
> intituled, nominated, or called, Don Adriano de Armado.
> HOLOFERNES. *Novi hominem tanquam te.* His humour is lofty,
> his discourse peremptory, his tongue filed, his eye ambitious, his
> gait majestical, and his general behaviour vain, ridiculous, and
> thrasonical. He is too picked, too spruce, too affected, too odd,
> as it were, too peregrinate, as I may call it.
> NATHANIEL. A most singular and choice epithet.
> HOLOFERNES. He draweth out the thread of his verbosity finer
> than the staple of his argument. I abhor . . . such rackers of
> orthography, as to speak "dout" fine, when he should say
> "doubt"; "det" when he should pronounce "debt";—d, e, b, t,
> not d, e, t. He clepeth a calf "cauf"; half, "hauf"; neighbour
> *vocatur* "nebour"; "neigh" abbreviated "ne". . . .
> NATHANIEL. *Laus Deo, bone intelligo.*
> HOLOFERNES. "Bone"?—"bone" for "bene." Priscian a little
> scratch'd; 'twill serve.
> *Enter Armado, Moth and Costard.*
> NATHANIEL. *Videsne quis venit?*
> HOLOFERNES. *Video, et gaudeo.* . . .
> ARMADO. Men of peace, well encount'red.

HOLOFERNES. Most military sir, salutation.
MOTH. [*Aside to Costard*] They have been at a great feast of languages and stol'n the scraps.

$$[5.1.1-34]$$

This cacophony serves as a kind of out-of-tune orchestral prelude to the dancing and playing of the Fifth Act. By its innocence of exigent meaning it emphasizes the leisure and security of the park, where life, freed from the demands of actuality, can mirror itself in language unburdened by the laconic necessities of communication.

Linguistic affectation and parody constitute one of comedy's more comprehensive themes. Language, like sex and money, is a social phenomenon, and like them, both holds society together and symbolizes society's understanding of itself. The abuse of language, therefore, is a staple of comedy. Many jokes, in fact, are told in dialect to reinforce their wit; and the inability of a foreigner to speak a language both draws the laughter of the society of native speakers, and simultaneously emphasizes their superiority and their common bond. The German, the French, the Italian pronunciation of English is found funny; as, indeed, is a high English accent in America, or an American accent in England. Linguistic abuse, moreover, is a particularly suitable substitute, in this and other of Shakespeare's comedies, for the absent theme of the abuse of money, which, associated with work and with the city, does not fit readily into the carefree world of pastoral.

The specific comic character of Holofernes's pedantry of Latin tags, accordingly, is elucidated by Bergson's general theoretical proposition that "we laugh at anything rigid, ready-made, mechanical in gesture, attitude and even facial expression. Do we find this kind of rigidity in language also? No doubt we do, since language contains ready-made formulas and stereotyped phrases. The man who always expressed himself in such terms would invariably be comic." The linguistic antics in *Love's Labour's Lost*, however, extend beyond mere rigidities. In coalescence with the motif of artifice-within-artifice, they permeate the drama from the low buffoonery of the "delightful ostentation, or show, or pageant, or antic, or firework" of the Nine Worthies (5.1.97-98) up to the serene and lovely songs of spring and winter that conclude the play. Linguistic subforms teem within the larger poetic form of the drama. Letters and poems abound, and take part in the repetitive symmetry of the action. Armado hands Costard a letter for Jaquenetta ("bear this significant to the country maid"—3.1.123–24) shortly before Berowne also hands him one for Rosaline ("And to her white hand see thou do commend / This seal'd-up counsel"—3.1.158–59). When, predictably, Costard misdelivers Armado's letter to the Princess, who causes great delight by reading it aloud, the repetitive series demands that Berowne's letter be likewise misdelivered, to fall into the hands of the King and thereby make complete the "sweet fellowship in shame."

As Armado's letters exploit the artifice-within-artifice motif in terms of prose, the lovers' poems exploit it in verse. The King composes and reads a love poem of sixteen lines:

> So sweet a kiss the golden sun gives not
> To those fresh morning drops upon the rose. . . .
>
> [4.3.22–23]

Longaville's is a fourteen-line sonnet:

> Did not the heavenly rhetoric of thine eye,
> 'Gainst whom the world cannot hold argument. . . .
>
> [4.3.56–57]

Dumain's contribution has more but shorter lines:

> Do not call it sin in me
> That I am forsworn for thee;
> Thou for whom Jove would swear
> Juno but an Ethiope were;
>
> [4.3.111–14]

Indeed, poems, or the threat of poems, preoccupy many of the characters. Armado, the "man of fire-new words," calls on the muse: "Assist me, some extemporal god of rhyme, for I am sure I shall turn sonnet. Devise, wit; write, pen; for I am for whole volumes in folio" (1.2.170–72). And Berowne—"so sweet and voluble is his discourse"—not only composes a sonnet ("If love make me forsworn, how shall I swear to love? / Ah, never faith could hold, if not to beauty vow'd!"—4.2.100–101), but delivers a great set speech in the Marlovian vein:

> . . . when Love speaks, the voice of all the gods
> Make heaven drowsy with the harmony.
> Never durst poet touch a pen to write

Until his ink were temp'red with Love's sighs;
O, then his lines would ravish savage ears,
And plant in tyrants mild humility.
From women's eyes this doctrine I derive.
They sparkle still the right Promethean fire;
They are the books, the arts, the academes,
That show, contain, and nourish all the world. . . .

[4.3.340–49]

This speech, which runs to seventy-five lines, is not only an ornamental piece of linguistic gaming; it also sums up the whole argument against the comic deviance: is the "salve for perjury" requested by the other lovers. As such, it is an integral part of the meaning of the drama as a whole. So, too, other linguistic artifices. The pageant of the Nine Worthies, as noted above, assists in the eviction of the heroic; but even more important, it serves, by bringing together the members of the subplot and the members of the main plot, as actors and audience, to assemble the whole society in one mutual happiness.

The final songs of spring and winter, in more subtle manner, reinforce the mood of mutual happiness. They are sung by the bumpkins with the elegance of the courtiers, and their rustic references ("While greasy Joan doth keel the pot," "And Marian's nose looks red and raw," and "Tom bears logs into the hall / And milk comes frozen home in pail") introduce the commonplaces of the bumpkins into the courtiers' realm.

And miracle of miracles, the sweet and mysterious limpidity of the songs reveals itself as the achievement of Holofernes and Sir Nathaniel, for the songs are "the dialogue that the two learned men have compiled" (5.2.873). The pedant and his foil, till now lost in babbling disharmonies of language, here symbolically project themselves, and the language of the play, into the paradisal community it now attains, and, behind its mock deviances, has always had. Earlier Holofernes, by his "extemporal epitaph on the death of the deer" (4.2.47–48), has fallen below even the ludicrous standards of Don Adriano:

The preyful Princess pierc'd and prick'd a pretty
    pleasing pricket;
Some say a sore; but not a sore till now made sore
    with shooting. . . .

[4.2.54–55]

His theorizing in retrospect of this disaster seemed to have removed forever the possibility that meaningful language might come within his reach:

> This is a gift that I have, simple, simple; a foolish extravagant spirit, full of forms, figures, shapes, objects, ideas, apprehensions, motions, revolutions. These are begot in the ventricle of memory, nourish'd in the womb of pia mater, and delivered upon the mellowing of occasion. But the gift is good in those in whom it is acute, and I am thankful for it.
>
> [4.2.62–69]

And then, from this "learned fool" and his dense companion, "upon the mellowing of occasion," issues forth, in the play's most exquisite playfulness, the sweetest and most gardenlike of all its language:

> When daisies pied and violets blue
> And lady-smocks all silver-white. . . .
> When all aloud the wind doth blow,
> And coughing drowns the parson's saw,
> And birds sit brooding in the snow. . . .
>
> [5.2.881–82, 908–10]

Yet the wonder might almost have been anticipated. The largest function of Holofernes and his foil, Sir Nathaniel, had been to make mockingly present the false future chosen by "Navarre and his book-men," that is, "painfully to pore upon a book" (1.1.74). "You two are book-men," says Dull to the pedant and the hedge-priest (4.2.32), thereby indicating their career down the King's wrong road. But all roads in paradise lead to happiness; so even Holofernes, by a botched Latin quotation from one of the pastoral eclogues of "good old Mantuan" (4.2.90), and a lopsided invocation of Ovid ("Ovidius Naso was the man. And why, indeed, 'Naso' but for smelling out the odoriferous flowers of fancy"—4.2.117–18), points to the involvement of the play in the ideal world where "shepherds pipe on oaten straws" (5.2.890).

That world controls all meanings of *Love's Labour's Lost*. The play's language is constantly alight with happiness. "Did not I dance with you in Brabant once?" (2.1.114); "Berowne they call him; but a merrier man, / Within the limit of becoming mirth, / I never spent an hour's talk withal" (2.1.66–68); "the merry mad-cap lord" (2.1.

214); "the curate and your sweet self are good at such eruptions and sudden breaking-out of mirth" (5.1.98–100); "To our sport, away" (5.1.135); "The third he caper'd, and cried 'All goes well' " (5.2.113); "Knowing aforehand of our merriment" (5.2.461); "like a merriment" (5.2.772); "A right description of our sport, my lord" (5.2.519).

Murmuring through this sunlit gambol flow old words of guilt and atonement, suggesting old thoughts of other gardens; but here without catastrophe. " 'Tis deadly sin to keep that oath, my lord, / And sin to break it" (2.1.104–5). "Guilty, my lord, guilty! I confess, I confess" 4.3.201). "You must be purged too, your sins are rack'd; / You are attaint with faults and perjury" (5.2.806–7). KING: "Teach us, sweet madam, for our rude transgression / Some fair excuse." PRINCESS: "The fairest is confession" (5.2.431–32).

But in this garden regained it is possible to "confess and turn it to a jest" (5.2.390). For here blooms the land of "Love, whose month is ever May" (4.3.98), where lovers act "like sweet roses in this summer air" (5.2.293). Mild and everlasting in its golden afternoon, the play looks upon that realm where "cuckoo-buds of yellow hue / Do paint the meadows with delight" (5.2.883–84). In the dear guiltiness of its inhabitants this glad enclosure finds a common factor of gentler meanings: in entreating excuse for the "liberal opposition of our spirits," the Princess says: "your gentleness / Was guilty of it" (5.2.721, 723–24). The separations of self-imposed law are repealed by a new awareness of community:

> Sweet lords, sweet lovers, O, let us embrace!
> As true we are as flesh and blood can be.
> The sea will ebb and flow, heaven show his face;
> Young blood doth not obey an old decree.

> [4.3.210–13]

The new community established, the edicts of still older law are now declared fulfilled:

> It is religion to be thus forsworn;
> For charity itself fulfills the law,
> And who can sever love from charity?

> [4.3.359–61]

And the golden world reverberates with the merriment that proves "Our loving lawful, and our faith not torn" (4.3.281).

III. And All Things Shall Be Peace

The Happiness of *A Midsummer-Night's Dream*

A Midsummer-Night's Dream is the happiest of Shakespeare's plays, and very possibly the happiest work of literature ever conceived. The merriment of *Love's Labour's Lost* is here reaffirmed, but the formal artifice of that play, which may be indicated by the word "labour" in the title, transforms itself now into a frolic less formed and more evanescent, as indicated by the word "dream." The merry sport of the earlier play becomes less verbal and teasing, more graceful and moonlit. Honeysuckle diction now veils environment and action in a tone softer and more luxuriant. "The reading of this play," says Hazlitt, "is like wandering in a grove by moonlight: the descriptions breathe a sweetness like odours thrown from beds of flowers." It is the moment of pure pastoral celebration.

The play, indeed, almost stills the conflicts of drama to achieve the static completeness of a painting. "Part of the delight of this poetry," says C. L. Barber, "is that we can enjoy without agitation imaginative action of the highest order" (*Shakespeare's Festive Comedy* [Cleveland and New York, 1963], p. 147). The language is virtually one long celebration. The comic deviances are not only artificial, but casual. Where *Love's Labour's Lost* fabricates its deviances and turns itself into a game, *A Midsummer-Night's Dream* moves in dreamlike sequences as if on the brink of an eternal bliss.

The setting, though nominally the Athens of myth and the woodland of dreams, is likewise a conflation of the sweetest aspects of the English countryside. And it is still further an unmistakable version of pastoral. As H. B. Charlton says in a notable passage:

England's cowslips were golden cups, spotted with rich rubies, and a pearl of dew hung in each. The woodlands were carpeted with thick primrose beds, and its springtime outrivalled that of Theocritus in greenery: the song of the lark in the season when wheat is green and hawthorn buds appear, roused English villages betimes to do observances to the month of May. The fields are asparkle with the dewdrop's liquid pearl: the woods are lighted with the fiery glow-worm's eyes. Morning has mountain top and western valley filled with music of the hounds. . . . And evening ushers in the midnight revels on hill, in dale, forest or mead, by paved fountain or by rushy brook, or in the beached margent of the sea, where ringlets are danced in quaint mazes to the whistling of the wind. This is the land of A *Midsummer Night's Dream* (*Shakespearian Comedy* [New York, (1966)], pp. 110–11).

Even the golden sun is too harsh a light for this play's happiness; and the moon shining down on a midsummer's night makes the darkness not a condition of anxiety, but a symbol of soft and benign exhilaration.

Where *Love's Labour's Lost* enlists the power of its king in the formal deviance of withdrawal from women, the mightier ruler, Theseus, clothed in centuries of mythical association, declares from the beginning the existence of a state of comic and pastoral grace. The words that begin the play, "Now, fair Hippolyta, our nuptial hour / Draws on apace" (1.1.1–2), reveal that the ultimate social confirmation already obtains, and that, under its protection, nobody can come to harm. In the opening speeches other motifs of happiness are revealed one by one:

> four happy days bring in
> Another moon; but, O, methinks, how slow
> This old moon wanes!
>
> [1.1.2–4]

The play's first line establishes the mood of nuptial anticipation; the second, the reality of happy days; the third, the soft moonlight that will suffuse the action. The language of the bride-to-be, thus kindled, attains a silvery lightness:

> Four days will quickly steep themselves in night;
> Four nights will quickly dream away the time;
> And then the moon, like to a silver bow
> New-bent in heaven, shall behold the night
> Of our solemnities.
>
> [1.1.7–11]

The anticipation of happiness in Hippolyta's lines, dreaming on things to come, is followed by Theseus's invocation of a similar bliss for society at large:

> Go, Philostrate,
> Stir up the Athenian youth to merriments;
> Awake the pert and nimble spirit of mirth;
>
> [1.1.11–13]

And he concludes, to Hippolyta, with words that decree the entire course of the play: "I will wed thee," he says—"With pomp, with triumph, and with revelling" (1.1.18–19).

It is difficult to imagine a comic opening to compare with this one in the benignity of its tone and in its absolute guarantee of gladness. The action of the play that follows can now be nothing other than a pretext for the continuing celebration of a joyous event, in a wondrous realm, in a timeless time. The attempt of Jan Kott to see darker themes of Dionysian orgy in the play is annulled by this tone, even if it were not discredited by the conjectures he finds necessary to support his surmise of a "cruel dream," of "a most truthful, brutal and violent play," of "brutal and bitter poetry." To be sure, the pastoral is closely allied with the erotic, but the eroticism here, as in the court comedies of Lyly, exists in the audience itself, and is articulated in the play only as a barely perceptible undercurrent, a kind of elegant hint of other things. Lyly's comedy, of whose tradition this play is the most beautiful avatar, emphasizes a near perversity both by the suggestive sexlessness of child actors and the flaunted artificiality of plot and setting. Whatever the sexual intricacies of the noble audience who first viewed Shakespeare's play in Southampton's house (or wherever it was in fact first performed), the play itself is an artifice that accentuates only by denying those very intricacies. To view it as a kind of Central European *Walpurgisnacht* is grossly to confuse it with other and alien motifs.

The deviances that provide the motives for the play's action are therefore presented lightly, their unreality stressed. There are two such deviances: the first that of Aegeus's arbitrary denial of Hermia's marriage choice, with Hermia's consequent defiance of his paternal authority; the second, Oberon and Titania's quarrel over the foundling Indian prince. But the first is so completely nominal that it seems, following as it does upon Theseus's command to "Stir up the Athenian youth to merriments," to dissolve in the act of its postulation. For

Lysander, Hermia's choice, is specifically presented as in every social way the duplicate of Demetrius, her father's choice:

> LYSANDER. I am, my lord, as well deriv'd as he,
> As well possess'd; my love is more than his;
> My fortunes every way as fairly rank'd,
> If not with vantage, as Demetrius's;
> And, which is more than all these boasts can be,
> I am belov'd of beauteous Hermia.
> Why should not I then prosecute my right?
>
> [1.1.99–105]

The disagreement between father and daughter is accordingly, from a social perspective, quite arbitrary, and promises the easiest sort of reconciliation.

Furthermore, Aegeus's threat is no threat at all, even though it emphasizes the perfection of the moonlit Athenian realm. It sounds as though it puts forward the possibility of death:

> Be it so she will not here before your Grace
> Consent to marry with Demetrius,
> I beg the ancient privilege of Athens:
> As she is mine I may dispose of her;
> Which shall be either to this gentleman
> Or to her death, according to our law. . . .
>
> [1.1.39–44]

This threat, which recalls the similar threat of death at the beginning of *The Comedy of Errors*, and in some sort prefigures the tormented world of *King Lear*, reveals itself as without purchase in this enchanted play. Two considerations prevail. One is that Theseus simply ignores the either/or proffered by Aegeus, and substitutes an unexcluded middle—retreat to a convent—which, moreover, is indicated as the real fate of Hermia should she persist in her defiance. Hermia asks,

> But I beseech your Grace that I may know
> The worst that may befall me in this case,
> If I refuse to wed Demetrius.
> THESEUS. Either to die the death, or to abjure
> For ever the society of men.
> Therefore, fair Hermia, question your desires,

> Know of your youth, examine well your blood,
> Whether, if you yield not to your father's choice,
> You can endure the livery of a nun,
> For aye to be in shady cloister mew'd,
> To live a barren sister all your life,
> Chanting faint hymns to the cold fruitless moon.
> Thrice-blessed they that master so their blood
> To undergo such maiden pilgrimage;
> But earthlier happy is the rose distill'd
> Than that which withering on the virgin thorn
> Grows, lives, and dies in single blessedness.
>
> [1.1.62–78]

The retreat to a convent, in such language, not only completely disarms the threat of death, but even asserts its own austere beauty.

A second consideration that takes the sting out of Aegeus's threat is that the world of death has been declared out of bounds by Theseus. His benign decree to "Awake the pert and nimble spirit of mirth" has as its coda the leaving behind of all awareness of mortality:

> Turn melancholy forth to funerals;
> The pale companion is not for our pomp.
>
> [1.1.14–15]

The world of sadness is transcended and so also is the world of strife. It is not without significance that Theseus's bride, Hippolyta, is in legend the warlike queen of the Amazons. Struggle, however, is now in the past:

> Hippolyta, I woo'd thee with my sword,
> And won thy love doing thee injuries;
> But I will wed thee in another key. . . .
>
> [1.1.16–18]

The cause of the quarrel between Oberon and Titania is even more unreal than the deviance provided by Hermia's defying her father in choosing her mate. The tiny Indian prince is a figure preposterously unexpected and yet peculiarly fitting in a world where wonder alone holds sway; his appearance, without any real explanation of his provenance, is in keeping with the dreamlike emergence of unsummoned images:

The King doth keep his revels here to-night;
Take heed the Queen come not within his sight;
For Oberon is passing fell and wrath,
Because that she as her attendant hath
A lovely boy, stolen from an Indian king.
She never had so sweet a changeling;
And jealous Oberon would have the child
Knight of his train, to trace the forests wild;
But she perforce withholds the loved boy,
Crowns him with flowers, and makes him all her joy.
And now they never meet in grove or green,
By fountain clear, or spangled starlight sheen,
But they do square, that all their elves for fear
Creep into acorn cups and hide them there.

[2.1.18–31]

The situation, described in such honeyed language, cannot be too serious; it is made clear that the quarrel between Oberon and Titania is not a rent, but merely a divided pattern, in the gossamer web. "The loved boy" is loved in either case (and if indeed he represents a kind of homosexual topicality, such a fact is not only muted in the language of the play but also is unavailable, to Kott or others, in the psychic configurations of its original audience).

With motivations so slight, the comic reclamation is almost unnecessary; the simplest actions eddy languidly in pastoral celebration. When Oberon prepares to squeeze the juice of the flower into Titania's eyes, he does not say, "I'll squeeze the juice into Titania's eyes"; he says rather:

I know a bank where the wild thyme blows,
Where oxlips and the nodding violet grows,
Quite over-canopied with luscious woodbine,
With sweet musk-roses, and with eglantine;
There sleeps Titania sometime of the night,
Lull'd in these flowers with dances and delight;
And there the snake throws her enamell'd skin,
Weed wide enough to wrap a fairy in;
And with the juice of this I'll streak her eyes,
And make her full of hateful fantasies.

[2.1.249–58]

Such is the moonlit forest world, somnolent, heavy, and luxuriant in its evocation. Titania's language frames the same reality as does Oberon's:

> These are the forgeries of jealousy;
> And never, since the middle summer's spring,
> Met we on hill, in dale, forest or mead,
> By paved fountain, or by rushy brook,
> Or in the beached margent of the sea,
> To dance our ringlets to the whistling wind,
> But with thy brawls thou hast disturb'd our sport. . . .
> The ox hath therefore stretch'd his yoke in vain,
> The ploughman lost his sweat, and the green corn
> Hath rotted ere his youth attain'd a beard;
> The fold stands empty in the drowned field,
> And crows are fatted with the murrion flock;
> The nine men's morris is fill'd up with mud,
> And the quaint mazes in the wanton green,
> For lack of tread, are undistinguishable. . . .
> The seasons alter: hoary-headed frosts
> Fall in the fresh lap of the crimson rose;
> And on old Hiems' thin and icy crown
> An odorous chaplet of sweet summer buds
> Is, as in mockery, set. The spring, the summer,
> The childing autumn, angry winter, change
> Their wonted liveries; and the mazed world,
> By their increase, now knows not which is which.
> And this same progeny of evils comes
> From our debate, from our dissension;
> We are their parents and original.

[2.1.81–117]

In this speech the overwhelmingly ideal setting of A *Midsummer-Night's Dream* is affirmed. Nothing could be less evil than the "progeny of evils" cataloged; it is in fact an account of paradise itself, though of paradise in a state of delicate and temporary desolation. The language is full of winsome nostalgia, and the perfection of "hoary-headed frosts / Fall in the fresh lap of the crimson rose, / And on old Hiems' thin and icy crown / An odorous chaplet of sweet summer buds / Is, as in mockery, set" recalls the similar perfection evoked in the "Hiems, Winter" song that concludes *Love's Labour's Lost*. But the painting-like perfection of the scene there is glimpsed as a prospect only at the end of the play, happy and sunlit though that play is; whereas the painting-like perfection of Titania's lines constitutes merely one of the evocations that overwhelms the senses at the beginning of the second act of the later play.

The realm of the moonlit forest requires such gorgeousness in order to function as the pastoral simplifier of the play's special version of an urban or courtly world. Where, in the earlier *The Two Gentlmen of Verona*, the forest had served to simplify and sort out the serious and real problems of Milan, and in the later *As You Like It* the forest of Arden simplified and muffled the problems of Duke Frederick's court, in the urban world of *A Midsummer-Night's Dream* there can be no such problems. That world, indeed, is safeguarded by the mythical prowess of Theseus, made benign and mirthful in the silvery moonlight by his nuptial happiness. It is, in short, a holy city. Athens in this play is already, at the outset, more benign by far than the sketchy forest of *The Two Gentlemen*, and also more benign even than the luxuriantly evoked forest of Arden. As Hermia says, Athens, before her love for Lysander, seemed "as a paradise to me" (1.1.205). Hence the necessity of pulling out all stops in order to sound notes more wondrous yet than those with which the play begins. And the forest notes are in fact more wondrous yet: "And in the wood, a league without the town, / Where I did meet thee once with Helena / To do observance to a morn of May" (1.1.165–67); "And in the wood, where often you and I / Upon faint primrose beds were wont to lie" (1.1.214–15); "Decking with liquid pearl the bladed grass" (1.1.211). None of this is indicated in Peter Brook's production, which is the stage embodiment of Kott's version of the play; yet the indication of a beautiful place is the pastoral tradition's primary concern. As Sir Thomas Elyot says of the *Georgics*, "Lord, what pleasant variety there is: ... reading therein, it seemeth to a man to be in a delectable gardein or paradise."

So perfect is the forest realm, piled Pelion-like on the splendor of dreaming Athens, that most of the vitality, as opposed to the beauty, of *A Midsummer-Night's Dream* resides, ironically, in the play-within-a-play and its preparation. This judgment holds true despite a recent tendency, in both criticism and performance, to emphasize the permutations of the paired lovers within the forest. To be sure, part of our pleasure stems from our awareness of the consummate foolishness displayed by the lovers, which is emphasized by analogy with the willful perverseness of Titania toward Oberon, and by contrast with the maturity of Theseus's love and the dignity of his speech and action. And the lovers' pastorally conventional mistakes and misfortunes are of course good stage business. But Lysander's saw, that "The course of true love never did run smooth" (1.1.134), must not be valued at too high a rate. Indeed, it is only apparently, not actually, exemplified by the main plot. To scramble about the enchanted forest for a single night, with none the loser, is hardly to experience the tragic obstacles of Romeo and Juliet, of Antony and Cleopatra. The main plot is only slightly more in its perplexity than a game of blindman's buff, and no more in its anxiety; while the subplot of the play-within-a-play and its preparation, though no more grave in tone, exhibits more nuance. For the comic deviation of the main plot, never serious from the first, is thoroughly reclaimed by the fourth act, and the play-within-a-play celebrates, as does its counterpart in *Love's Labour's Lost*, the coming together of all elements of the society in mutual happiness, and signifies as well the absence of problems.

Indeed, the Pyramus and Thisby episode is even more carefree than the Nine Worthies, for the skit of the Worthies served to deflate heroism, whereas the Pyramus episode seems to serve not even that confirming function (although it lightly mocks the love theme of the main plot). It is, in consequence, more risible than the skit of the Worthies, and the interlaced comment of the noble audience is more gentle than in *Love's Labour's Lost*. Shakespeare still frolics with linguistic parody; Pyramus's entrance mocks Hieronimo's "O eyes! no eyes, but fountains fraught with tears; / O life! no life, but lively form of death; / O world! no world, but mass of public wrongs . . . ," and, indeed, the idiosyncratically repetitive technique that runs all through Kyd's tragic prosody:

> O grim-look'd night! O night with hue so black!
> O night, which ever art when day is not!
> O night, O night, alack, alack, alack,
> I fear my Thisby's promise is forgot!
> And thou, O wall, O sweet, O lovely wall,
> That stand'st between her father's ground
>   and mine;
> Thou wall, O wall, O sweet and lovely wall,

Show me thy chink, to blink through with
    mine eyne.

[5.1.168–75]

The passage is wickedly funny. The threefold "alack," so as to rhyme
with "black," shows an unabashed paucity of invention; the witless
fixing of night as "when day is not"; the rhyme of "mine" and "eyne,"
thrown askew by the adjectival repetition of "mine"; the improperly
placed rhyme of "chink" and "blink"; and most of all, the inspired
personification of Wall—all these ludicrous elements are masterfully
realized.

Another parody exists in the title of the skit, "The most Lamentable
Comedy and most Cruel Death of Pyramus and Thisby" (1.2.10–12),
for the oxymoronic title catches up the much ridiculed title of *Cam-
bises*: "A Lamentable Tragedie, Mixed Full of Pleasant Mirth," and
also that title's greedy claim to cater for all aspects of popular taste.

Both the parody of Kyd and that of Preston, however, suggest more
than a merely random laugh at earlier plays. For both parodies flaunt
A Midsummer-Night's Dream's hermetic security from mortality's
threat: from such historical horror as Preston's Herodotean monster
tale represents, and from the Senecan bloodiness of Kyd's tragedy. The
play-within-a-play goes against the grain of its larger context; in its
explicit summoning up of a tragic story of love, it tests the enchanted
world. But as pointedly as the Romeo-and-Juliet-like outcome of sexual
attraction is suggested, equally pointedly is that tragic possibility disarmed. And not merely disarmed, but dismantled, made ludicrous,
overwhelmed. The spectators laughing at the tragedy of Pyramus and
Thisby confirm their existence in paradise. "Marry, if he that writ it
had played Pyramus, and hang'd himself in Thisby's garter," says
Theseus, "it would have been a fine tragedy. And so it is, truly; and
very notably discharg'd" (5.1.347–49). And in the same breath his
language changes to poetry, as the true reality of the moonlit society
supervenes:

Lovers, to bed; 'tis almost fairy time. . . .
This palpable-gross play hath well beguil'd
The heavy gait of night. Sweet friends, to bed.
A fortnight hold we this solemnity,
In nightly revels and new jollity.

[5.1.353–59]

In this realm tragedy is ludicrous and not serious; those things that are serious—"solemnity"—involve "nightly revels and new jollity." "We'll hold a feast in great solemnity" (4.1.182). The "night of our solemnities," as Hippolyta calls it, involves "pomp," "triumph," and "revelling" (1.1.11, 19). In this interpretation of the meaning of seriousness, we are almost transformed to that other realm celebrated by Plato: "Of the place beyond the heavens none of our earthly poets has yet sung. . . . It is there that true being dwells" (*Phaedrus* 247C). As Cassirer says, "Plato's vision of the world is characterized by the sharp division he makes between the sensible and the intelligible world. . . . The two worlds . . . do not lie on the same plane and, therefore admit of no immediate comparison. Rather, each is the complete opposite, the ἕτερον, of the other. Everything predicated of the one must be denied to the other" (*The Individual and the Cosmos in Renaissance Philosophy*, trans. M. Domandi [New York, 1963], p. 16).

In Shakespeare's play a dreaming other world is shaped, and at the beginning of the fifth act Theseus, idly in his context, but startlingly in view of Shakespeare's own customary reticence about his art, toys with the potentialities of the poetic imagination:

> I never may believe
> These antique fables, nor these fairy toys.
> Lovers and madmen have such seething brains,
> Such shaping fantasies, that apprehend
> More than cool reason ever comprehends.
> The lunatic, the lover, and the poet,
> Are of imagination all compact. . . .
> The poet's eye, in a fine frenzy rolling,
> Doth glance from heaven to earth, from earth to heaven;
> And as imagination bodies forth
> The forms of things unknown, the poet's pen
> Turns them to shapes, and gives to airy nothing
> A local habitation and a name.
>
> [5.1.2–17]

Glancing from "heaven to earth, from earth to heaven," Shakespeare in this play "gives to airy nothing / A local habitation and a name"; and that local habitation is elsewhere named paradise. If a mundane realist protests that the other world, paradise, does not exist, the play answers with images that "apprehend / More than cool reason ever comprehends."

The imagination here playfully defies the world of intractable objectivity, and the zany personification of "wall" is an inspired assertion of imagination's power to transcend the mundane. For the wall, symbol of obdurate thingness, symbol of the separation of humans from one another, symbol of all blockings, holdings back, keepings out, pennings in, is here—wondrously—not a wall. Not a thing at all, but a person:

> This man, with lime and rough-cast, doth present
> Wall, that vile Wall which did these lovers sunder;
> And through Wall's chink, poor souls, they are
>   content
> To whisper.
>
> [5.1.130–33]

Through its grotesque and Bergsonian humor, the wall is insistently put forward as the most significant role in this tender, happy, and ultimately meaningful play-within-a-play:

> In this same interlude it doth befall
> That I, one Snout by name, present a wall;
> And such a wall as I would have you think
> That had in it a crannied hole or chink,
> Through which the lovers, Pyramus and Thisby,
> Did whisper very often secretly.
> This loam, this rough-cast, and this stone,
>   doth show
> That I am that same wall; the truth is so;
> And this the cranny is, right and sinister,
> Through which the fearful lovers are to whisper.
>
> [5.1.154–63]

It is the fulfillment of that most primitive and most childlike of all longings, that things be swayed by thoughts. Ludicrously, a request is made:

> Thou wall, O wall, O sweet and lovely wall,
> Show me thy chink, to blink through with mine eyne.

And, magically, the wall does just that. Snout holds up his fingers:

> Thanks, courteous wall. Jove shield thee well for this!
>
> [5.1.174–76]

The magical transformation of thing to person is witnessed again, in broad Freudian humor, by Thisby's hilarious reply to Pyramus:

> PYRAMUS. O, kiss me through the hole of this vile wall.
> THISBY. I kiss the wall's hole, not your lips at all.
>
> [5.1.199–200]

And the relationship of all this mirth to the deeper transformations wrought by the paradisal imagination is acknowledged by Theseus. Wall exits:

> Thus have I, Wall, my part discharged so;
> And being done, thus Wall away doth go.
>
> [5.1.204–5]

Whereupon Hippolyta says,

> This is the silliest stuff that ever I heard.
> THESEUS. The best in this kind are but shadows; and the worst are no worse, if imagination amend them.
> HIPPOLYTA. It must be your imagination then, and not theirs.
> THESEUS. If we imagine no worse of them than they of themselves, they may pass for excellent men.
>
> [5.1.208–14]

Imagination, in short, not only bodies forth the forms of things unknown, but sees beneath the piglike exterior of a lout the dignity of a human soul. Indeed, as Shelley saw, "Reason respects the differences, and imagination the similitudes of things"—"A man, to be greatly good, must imagine intensely and comprehensively: he must put himself in the place of another and of many others; the pains and pleasures of his species must become his own."

The play-within-a-play thus becomes, in its mirthful good fellowship, a testament to a society in bliss. It evokes words from Theseus that hauntingly reverberate beyond their immediate occasion: rejecting other forms of entertainment as "not sorting with a nuptial ceremony" (5.1.55), he comes to the possibility of the loutish play:

"A tedious brief scene of young Pyramus
And his love Thisby; very tragical mirth."
Merry and tragical! tedious and brief!
That is hot ice and wondrous strange snow.
How shall we find the concord of this discord?

[5.1.56–60]

But Theseus's question is answered by the play's unfolding. The discord of the loutish grotesquerie results in the concord of a blessed society. The "tragical mirth," in a play that glances from "heaven to earth, from earth to heaven," welds together the two realms into a Cusanan *coincidentia oppositorum*. The presentation of the skit allows the benignity of Theseus to establish its absolute spiritual hegemony:

THESEUS. What are they that do play it?
PHILOSTRATE. Hard-handed men that work in Athens here.
Which never labour'd in their minds till now,
And now have toil'd their unbreathed memories
With this same play against your nuptial.
THESEUS. And we will hear it.
PHILOSTRATE.   No, my noble lord,
It is not for you. I have heard it over,
And it is nothing, nothing in the world;
Unless you can find sport in their intents,
Extremely stretch'd and conn'd with cruel pain
To do you service.

[5.1.71–81]

But Theseus's answer confirms how courteously gentle that sport will be:

I will hear that play;
For never anything can be amiss,
When simpleness and duty tender it.
Go, bring them in; and take your places,
    ladies. . . .
Our sport shall be to take what they
    mistake. . . .

[5.1.81–90]

Indeed, everything about the play by the "crew of patches, rude mechanicals" (3.2.9) mysteriously trails behind it a cloud of final assurance. After the "wittiest partition" has long departed the scene, Wall's symbolic function is startlingly pointed out by Bottom at the end of both plays:

> THESEUS. Moonshine and Lion are left to bury the dead.
> DEMETRIUS. Ay, and Wall too.
> BOTTOM. No. I assure you; the wall is down that parted their fathers.
>
> [5.1.339–42]

And remarks of similar reverberation occur in the skit's rehearsal:

> BOTTOM. There are things in this comedy of Pyramus and Thisby that will never please. First, Pyramus must draw a sword to kill himself; which the ladies cannot abide. . . .
> SNOUT. By'r lakin, a parlous fear.
> STARVELING. I believe we must leave the killing out, when all is done.
> BOTTOM. Not a whit; I have a device to make all well. Write me a prologue; and let the prologue seem to say we will do no harm with our swords, and that Pyramus is not kill'd indeed; and, for the more better assurance, tell them that I Pyramus am not Pyramus but Bottom the weaver. This will put them out of fear.
>
> [3.1.8–20]

"I believe we must leave the killing out, when all is done"—so says the bumpkin, and so say more elevated hopes. The "parlous fear" of existence is healed by Bottom's "device to make all well." The thought that "Pyramus is not kill'd indeed" taps the same hope as the thought that "Lycidas your sorrow is not dead." "If that may be, then all is well," says Peter Quince in benediction, when Bottom decrees that "some man or other must present Wall" (3.1.64, 60).

The subject of the skit, Pyramus and Thisby, accords with still another persisting motif of A Midsummer-Night's Dream. For the story comes from Ovid's Metamorphoses, and the metamorphoses of the lovers' affections for one another constitute the chief business of the main plot. Metamorphosis of affection becomes openly Ovidian in Titania's love for Bottom, for there the transformation is accompanied by the visual symbol of Bottom's transformation to an ass:

> QUINCE. Bless thee, Bottom, bless thee! Thou art translated.
> BOTTOM. I see their knavery: this is to make an ass of me; to

fright me, if they could. But I will not stir from this place, do
what they can; I will walk up and down here, and I will sing,
that they shall hear I am not afraid.

[3.1.109–13]

The alacrity with which Bottom accustoms himself to his unthinkable
eminence as the beloved of Titania offers the same testimony to humankind's limitless vanity as does the hilarious complacency of Chris-
topher Sly:

> SLY. Am I a lord and have I such a lady?
> Or do I dream? Or have I dream'd till now? . . .
> Upon my life, I am a lord indeed,
> And not a tinker, nor Christopher Sly.
> Well, bring our lady hither to our sight;
> and once again, a pot o' th' smallest ale. . . .
> SLY. Madam wife, they say that I have dream'd
> And slept above some fifteen year or more.
> PAGE. Ay, and the time seems thirty unto me,
> Being all this time abandon'd from your bed.
> SLY. 'Tis much. Servants, leave me and her alone.
> Madam, undress you, and come now to bed.
> [*The Taming of the Shrew*, Induction, 2.66–83, 110–15]

Bottom differs mainly in the paradisal language that cascades around
his grotesqueness:

> TITANIA. Be kind and courteous to this gentleman;
> Hop in his walks and gambol in his eyes;
> Feed him with apricocks and dewberries,
> With purple grapes, green figs, and mulberries;
> The honey bags steal from the humble-bees,
> And for night-tapers crop their waxen thighs,
> And light them at the fiery glow-worm's eyes,
> To have my love to bed and to arise;
> And pluck the wings from painted butterflies,
> To fan the moonbeams from his sleeping eyes.
> Nod to him, elves, and do him courtesies.

[3.1.150–60]

His complacent acceptance of these marvels, however, is no less laughable than that of Sly:

BOTTOM. Where's Peaseblossom?

PEASEBLOSSOM. Ready.

BOTTOM. Scratch my head, Peaseblossom. Where's Mounsieur Cobweb?

COBWEB. Ready.

BOTTOM. Mounsieur Cobweb; good mounsieur, get you your weapons in your hand and kill me a red-hipp'd humble-bee on the top of a thistle; and, good mounsieur, bring me the honey-bag. Do not fret yourself too much in the action, mounsieur; and, good mounsieur, have a care the honey-bag break not; I would be loath to have you overflowen with a honey-bag, signior. Where's Mounsieur Mustardseed?

[4.1.5–16]

The humor, and the exquisite gentleness, of the passage, almost defy analysis ("I imagine Titania's court," says Kott, relinquishing his hold on the text of the play, "as consisting of old men and women, toothless and shaking, their mouths wet with saliva . . ."). Much depends on the two appearances of the timeless response: "Ready"—the tiny attendants take their ludicrous and whimsical duties with vast seriousness. At the same time, the statement "ready" is an unchanging part of childhood games. Much also depends on Bottom's formality as indicated by the word "Mounsieur." And the quality of the whole passage is an effect of the relationship so unquestioningly and quickly established between the bumpkin and his wonderful retainers.

The combination of physical metamorphosis and flower-laden language in Bottom's transformation brings Shakespeare closer to Ovid in this episode than at any other point in his career as a playwright, and justifies the statement of Meres that "the sweete wittie soule of *Ouid* liues in mellifluous and hony-tongued *Shakespeare*." The point should be emphasized, because Kott interprets Bottom's transformation as the symbol of a *Walpurgisnacht* of "animal eroticism," and he finds relevant the fact that the ass "among all the quadrupeds is supposed to have the longest and hardest phallus." Shakespeare's play, however, is not the representation of a Dionysian orgy; on the contrary it is—even if not entirely—an Apollonian, that is, Ovidian, suppression of such motifs.

In this regard, the metamorphosis most significant for the final meaning of the play is the Ovidian change of Oberon. In a startling evocation of pastoral, Titania reveals that world as a metamorphosis of the fairy realm; and conversely, the fairy realm as a version of the pastoral symbol. As she says to Oberon,

> I know
> When thou hast stolen away from fairy land,
> And in the shape of Corin sat all day,
> Playing on pipes of corn, and versing love
> To amorous Phillida.
>
> [2.1.64–68]

With such conclusive, even though brief, pastoral authentication, Oberon presides in still deeper benignity than does Theseus; indeed, Theseus is Duke but Oberon is King. His reconciling fiat, therefore, occurring as early as the third act, stills all possibility of struggle and travail:

> And back to Athens shall the lovers wend
> With league whose date till death shall never end.
> Whiles I in this affair do thee employ,
> I'll to my queen, and beg her Indian boy;
> And then I will her charmed eye release
> From monster's view, and all things shall be peace.
>
> [3.2.372–77]

Both comic motivations—the misunderstandings between the lovers, and the quarrel between Oberon and Titania over the Indian boy, representing respectively the motive deviance for Athens and that for the moonlit forest—are here resolved and stilled by one magical utterance, and the future is divinely cast into a joyous mold: "and all things shall be peace."

The goodness, happiness, and benignity emanating from Oberon's presence are accentuated by his reply to Puck's reference to the relation of ghosts and daylight:

> PUCK. My fairy lord, this must be done with haste.
> For night's swift dragons cut the clouds full fast;
> And yonder shines Aurora's harbinger,
> At whose approach ghosts, wand'ring here and there,
> Troop home to churchyards. Damned spirits all. . . .

Puck's anxiety gives only superficial countenance to Kott's demonological emphasis (". . . the devilish origin of Puck. Puck has simply been one of the names for the devil"), for demonic threats cannot survive in the pastoralism of the play. Soaring and mysteriously exultant, Oberon's reply frees the imagination from all such fear:

> But we are spirits of another sort:
> I with the Morning's love have oft made sport;
> And, like a forester, the groves may tread
> Even till the eastern gate, all fiery red,
> Opening on Neptune with fair blessed beams,
> Turns into yellow gold his salt green streams.
>
> [3.2.378–82, 387–93]

Dawn-lit by such images and shadows of divine things, the action of the play becomes even more exhilarated. Oberon affirms to Titania the rule of "amity," "prosperity," and "jollity":

> Now thou and I are new in amity,
> And will to-morrow midnight solemnly
> Dance in Duke Theseus's house triumphantly,
> And bless it to all fair prosperity.
> There shall the pairs of faithful lovers be
> Wedded, with Theseus, all in jollity.
>
> [4.1.84–89]

Theseus, the play's language now totally serene and blissful, adds the realities of "joy," "mirth," and "love":

> Here come the lovers, full of joy and mirth.
> Joy, gentle friends, joy and fresh days of love
> Accompany your hearts!
>
> [5.1.28–30]

His words, looking forward to the play-within-a-play, are a further assurance of ineffable well-being:

> Come now; what masques, what dances shall we have, . . .
> Where is our usual manager of mirth?
> What revels are in hand? . . .
> What masque? what music? How shall we beguile
> The lazy time, if not with some delight?
>
> [5.1.32–41]

And with such a benediction, this extended arabesque of hope and joy sweeps to its end. Where, in *Love's Labour's Lost*, a playful check had been put upon final happiness in that "Jack hath not Jill" (5.2.863), in this still more radiant realm "Jack shall have Jill; / Nought shall go ill" (3.2.461–62). The hempen homespuns' play proudly participates in the world of pastoral bliss: "This green plot shall be our stage, this hawthorn brake our tiring-house" (3.1.3–4). And the converging delights compel universal assent to Bottom's prophecy: "I do not doubt but to hear them say it is a sweet comedy" (4.2.37–38).

IV. For Other Than for Dancing Measures

The Complications of *As You Like It*

*T*o approach *As You Like It* immediately after *Love's Labour's Lost* and *A Midsummer-Night's Dream* is to encounter a darkening of action and tone. The pastoral realm into which it enters has, in marked contrast to the moonlit forest outside Athens, genuine problems to ameliorate. The moment of pure pastoral celebration in Shakespeare's art is now forever gone. The motif of criminal action, which had been tentatively put forward in *The Two Gentlemen of Verona*, only to be banished from the golden confines of Navarre's park and Oberon's forest, now reasserts itself. *As You Like It* is a play that labors to keep its comic balance, and for this reason the comic reclamation in the Forest of Arden involves complicated character interactions and severe criticisms of behavior. The play exhibits more humor, but much less happiness, than its two great pastoral predecessors.

The situation at the start of *As You Like It* could, indeed, as well serve for a tragedy as for a comedy. The index to the state of moral well-being in Shakespeare's comedies is usually provided by the character and circumstances of the ruler. The mysterious illness of the King in *All's Well* casts that whole play into deviation from an ideal state; the lovesickness of Orsino at the beginning of *Twelfth Night* forebodes maladjustments throughout the Illyrian society. Conversely, the youth and magnanimity of Navarre, the puissance and benignity of Theseus, authenticate a pervasive well-being in their two realms. It is significant, therefore, that the world of *As You Like It* is presented at the outset as severely disfigured, for its ruler has been banished and his power usurped.

Grave though usurpation is, it is rendered still more grave by the fact that the usurper, as in *The Tempest*, is the brother of the true ruler, and the action of usurpation therefore reverberates with the archetypal crime of Cain. When Claudius faces his own offense, he says: "O my offence is rank, it smells to heaven; / It hath the primal eldest curse upon't, / A brother's murder" (*Hamlet*, 3.3.36–38). Neither in *As You Like It* nor in *The Tempest* does the crime of brother against brother proceed to murder; for such an outcome would put the actions of the two plays irrevocably beyond the power of comedy to heal. But usurpation and banishment represent the most serious kind of transgression. We recall the word that, in opening the somber action of *The White Devil*, casts all within that play into a nightmare of alienation: "Banished?" Or we recall Romeo's agony:

> They are free men, but I am banished.
> Hadst thou no poison mix'd, no sharp-ground knife,
> No sudden mean of death, though ne'er so mean,
> But "banished" to kill me?—"banished"?
> O friar, the damned use that word in hell;
> Howling attends it.
>
> [*Romeo and Juliet*, 3.3.42–48]

When, therefore, we learn that "the old Duke is banished by his younger brother the new Duke" (1.1.91–92), a mood of intense alienation settles over *As You Like It*. The mood is deepened by its foreshadowing in the relationship of Orlando and Oliver. "He lets me feed with his hinds, bars me the place of a brother," says Orlando (1.1.17–18). Indeed, it is bitter irony that in this play the comic motif of repetition doubles the Cain-and-Abel motif by extending it from Oliver and Orlando to the young Duke and the old Duke. In the supporting trope of Orlando and Oliver, moreover, the trouble between the brothers specifically involves, as does that of Cain and Abel, the relationship between father and son:

> My father charg'd you in his will to give me good education: you have train'd me like a peasant, obscuring and hiding from me all gentleman-like qualities. The spirit of my father grows strong in me, and I will no longer endure it. . . .
>
> [1.1.60–65]

Their father being dead, the old servant Adam fills his place in the psychodramatic struggle, his name reinforcing the motif of "primal eldest curse." It can hardly be without significance that Shakespeare here slightly alters his source, for in Lodge's *Rosalynde* the retainer is called "*Adam Spencer, the olde servaunt of Sir John of Bordeaux,*" and is almost always referred to by both given and surname. In changing "Adam Spencer" to simple "Adam" in the struggle of brother against brother, *As You Like It* conveys the sense of old woe ever renewed.

Beset from its beginning by such clouds of gloom and disharmony, the play must stake its claim to comic redemption very early. In the same conversation in which Oliver, fresh from his mistreatment of his brother and old Adam, learns from the wrestler Charles the "old news" of the old Duke's banishment (1.1.90), he, and the cosmos of the play, also learn of the existence of the land of pastoral wonder:

> OLIVER. Where will the old Duke live?
> CHARLES. They say he is already in the Forest of Arden. . . .
> many young gentlemen flock to him every day, and fleet the
> time carelessly, as they did in the golden world.
>
> [1.1.104–9]

It is interesting that the play here invokes, instead of the Theocritan iconology of formal pastoral, the separate but intertwined tradition of the Golden Age; for the latter, by being more explicitly paradisal, more explicitly repels tragic possibility. Rapin urges in 1659, in his "Dissertatio de carmine pastorali," that pastoral poetry "is a product of the Golden Age." To Rapin, pastoral itself is "a perfect image of the state of Innocence, of that golden Age, that blessed time, when Sincerity and Innocence, Peace, Ease, and Plenty inhabited the Plains." So, to bring in the golden world so early, and entrust the message to such an unexpected source as Charles, is to go—not historically but semiotically —to the very fountainhead of the pastoral myth and thereby to concede the dire need for alleviation of the alienated mood.

Secure, then, in the promise of Arden's redemption, the play indulges in a still closer approach to tragic irrevocability. "I had as lief thou didst break his neck as his finger," says Oliver to Charles, perverting the latter's honorable intentions in the proposed wrestling match against Orlando (1.1.132). Oliver adorns the malignant proposal by language of studied villainy:

> And thou wert best look to't; for if thou dost him any slight
> disgrace, or if he do not mightily grace himself on thee, he will
> practise against thee by poison, entrap thee by some treacherous
> device, and never leave thee till he hath ta'en thy life by some

indirect means or other; for, I assure thee, and almost with tears I speak it, there is not one so young and so villainous this day living. I speak but brotherly of him; but should I anatomize him to thee as he is, I must blush and weep, and thou must look pale and wonder.

[1.1.132–40]

Such brotherly betrayal prefigures the relationship of Edmund and Edgar. And when Charles departs, Oliver's musing to himself suggests also the selfless dedication of Iago's hatred:

I hope I shall see an end of him; for my soul, yet I know not why, hates nothing more than he.

[1.1.144–46]

This play, then, involves the first massive assault of the forces of bitterness and alienation upon the pastoral vision of Shakespeare, and its action glances off the dark borders of tragedy. Indeed, the motif of repeated abandonment of the court, first by Orlando and Adam, then by Rosalind, Celia, and Touchstone, is prophetic of the departings and rejections of Cordelia, Kent, and Edgar at the beginning of *King Lear's* quest for essential being.

It is, accordingly, both fitting and necessary that the second act of *As You Like It* opens with an equally massive attempt to restore comic benignity and to check the tragic tendency. For the rightful ruler, Duke Senior, without preliminary of action, invokes the pastoral vision and the idea of a new society in extraordinarily specific terms. In fact, the social assurance of comedy, the environmental assurance of pastoral, and the religious implication of both, are all established by the Duke's speech:

Now, my co-mates and brothers in exile,
Hath not old custom made this life more sweet
Than that of painted pomp? Are not these woods
More free from peril than the envious court?
Here feel we not the penalty of Adam,
The seasons' difference; as the icy fang
And churlish chiding of the winter's wind,
Which when it bites and blows upon my body,
Even till I shrink with cold, I smile and say,
"This is no flattery; these are counsellors

That feelingly persuade me what I am."
Sweet are the uses of adversity;
Which, like the toad, ugly and venomous,
Wears yet a precious jewel in his head;
And this our life, exempt from public haunt,
Finds tongues in trees, books in the running brooks,
Sermons in stones, and good in everything.

[2.1.1–17]

But "good," despite the Duke's statement, is not "in everything" as it is in *Love's Labour's Lost* and *A Midsummer-Night's Dream*; and the early promise of a "golden world" is not entirely fulfilled. The Forest of Arden, though a paradise, is not an unequivocal paradise; the "churlish chiding of the winter's wind," even if not painfully felt, is present. "Arden," as Helen Gardner notes in her well-known essay on *As You Like It*, "is not a place where the laws of nature are abrogated and roses are without their thorns." The gall of the court, before it is flushed away by the Arethusan waters, mingles and dissolves itself into the pastoral limpidity. Hence the existence of natural danger in the forest makes it a place halfway between reality and paradise. As Oliver says of his encounter with Orlando there:

A wretched ragged man, o'ergrown with hair,
Lay sleeping on his back. About his neck
A green and gilded snake had wreath'd itself,
Who with her head nimble in threats approach'd
The opening of his mouth; but suddenly,
Seeing Orlando, it unlink'd itself,
And with indented glides did slip away
Into a bush. . . .

[4.3.105–12]

The presence of the serpent, potentially dangerous, indicates a certain admixture of harsh reality in this version of a golden world, for of that world Virgil stipulates that "occidet et serpens, et fallax herba veneni occidet"—both the serpent and the false poison plant shall die (*Eclogues*, 4.24–25). And in the Forest of Arden, an unpastoral danger is brought still closer by the lioness that almost kills Oliver:

A lioness, with udders all drawn dry,
Lay crouching, head on ground, with catlike watch,

When that the sleeping man should stir. . . .
This seen, Orlando did approach the man,
And found it was his brother, his elder brother. . . .
. . . kindness, nobler ever than revenge,
And nature, stronger than his just occasion,
Made him give battle to the lioness,
Who quickly fell before him. . . .
In brief, he led me to the gentle Duke,
Who gave me fresh array and entertainment,
Committing me unto my brother's love;
Who led me instantly into his cave,
There stripp'd himself, and here upon his arm
The lioness had torn some flesh away,
Which all this while had bled. . . .

[4.3.113–47]

The function of the serpent and the lioness are clearly revealed in these lines: as figures of venom and fury, they symbolically accept the burden of the venom and fury generated by the Cain and Abel contest of Oliver and Orlando. The two brothers, their rage displaced into the iconic beasts, are ready for reconciliation:

CELIA. Are you his brother?
ROSALIND.   Was't you he rescu'd?
CELIA. Was't you that did so oft contrive to kill him?
OLIVER. 'Twas I; but 'tis not I. I do not shame
To tell you what I was, since my conversion
So sweetly tastes, being the thing I am. . . .
When from the first to last, betwixt us two,
Tears our recountments had most kindly bath'd,
As how I came into that desert place—
In brief, he led me to the gentle Duke.

[4.3.132–41]

Thus the Cain-against-Abel tragic disharmony gives way to the legendary Roland-for-an-Oliver togetherness implied by the brothers' names.

The seriousness of the deviances to be reclaimed is to be found not only in a slight deterioration in the pastoral environment, but also in the introduction of Jaques, a pastorally untypical character. Jaques is a humor figure representing the type of the malcontent; he is a member of the tribe not only of Marston's Malevole but, in a sense, of Hamlet himself. Like Hamlet, he calls into question all aspects of life that fall below an exalted ideal of human conduct. It is significant that the first mention of his name refers to his awareness of this less-than-ideal pastoral environment. The old Duke says:

> Come, shall we go and kill us venison?
> And yet it irks me the poor dappled fools,
> Being native burghers of this desert city,
> Should, in their own confines, with forked heads
> Have their round haunches gor'd.
> FIRST LORD.   Indeed, my lord,
> The melancholy Jaques grieves at that;
> And, in that kind, swears you do more usurp
> Than doth your brother that hath banish'd you.
>
> [2.1.21–28]

It is emphasized that the Forest of Arden is a version of pastoral like Robin Hood's Sherwood Forest (Charles had said at the outset that "in the forest of Arden" the Duke and his retainers "live like the old Robin Hood of England" [1.1.105–9]). The specification not only prefigures Jonson's pastoral variant, whose "scene is Sherwood" (*The Sad Shepherd*, Prologue, line 15), but it also indicates a world somewhat less perfect than Ovid's golden age. Indeed, as Elizabeth Armstrong points out, "Peace between man and the animal creation" was "a traditional feature of the Age of Gold"; and the "existence of this tradition" may have deterred Ronsard "from allowing his Age of Gold people to slay animals for food or sport" (*Ronsard and the Age of Gold* [Cambridge, 1968], p. 189). The continuation of the First Lord's report suggests, in direct ratio to its length, the deficiencies of this only partly golden world:

> To-day my Lord of Amiens and myself
> Did steal behind him as he lay along
> Under an oak whose antique root peeps out
> Upon the brook that brawls along this wood!
> To the which place a poor sequest'red stag,
> That from the hunter's aim had ta'en a hurt,
> Did come to languish; and indeed, my lord,
> The wretched animal heav'd forth such groans

That their discharge did stretch his leathern coat
Almost to bursting; and the big round tears
Cours'd one another down his innocent nose
In piteous chase; and thus the hairy fool. . . .
Stood on th' extremest verge of the swift brook,
Augmenting it with tears.
DUKE SENIOR.   But what said Jaques?
Did he not moralize this spectacle?
FIRST LORD. O, yes, into a thousand similes. . . .
                              swearing that we
Are mere usurpers, tyrants, and what's worse,
To fright the animals and to kill them up
In their assign'd and native dwelling-place.
DUKE SENIOR. And did you leave him in this contemplation?
SECOND LORD. We did, my lord, weeping and commenting
Upon the sobbing deer.*

[2.1.29–66]

The import of the passage can hardly be mistaken: the deer, with its human coordinates of feeling ("The wretched animal . . . the big round tears . . . his innocent nose . . ."), brings the reality of human pain into the forest; and Jaques's moral criticism, by linking the killing of the deer with usurpation and tyranny,** indicates that the forest is not completely divorced from the reality of the urban spectacle. Jaques, indeed, links city, court, and pastoral forest together by his criticism.

---

* For a comprehensive discussion of the tradition of human lament for the death of animals, see D. C. Allen, "Marvell's 'Nymph,'" *ELH*, 23 (1956): 93–111; see especially note 19, pp. 100–101, for the deer as "the symbol of Christ," as "good Christian," as "repentant man." For the ancient association of a deer with "metaphors of love" see pp. 102–3. See further Herrlinger, *Totenklage um Tiere in der antiken Dichtung* (Stuttgart, 1929).

** See further Claus Uhlig, "Der weinende Hirsch: *As You Like It*, II.i.21–66, und der historische Kontext," in *Deutsche Shakespeare-Gesellschaft West; Jahrbuch 1968*, pp. 141–68. Uhlig places the "emblematic" passage of Jaques's "weeping and commenting/ Upon the sobbing deer" (2.1.65–66) in a tradition of "hunt criticism" extending from Roman antiquity to the late eighteenth century, with special attention to John of Salisbury's *Policraticus*, More's *Utopia*, and, as direct progenitor of Shakespeare's passage, Sidney's *Arcadia*. By his "lament over the tyrannical cruelty of the hunt," Jaques reveals himself as not only a "malcontent" but a "humanist" as well. But Jaques "does not stop to think that the banished men pursue the hunt out of bitter necessity, which is permitted in both the *Policraticus* and the *Utopia*." By this lack of realism, therefore, Jaques's high moral earnestness is kept within the bounds of comedy and out of the realm of tragic criticism.

Although a pastorally atypical figure in the play, Jaques is nevertheless in a sense its central figure, or at least the figure who does most to
define the idiosyncratic strain of malaise. But the type of the malcontent can imply not only Hamlet's idealism but Bosola's cynicism, and
Jaques's presence threatens as well as criticizes the pastoral environment. It is therefore necessary to provide him a counterweight, so that
the unchecked burden of malcontentment may not become so heavy
as to break up entirely the fragilities of the pastoral vision. That counterweight the play summons up in the character of Touchstone, the
fool. Replacing the "hairy fool / Much marked of the melancholy
Jaques" (that is, the deer whose travail brings out Jacques's role as in
part the emissary of a realm of more beatific feeling), Touchstone re-
minds us, perhaps subliminally, of Jaques's compassion and at the
same time dissolves the accompanying melancholy into a language of
ridicule and jest more fitting to comic aims. The function of the fool
is to redeem Jaques from the melancholy that is so dangerous to the
comic-pastoral aspiration:

> DUKE SENIOR. What, you look merrily!
> JAQUES. A fool, a fool! I met a fool i' th' forest,
> A motley fool. A miserable world!
> As I do live by food, I met a fool,
> Who laid him down and bask'd him in the sun,
> And rail'd on Lady Fortune in good terms,
> In good set terms—and yet a motley fool.
> "Good morrow, fool," quoth I. "No, sir," quoth he,
> "Call me not fool till heaven hath sent me fortune."
> And then he drew a dial from his poke,
> And, looking on it with lack-lustre eye,
> Says very wisely, "It is ten o'clock;
> Thus we may see," quoth he, "how the world wags;
> 'Tis but an hour ago since it was nine;
> And after one hour more 'twill be eleven;
> And so, from hour to hour, we ripe and ripe,
> And then, from hour to hour, we rot and rot;
> And thereby hangs a tale." When I did hear
> The motley fool thus moral on the time,
> My lungs began to crow like chanticleer,
> That fools should be so deep contemplative;

And I did laugh sans intermission
An hour by his dial. O noble fool!
A worthy fool! Motley's the only wear.

[2.7.11–34]

Thus, whilst Jaques criticizes the world, Touchstone gently and unintentionally mocks that criticism. Touchstone's own railing "on Lady
Fortune in good set terms" reveals to Jaques the dimension of the absurd in all human seriousness. To hear a "motley fool thus moral on
the time" is to suggest that to moral on the time is to be a motley fool.
If a fool is "deep contemplative," then perhaps the "deep contemplative" is the foolish. Touchstone is a mirror that not only reflects, but
lightens, the malcontentment of Jaques. Indeed, garbed in fool's motley, such criticisms as those of Jaques can safely be allowed in the pastoral realm. "Invest me in my motley," says Jaques:

give me leave
To speak my mind, and I will through and through
Cleanse the foul body of th' infected world. . . .

[2.7.58–60]

But only if he accepts the dimension of the ludicrous as supplied by the
fool can Jaques fit into the comic scheme:

JAQUES. Yes, I have gain'd my experience.
ROSALIND. And your experience makes you sad. I had rather have
a fool to make me merry than experience to make me sad. . . .

[4.1.23–25]

Touchstone himself serves the same large function as his counterpart in *King Lear*, although his role is less wonderfully developed. The
fool, in either comedy or tragedy, tends to criticize arrogance and pretense on the part of other characters (he can make no claim to wisdom,
but he is, notwithstanding, no less wise than the others). In comedy,
moreover, his benign good nature provides an added depth of social
criticism of the individual: the fool, who is isolated by his motley garb
and supposed mental limitations, refuses to be alienated. Whereas
Jaques, the malcontent, endlessly finds the world a woeful place,
Touchstone accepts existence as he finds it. And most importantly,
either here or in *King Lear*, the fool constantly urges the paradox of
St. Paul: "If any man among you seemeth to be wise in this world, let
him become a fool, that he may be wise" (I Cor. 3:18).

Thus, as Jaques says, "The wise man's folly is anatomiz'd / Even by the squand'ring glances of the fool" (2.7.56–57). "The more pity," says Touchstone,

> that fools may not speak wisely what wise men do foolishly.
> CELIA. By my troth, thou sayest true; for since the little wit that fools have was silenced, the little foolery that wise men have makes a great show.
>
> [1.2.78–82]

And as Touchstone emphasizes, " 'The fool doth think he is wise, but the wise man knows himself to be a fool' " (5.1.29–30). By thus paradoxically collapsing the original juxtaposition of wisdom and folly into a playful equation where they are interchangeable, the fool reinforces those attitudes of Plotinus and Plato, mentioned in the first chapter, by which we are urged to realize that human life, when all is done, is not a very serious matter.

This implication of the fool's influence is made explicit in the famous speech of Jaques, uttered after he has met Touchstone and expressed the desire "that I were a fool! / I am ambitious for a motley coat" (2.7.42–43); for the speech constitutes a change from Jaques's customary black melancholy:

> All the world's a stage,
> And all the men and women merely players;
> They have their exits and their entrances;
> And one man in his time plays many parts,
> His acts being seven ages. At first the infant,
> Mewling and puking in the nurse's arms,
> Then the whining school-boy, with his satchel
> And shining morning face, creeping like snail
> Unwillingly to school. And then the lover,
> Sighing like furnace, with a woeful ballad
> Made to his mistress' eyebrow. Then a soldier,
> Full of strange oaths, and bearded like the pard,
> Jealous in honour, sudden and quick in quarrel,
> Seeking the bubble reputation
> Even in the cannon's mouth. And then the justice,
> In fair round belly with good capon lin'd,
> With eyes severe and beard of formal cut,

Full of wise saws and modern instances;
And so he plays his part. The sixth age shifts
Into the lean and slipper'd pantaloon,
With spectacles on nose and pouch on side,
His youthful hose, well sav'd, a world too wide
For his shrunk shank; and his big manly voice,
Turning again toward childish treble, pipes
And whistles in his sound. Last scene of all,
That ends this strange eventful history,
Is second childishness and mere oblivion;
Sans teeth, sans eyes, sans taste, sans every thing.

[2.7.139–66]

The lines achieve simultaneously a vision of life and a wry, rather than melancholy or despairing, perspective on its mystery. The tears of Jaques's contemplation of the wounded stag, mingled with the merry wonder of Touchstone's motley, become now an equivocal smile. Jaques's attitude, accordingly, is reclaimed from tragedy; and as a mark of this reclamation it sees the vanity of human life in terms of social roles—schoolboy, lover, soldier, justice—rather than in terms of individual agonies.

Jaques's moralizing, however, is here, as in the instance of the sobbing deer, somewhat blunted by a certain misunderstanding of reality. In the earlier instance, he did not consider that the hunters were killing out of necessity and not for sport; now the generalities of his cynical seven ages speech do not relate to the actuality around him. For Adam, who by Jaques's speech should be in "second childishness and mere oblivion . . . sans every thing," is instead—and the point is made by Orlando just before Jaques begins to speak—an "old poor man, / Who after me hath many a weary step / Limp'd in pure love." Adam is not "sans every thing," but full of "pure love." Jaques's speech, in short, does not recognize the facts of human community and mutual concern, and flies in the face of the reality before him:

ORLANDO. I almost die for food, and let me have it.
DUKE SENIOR. Sit down and feed, and welcome to our table.
ORLANDO. Speak you so gently? Pardon me, I pray you;
I thought that all things had been savage here. . . .

[2.7.104–7]

The Duke's answer serves both as a repudiation of Jaques's antisocial cynicism and as a sacramental affirmation of human community:

> True is it that we have seen better days,
> And have with holy bell been knoll'd to church,
> And sat at good men's feasts, and wip'd our eyes
> Of drops that sacred pity hath engend'red;
> And therefore sit you down in gentleness,
> And take upon command what help we have
> That to your wanting may be minist'red.
>
> [2.7.120–26]

Then, immediately after Jaques's interruption, the Duke reaffirms the holy sense of mutual concern: he pointedly includes the aged Adam in the communal meal:

> Welcome. Set down your venerable burden.
> And let him feed.
>
> [2.7.167–68]

In the midst of gentleness, welcoming, help, and veneration Jaques has revealed himself as deficient in the sympathies shared by "co-mates and brothers," and is therefore finally excluded from the community achieved by comic resolution. He is not only counterbalanced, but humanized, by Touchstone; yet in a sense he is and remains more a fool than does the man in motley.

Although not so profound a creation as Lear's fool, Touchstone is clearly closely related:

> ROSALIND. Well, this is the forest of Arden.
> TOUCHSTONE. Ay, now am I in Arden; the more fool I; when I was at home, I was in a better place; but travellers must be content.
>
> [2.4.12–14]

The combination of childlike apprehension and childlike acceptance marks Lear's fool too. Moreover, in this play the fool's apprehension and acceptance upon entering the Forest of Arden are still another way of suggesting that here is a golden world manqué. Like his counterpart in *King Lear*, Touchstone speaks truer than supposedly more intelligent figures: "Thou speak'st wiser than thou art ware of," says Rosalind (2.4.53). So when he anatomizes the "seven causes" of dueling, the old Duke finds it appropriate to say, "He uses his folly like a stalking-horse, and under the presentation of that he shoots his wit" (5.4.100–101). The attack on the folly and pretense of dueling, however, is not mere random wit; dueling is a social abuse, and by making it ridiculous, at the end of the fifth act (compare *The Alchemist*, 4.2.67–68), Touchstone symbolically makes ridiculous all the verbal duelings and disharmonies that have occupied the inhabitants of the pastoral forest.

These duelings interweave themselves into the encounters of almost all the characters. Orlando, for instance, escapes the deadly duel with Oliver, which is made concrete by his wrestling duel with Charles, only to engage in a duel of wits with Rosalind-Ganymede, and another with Jaques. Indeed, as a recent critic has emphasized, meetings or encounters (of which such duelings are a version) substitute for conventional plot in the play's middle portion and thereby invest the action with a special lightness of tone: ". . . such is the ease and rapidity with which pairs and groups break up, re-form, and succeed one another on the stage that there is a sense of fluid movement. All is done with the utmost lightness and gaiety, but as the lovers move through the forest, part and meet again, or mingle with the other characters in their constantly changing pairs and groups, every view of life seems, sooner or later, to find its opposite." *

Such an opposition, playfully cast into dueling's artifice of thrust and riposte, is the encounter between Jaques and Orlando:

> JAQUES. I thank you for your company; but, good faith, I had as lief have been myself alone.
> ORLANDO. And so had I; but yet, for fashion sake, I thank you too for your society.
> JAQUES. God buy you; let's meet as little as we can.
> ORLANDO. I do desire we may be better strangers.
> JAQUES. I pray you, mar no more trees with writing love songs in their barks.
> ORLANDO. I pray you, mar no moe of my verses with reading them ill-favouredly.
> JAQUES. Rosalind is your love's name?
> ORLANDO. Yes, just.
> JAQUES. I do not like her name.

* Harold Jenkins, "As You Like It," *Shakespeare Survey* 8 (Cambridge, 1968), p. 50.

ORLANDO. There was no thought of pleasing you when she was christen'd. . . .

JAQUES. You have a nimble wit; I think 'twas made of Atalanta's heels. Will you sit down with me? and we two will rail against our mistress the world, and all our misery.

ORLANDO. I will chide no breather in the world but myself, against whom I know most faults.

JAQUES. The worst fault you have is to be in love.

ORLANDO. 'Tis a fault I will not change for your best virtue. I am weary of you.

JAQUES. By my troth, I was seeking for a fool when I found you.

ORLANDO. He is drown'd in the brook; look but in, and you shall see him.

JAQUES. There I shall see mine own figure.

ORLANDO. Which I take to be either a fool or a cipher.

JAQUES. I'll tarry no longer with you; farewell, good Signior Love.

ORLANDO. I am glad of your departure; adieu, good Monsieur Melancholy.

[3.2.238–77]

In such a staccato combat, the elegance of which depends on the tension between the content of antagonism and the form of social courtesy, both participants are rebuked for social deviance: Orlando for his lovesickness, Jaques for his misanthropic melancholy; and each, kept within social bounds by the form of courtesy, serves as a comic nullifier of the other's deviance.

Neither, however, is wholly reclaimed. Jaques is never entirely redeemed by the play's action, and Orlando is reclaimed only after complicated and lengthy criticism by Rosalind-Ganymede. Indeed, this comedy, even more than *Twelfth Night*, rejects romantic love as social sickness. In the Forest of Arden romantic love replaces, and thereby almost seems to participate in the antisocial nature of, the darker motif of Cain against Abel that had characterized the action at court.

Orlando indicates his lovesickness by carving his emotion into the bark of forest trees:

O Rosalind! these trees shall be my books
And in their barks my thoughts I'll character; . . .

Run, run, Orlando; carve on every tree
The fair, the chaste, and unexpressive she.

[3.2.5–10]

Such a proposal echoes a motif from Virgil's pastorals:

certum est in silvis, inter spelaea ferarum
malle pati tenerisque meos incidere amores
arboribus: crescent illae, crescetis, amores.

it is certain that in the forest, among the caves of the wild
beasts, it is better to suffer and carve my love on the young
trees; when they grow, you will grow, my love.

The lines are from the tenth eclogue, which is where the pain of romantic love is most specifically recognized. In *As You Like It*, however,
it is not the case that "vincit omnia Amor"; for the comic society rebukes the pain and despair of a pastoral Gallus-like lover.

A second significance of the love-carving is that it reinforces still
further the sense of Arden as something less than the pastoral ideal.
Thomas Rosenmeyer, in his *The Green Cabinet: Theocritus and the
European Pastoral Lyric*, points out that this "pretty vulgarism"—the
"self-defeating attack upon the surface of trees"—which had its inception in Callimachus rather than in Theocritus, actually damages rather
than honors the sacred environment of pure pastoral (p. 203). The
play makes clear, nonetheless, that the change from the motif of social
sickness as brother-against-brother to the motif of social sickness as
romantic love corresponds to a change from a courtly to a pastoral environment. It is, accordingly, noteworthy that Orlando's proposal to
carve on the trees is directly followed by a change in the tone of
Arden: it promptly becomes less an English Sherwood Forest and more
a Latinate shepherd's world. As though a signal has been given, Orlando's proposal is followed by the entrance of Touchstone and of
Corin, a shepherd. They duel:

CORIN. And how like you this shepherd's life, Master Touchstone?
TOUCHSTONE. Truly, shepherd, in respect of itself, it is a good
life; but in respect that it is a shepherd's life, it is nought. In
respect that it is solitary, I like it very well; but in respect that
it is private, it is a very vile life. Now in respect it is in the

fields, it pleaseth me well; but in respect it is not in the court, it is tedious. . . . Hast any philosophy in thee, shepherd?

CORIN. No more but that I know the more one sickens the worse at ease he is; . . . that good pasture makes fat sheep; and that a great cause of the night is lack of the sun; . . .

TOUCHSTONE. Such a one is a natural philosopher. Wast ever in court, shepherd?

CORIN. No, truly. . . .

TOUCHSTONE. Why, if thou never wast at court, thou never saw'st good manners. . . . Thou art in a parlous state, shepherd.

CORIN. Not a whit, Touchstone. Those that are good manners at the court are as ridiculous in the country as the behaviour of the country is most mockable at court.

[3.2.11–43]

Such extended badinage both confirms the equivocal nature of the pastoral realm in *As You Like It,* and establishes that realm as in fact pastoral. The shepherd's world is somewhat criticized as against the court; the court is somewhat criticized as against the shepherd's world.

In the shepherd's world, Orlando's love is attacked from many quarters. It is, first of all, divested of its claim to uniqueness by being ironically echoed in the pastoral lovesickness of Silvius for Phebe. It is lowered in its claim to dignity by being distortedly reflected in the bumpkin love of Touchstone for Audrey. And it is shown as a diminution, rather than a heightening, of awareness by the fact that Orlando does not know that Ganymede, to whom he laments the absence of Rosalind, is actually that Rosalind whom he so extravagantly loves. His emotion, furthermore, is made to appear moist and ludicrous by the dry criticism of Rosalind. "Then in mine own person I die," sighs Orlando. Rosalind replies:

No, faith, die by attorney. The poor world is almost six thousand years old, and in all this time there was not any man died in his own person, videlicet, in a love-cause. Troilus had his brains dash'd out with a Grecian club; yet he did what he could to die before, and he is one of the patterns of love. Leander, he would have liv'd many a fair year, though Hero had turn'd nun, if it had not been for a hot midsummer night; for, good youth, he went but forth to wash him in the Hellespont, and, being taken with the cramp, was drown'd; and the foolish chroniclers of that age found it was—Hero of Sestos. But these are all lies: men have died from time to time, and worms have eaten them, but not for love.

[4.1.82–95]

The last justly famous sentence establishes the absolute norm of comedy's rebuke to romantic love. And the invocation of Hero and Leander directs attention to Marlowe's poem. Indeed, Marlowe's anti-social life, as well as the unacceptability of romantic love's exclusiveness, are focused by reference to Marlowe's death and by direct quotation of a line from *Hero and Leander*: "Dead shepherd, now I find thy saw of might,/ 'Who ever lov'd that lov'd not at first sight?'" (3.5.80–81; *Hero and Leander*, 1.176). The question is asked, however, by the pastoral Phebe as she embarks upon a course of patent folly: blind love for Ganymede, who, in reality a woman, represents a social impossibility for the shepherdess.

Phebe's folly is underscored by her "love at first sight" infatuation; her pastoral lover, Silvius, is equally foolish, for love makes him less than a man:

> Sweet Phebe, do not scorn me; do not, Phebe.
> Say that you love me not; but say not so
> In bitterness.

[3.5.1–3]

Both Phebe and Silvius are accordingly dry-beaten with Rosalind's scoff, which is the curative of such extravagant and socially unsettling emotion. To Phebe she says:

> I see no more in you than in the ordinary
> Of nature's sale-work. 'Od's my little life,
> I think she means to tangle my eyes too!
> No, faith, proud mistress, hope not after it;
> 'Tis not your inky brows, your black silk hair,
> Your bugle eyeballs, nor your cheek of cream,
> That can entame my spirits to your worship.

[3.5.42–48]

Having demolished Phebe's pretensions to uniqueness, she then turns her scorn on Silvius:

You foolish shepherd, wherefore do you follow her,
Like foggy south, puffing with wind and rain?
You are a thousand times a properer man
Than she a woman. 'Tis such fools as you
That makes the world full of ill-favour'd children.

[3.5.49-53]

Even more explicit, and much more prolonged, are the rebukes administered to Orlando. His romantic extravagance is repeatedly denigrated by being referred to in the language of sickness, and his dramatically pastoral emotion is withered by Rosalind's scorn:

There is a man haunts the forest that abuses our young plants with carving "Rosalind" on their barks; hangs odes upon hawthorns and elegies on brambles; all, forsooth, deifying the name of Rosalind. If I could meet that fancy-monger, I would give him some good counsel, for he seems to have the quotidian of love upon him.

ORLANDO. I am he that is so love-shak'd; I pray you tell me your remedy.

ROSALIND. There is none of my uncle's marks upon you; he taught me how to know a man in love; in which cage of rushes I am sure you are not prisoner.

ORLANDO. What were his marks?

ROSALIND. A lean cheek, which you have not; a blue eye and sunken, which you have not; an unquestionable spirit, which you have not; a beard neglected, which you have not. . . . Then your hose should be ungarter'd, your bonnet unbanded, your sleeve unbutton'd, your shoe untied, and every thing about you demonstrating a careless desolation. . . .

ORLANDO. Fair youth, I would I could make thee believe I love. . . .

ROSALIND. But are you so much in love as your rhymes speak?

ORLANDO. Neither rhyme nor reason can express how much.

ROSALIND. Love is merely a madness. . . .

ORLANDO. I would not be cured, youth.

ROSALIND. I would cure you, if you would but call me Rosalind, and come every day to my cote and woo me.

[3.2.334-92]

The artifice of Rosalind pretending to be Ganymede, and Ganymede pretending to be Rosalind again, grants the audience an insight immensely superior to that of Orlando, while equating his exaggerated love with his ignorance; and it also satisfies dramatically the idea that love is a mistaking of reality. Once love comes under the control supplied by Rosalind's criticism, however, the play begins to frolic in the dance-like patterns of *Love's Labour's Lost*. The Cain-against-Abel situation of the two dukes, like that of Orlando and Oliver, had from the first involved the play in doublings; and these, together with the doubling of Rosalind by Celia, and the Ganymede disguise by the Aliena disguise, become, as the action of the play lightens, the symmetrical doublings and repetitions of comedy's artifice. Indeed, perhaps no single place in Shakespeare's comedy achieves a more perfect coordination of symmetry, repetition, and comic inevitability than the merry-go-round of the love doctor's final social disposition of the disease of romantic love. Rosalind says to Orlando:

> Therefore, put you in your best array, bid yours friends; for if you will be married tomorrow, you shall; and to Rosalind, if you will.

At this point Silvius and Phebe enter:

> PHEBE. Youth, you have done me much ungentleness. . . .
> ROSALIND. I care not if I have. . . .
> You are there follow'd by a faithful shepherd;
> Look upon him, love him; he worships you.
> PHEBE. Good shepherd, tell this youth what 'tis to love.
> SILVIUS. It is to be all made of sighs and tears;
> And so am I for Phebe.
> PHEBE. And I for Ganymede.
> ORLANDO. And I for Rosalind.
> ROSALIND. And I for no woman.
> SILVIUS. It is to be all made of faith and service;
> And so am I for Phebe.
> PHEBE. And I for Ganymede.
> ORLANDO. And I for Rosalind.
> ROSALIND. And I for no woman.
> SILVIUS. It is to be all made of fantasy.
> All made of passion, and all made of wishes;

All adoration, duty, and observance,
All humbleness, all patience, and impatience,
All purity, all trial, all obedience;
And so am I for Phebe.

PHEBE. And so am I for Ganymede.

ORLANDO. And so am I for Rosalind.

ROSALIND. And so am I for no woman.

PHEBE. If this be so, why blame you me to love you?

SILVIUS. If this be so, why blame you me to love you?

ORLANDO. If this be so, why blame you me to love you? . . .

ROSALIND. Pray you, no more of this; 'tis like the howling of Irish wolves against the moon. [*To Silvius*] I will help you, if I can. [*To Phebe*] I would love you, if I could.—To-morrow meet me all together. [*To Phebe*] I will marry you if ever I marry woman, and I'll be married to-morrow. [*To Orlando*] I will satisfy you if ever I satisfied man, and you shall be married to-morrow. [*To Silvius*] I will content you if what pleases you contents you, and you shall be married to-morrow.

[5.2.66–109]

And thus the play dances to its final resolution. Hymen announces that "Then is there mirth in heaven, / When earthly things made even / Atone together" (5.4.102–4), and his beautiful song pours comic benignity lavishly over the concluding action:

Wedding is great Juno's crown
 O blessed bond of board and bed!
'Tis Hymen peoples every town;
 High wedlock then be honoured.
Honour, high honour, and renown,
To Hymen, god of every town!

[5.4.135–40]

The song provides one of literature's most elevated and explicit salutations to the aim and justification of comedy. Under its assurance, the old Duke commands his society to

fall into our rustic revelry.
Play, music; and you brides and bridegrooms all,
With measure heap'd in joy, to th' measures fall.

[5.4.171–73]

And yet even this comic happiness cannot totally sweeten the trace of the bitter root in *As You Like It*. Both the usurping Duke and the melancholy Jaques are ejected from, rather than reconciled to, the new society. As Jaques de Boys—the new Jaques—says:

> Duke Frederick, hearing how that every day
> Men of great worth resorted to this forest,
> Address'd a mighty power; which were on foot,
> In his own conduct, purposely to take
> His brother here, and put him to the sword;
> And to the skirts of this wild wood he came,
> Where, meeting with an old religious man,
> After some question with him, was converted
> Both from his enterprise and from the world;
> His crown bequeathing to his banish'd brother,
> And all their lands restor'd to them again
> That were with him exil'd.
>
> [5.4.148–59]

And Jaques, the malcontent, is, like Molière's Alceste, equally irredeemable by the comic therapy:

> JAQUES. Sir, by your patience. If I heard you rightly,
> The Duke hath put on a religious life
> And thrown into neglect the pompous court.
> JAQUES DE BOYS. He hath.
> JAQUES. To him will I. Out of these convertites
> There is much matter to be heard and learn'd.
> . . . So to your pleasures;
> I am for other than for dancing measures.
>
> [5.4.174–87]

Jaques, indeed, though necessary to the process of comic catharsis in the play, has always exerted counter-pressure against the pastoral ideal. When Amiens sings the lovely song that declares Arden's version of pastoral carefreeness, Jaques immediately seeks to cloud its limpidity:

> AMIENS. Under the greenwood tree
> Who loves to lie with me,
> And turn his merry note
> Unto the sweet bird's throat,

Come hither, come hither, come hither.
> Here shall he see
> No enemy
> But winter and rough weather.

JAQUES. More, more, I prithee more.

AMIENS. It will make you melancholy, Monsieur Jaques.

JAQUES. I thank it. More, I prithee, more. I can suck melancholy out of a song, as a weasel sucks eggs.

[2.5.1–13]

And then Jaques produces his own song, which, in its cynicism, superimposes itself like a blotter on that of Amiens:

> If it do come to pass
> That any man turn ass,
> Leaving his wealth and ease
> A stubborn will to please,
> Ducdame, ducdame, ducdame;
> Here shall he see
> Gross fools as he,
> An if he will come to me.

AMIENS. What's that "ducdame"?

JAQUES. 'Tis a Greek invocation, to call fools into a circle.

[2.5.46–56]

If the coming together of individuals into social happiness is for Jaques a calling of "fools into a circle," it is clear that his own deviation is as impervious to comic reclamation as that of the wicked younger duke.

Thus Duke Frederick and Jaques are "for other than for dancing measures," and by that fact they show that certain persisting threads of action and tone in this play are alien to the comic vision. By leaving Frederick and Jaques out of the social resolution, *As You Like It* intensifies the strain on comic limits that the villainous Don John had exerted in *Much Ado About Nothing*. That play, like this one, concludes equivocally. Benedick recites the comic benediction: "Come, come, we are friends. Let's have a dance ere we are married" (*Much Ado*, 5.4.113–14); but Don John is a loose end:

MESSENGER. My lord, your brother John is ta'en in flight,
And brought with armed men back to Messina.

BENEDICK. Think not on him till to-morrow. I'll devise thee brave punishments for him. Strike up, pipers.

[*Much Ado*, 5.4.120–24]

In *As You Like It*, Hymen's song provides a more radiant measure of comic well-being than any statements at the end of *Much Ado*, but even so the complications have moved nearer to tragedy, and Hymen cannot eradicate all the signs of strain. And after *As You Like It*, Shakespeare not only forgoes pastoral therapy for a while, but his comic vessels, leaving behind the clear waters sailed by *Twelfth Night* and *The Merry Wives of Windsor*, begin increasingly to labor in heavy seas of bitterness. The idea of the joyous society tends henceforth to be more difficult to achieve or maintain. In *The Winter's Tale*, great cracks run through the artifice of happiness, and are caulked only with difficulty. Not until *The Tempest* does Shakespeare's art, having traversed the bitter complications of the middle and late comedies, find quiet harbor in a renewed paradisal hope. There at last, in the enchanted island's golden world, the storm of cynicism and tragic disharmony, with a final rage, blows itself out.

V. We Must Be Gentle

Disintegration and Reunion in
The Winter's Tale

"*A* sad tale's best for winter." The melancholy words of the doomed child Mamillius (2.1.25) set the tone, and ordain the comic reality, of *The Winter's Tale*. For demonic forces are loose within this play, and the redemption provided by pastoral is as bittersweet as the idea of winter's beauty itself. Indeed, the very conception of a winter pastoral evokes an ambivalence; the Ovidian golden age was specifically one where "ver erat aeternum"— spring was eternal. A pastoral simplification of winter, no matter what its beauty, must incorporate something less than the perfect fulfillment of the paradisal vision.

To be sure, a winter pastoral can be as lovely as a spring or summer pastoral. The *Hiems* song that concludes *Love's Labour's Lost* is no less limpidly perfect than the *Ver* song that is its counterpart. But that limpid perfection, when set into metaphors of winter, must always imply meanings that hint of sadness. "Thou barrein ground," laments Spenser's Colin Cloute, "whome winters wrath hath wasted, / Art made a myrrhour to behold my plight. . . . Such rage as winters reigneth in my heart, / My life bloud friesing with unkindly cold" (*The Shepheardes Calendar*, 1.19–20, 25–26). And in the December eclogue, the lament is raised that "Winter is come, that blows the balefull breath, / And after winter commeth timely death" (12.149–50).

In *The Winter's Tale*, death, and other aspects of diminished being that herald it, dominate the first three acts. In its motifs of restlessness, sudden hatred, troubled journeys, deadly pursuit, and broken faith, the play in these acts affirms the bitter cosmos of *Pericles*. And death is everywhere: in the King's intentions toward Polixenes, in his attitude toward Hermione's baby, in the wasting away of Mamillius, in the seeming death of Hermione, and, most grotesquely, in the devouring of Antigonus. The sixteen-year hiatus between the third and fourth act, which so fascinated Coleridge, and which so utterly repudiates the dramatic unities of the French classical mode, is a sign of the play's tormented wrenching of comedy out of its normal symmetries, and is also a psychological necessity. For only a new generation, and many years to soften old hatred, can make acceptable a comic resolution to the madness of Leontes.

The first enunciation of his inner rage erupts, startlingly, into a seemingly ideal social situation of happy marriage and longtime friendship. Indeed, if this play looks back, in its pastorally redeemed fourth and fifth acts, to a torment sixteen years gone, such curious preoccupation with the past is not unique. For the torment of Leontes, and the destruction it causes, themselves look back to a still earlier time when pastoral bliss was the norm. As Northrop Frye says, "We begin with reference to an innocent childhood when Leontes and Polixenes were 'twinned lambs,' and then suddenly plunge from the reminiscence of this pastoral paradise into a world of superstition and obsession" (*A Natural Perspective: The Development of Shakespearean Comedy and Romance* [New York and London, 1965], p. 114).

This play, in fact, attacks pastoral bliss at its very heart, for childhood is the persistent object of the action's dramatic rage. Leontes repudiates the childhood friendship he bore for Polixenes, frightens the boy Mamillius to death, rejects the infant Perdita and abandons her to die. His rejection of his newborn child shockingly epitomizes his madness. Emilia notes that Hermione "is, something before her time, deliver'd. . . . A daughter, and a goodly babe, / Lusty and like to live" (2.2.25–27). Paulina, relying on society's universal love for children, says, "I'll show't the King, and undertake to be / Her advocate to th' loud'st. We do not know / How he may soften at the sight o' th' child" (2.2.38–40). But this tactic only elicits a language of the most twisted and grotesque hatred: "Give her the bastard"; "Take up the bastard; . . . giv't to thy crone"; "This brat is none of mine"; "My child! Away with't! . . . take it hence, / And see it instantly consum'd with fire"; "Shall I live on to see this bastard kneel / And call me father? Better burn it now / Than curse it then" (2.3.73, 75–76, 92, 131–33, 154–56).

Scarcely less grotesque is his altered decision to stop just short of murdering the infant:

> You, sir, come you hither.
> You that have been so tenderly officious
> With Lady Margery, your midwife there,

To save this bastard's life—for 'tis a bastard,
So sure as this beard's grey—what will you adventure
To save this brat's life? . . .
                              We enjoin thee,
As thou art liegeman to us, that thou carry
This female bastard hence; and that thou bear it
To some remote and desert place, quite out
Of our dominions; and that there thou leave it,
Without more mercy, to its own protection
And favour of the climate. As by strange fortune
It came to us, I do in justice charge thee. . . .
That thou commend it strangely to some place
Where chance may nurse or end it.

                                        [2.3.157–82]

The attack on childhood signifies everything that is sick, inhuman, antisocial, and opposed to the express values of the paradisal vision. Leontes's rage, indeed, erupts like lava from a nether region, and in its intensity, its awesome suddenness, suggests vast subliminal depths of torment and anguish. Often noted as one of the most startling of all dramatic volte-faces, the change from mellow friendliness to seething hatred never loses its power to shock. We retrace the process:

POLIXENES.   . . . I have stay'd
to tire your royalty. . . . No longer stay.
LEONTES. One sev'night longer.
POLIXENES. Very sooth, to-morrow.
LEONTES. We'll part the time between's then. . . .
Tongue-tied our Queen? Speak you.
HERMIONE. I had thought, sir, to have held my peace until
You had drawn oaths from him not to stay. You, sir,
Charge him too coldly. . . .
LEONTES. Well said, Hermione. . . .
HERMIONE.   Not your gaoler, then.
But your kind hostess. Come, I'll question you
Of my lord's tricks and yours when you were boys.
You were pretty lordings then!

And this elegant and archetypal situation, of a husband and wife entreating an old friend to prolong a visit, expands in its good feeling to include an Edenic claim of more happiness than life, its childhood paradise lost, can sustain:

> POLIXENES.   We were, fair Queen,
> Two lads that thought there was no more behind
> But such a day to-morrow as to-day,
> And to be boy eternal. . . .
> We were as twinn'd lambs that did frisk i' th' sun,
> And bleat the one at th' other. What we chang'd
> Was innocence for innocence; we knew not
> The doctrine of ill-doing, nor dream'd
> That any did. Had we pursu'd that life,
> And our weak spirits ne'er been higher rear'd
> With stronger blood, we should have answer'd heaven
> Boldly "Not guilty," the imposition clear'd
> Hereditary ours.
>
>   [1.2.14–75]

But the Pelagian thought of heavenly innocence in this our life is ironically and mightily rebuked by the eruption from the Augustinian depths of man's corrupt and fallen nature:

> LEONTES.   Is he won yet?
> HERMIONE. He'll stay, my lord.
> LEONTES. At my request he would not.
> Hermione, my dearest, thou never spok'st
> To better purpose.
>
>   [1.2.86–89]

And after some banter Hermione answers:

> Why, lo you now, I have spoke to th' purpose twice:
> The one for ever earn'd a royal husband;
> Th' other for some while a friend.
>
>   [1.2.106–8]

Then she gives her hand to Polixenes, and Leontes, aside, utters those words of agonized hatred that give the lie to all optimism about human affairs:

> Too hot, too hot!
> To mingle friendship far is mingling bloods.
> I have tremor cordis on me; my heart dances,

> But not for joy, not joy. This entertainment
> May a free face put on; derive a liberty
> From heartiness, from bounty, fertile bosom,
> And well become the agent. 'T may, I grant;
> But to be paddling palms and pinching fingers,
> As now they are, and making practis'd smiles,
> As in a looking-glass; and then to sigh, as 'twere
> The mort o' th' deer.
>
> [1.2.108–18]

The sexual fury and disgust that seethed in Hamlet when he thought about Claudius and his mother are echoed in these words; and as Leontes goes on, he begins to croak in the tones of Othello's Iago-induced prurience and suspicion:

> Is whispering nothing?
> Is leaning cheek to cheek? Is meeting noses?
> Kissing with inside lip? Stopping the career
> Of laughter with a sigh?—a note infallible
> Of breaking honesty. Horsing foot on foot?
> Skulking in corners? Wishing clocks more swift;
> Hours, minutes; noon, midnight? And all eyes
> Blind with the pin and web but theirs, theirs only,
> That would unseen be wicked—is this nothing?
>
> [1.2.284–92]

The reason for such molten torment may seem, to an industrious and mechanical scholar, sitting comfortably in his study, to be only a matter of dramatic license or Jacobean convention; it will not seem so to those whose misfortune has been actually to experience such agony. For the probabilities in such situations all too often support the fact of guilt. "There have been," says Leontes in recognition of the world's way, ". . . cuckolds ere now; / And many a man there is, even at this present, / Now while I speak this, holds his wife by th' arm / That little thinks she has been sluic'd in's absence, / And his pond fish'd by his next neighbor, by / Sir Smile, his neighbour" (1.2.190–96). "For aught I know," says Beaumont and Fletcher's Amintor, "all husbands are like me; / And every one I talk with of his wife /Is but a well dissembler of his woes" (The Maid's Tragedy, 3.2.49–51).

Such are the dramatic probabilities, and such too are the probabilities in lived experience. A newspaper report (and perhaps the more ephemeral the document, the more depressingly timeless the statistic) on the day this page is being written, estimates that in America "60 per cent of all husbands and 35 to 40 per cent of all wives cheat on their spouses"; and although much of this infidelity is casual, as uncared about as it is uncaring, some of it inflicts soul-shaking pain. And this is not to mention the other forms of betrayal, unrecorded and unestimated, that harrow human relationships.

The most persistent theme in all Shakespeare, in fact, is that of human faithlessness. It is the very substance of the history plays, the most tormented preoccupation of the tragedies, the chief ingredient of the bitterness in the middle and late comedies, all haunted by the theme of sonnet 92: "Thou mayst be false, and yet I know it not." Othello's suspicions, like those of Leontes, are in the instance unjustified, but they derive motive power from the high probability of a young wife's betrayal; and Othello is, indeed, betrayed, by his friend Iago if not by his wife Desdemona, just as Desdemona, though faithful to her husband, betrays her father. Elsewhere the probability of betrayal is more directly realized. The pain suffered by Troilus corresponds to his actual betrayal by Cressida, and the language of that play mocks all human idealism as alternating between illusion and treachery. Indeed, when Shakespeare deals with the ideas of loyalty and broken faith, the betrayal of human commitment is far more often represented as simple fact than as mistaken suspicion. The betrayal of friendship by Rosencrantz and Guildenstern, of love by Ophelia, of wifehood by Gertrude, of brotherhood by Claudius—these motifs form the central meaning of *Hamlet*. Macbeth's betrayal of Duncan, Enobarbus's of Antony, Rome's of Coriolanus, Caesar's of Rome and the conspirators of Caesar, Angelo's of the Duke, Prince Hal's of Falstaff, and above all, Lear's betrayal by his daughters—these and other instances testify to the prevalence of the themes of betrayal and broken faith in Shakespeare's art.

It is, in the light of this preoccupation, not unfitting that *Timon of Athens* should seem so important a play in the estimation of G. Wilson Knight. For, although one cannot wholly agree with his high estimate of it as a work of art, there can be little doubt that its emotional attitudes represent, in extreme form, the most powerful and pervasive of Shakespeare's dramaturgic conceptions. Indeed, the very inadequacy of *Timon* as art seems to authenticate the bitter personal intensity of its statements, as though Shakespeare here cannot remove himself far enough from the torments of betrayed trust to achieve the tragic clarities of *Hamlet* and *Lear*:

> There's nothing level in our cursed natures
> But direct villainy. Therefore be abhorr'd
> All feasts, societies, and throngs of men!
> His semblable, yea, himself, Timon disdains.
> Destruction fang mankind!
>
> [*Timon of Athens*, 4.3.19–23]

Let no assembly of twenty be without a score of villains. If there sit twelve women at the table, let a dozen of them be—as they are.

> [*Timon of Athens*, 3.6.78–80]

> Most smiling, smooth, detested parasites,
> Courteous destroyers, affable wolves, meek bears,
> You fools of fortune, trencher friends, time's flies,
> Cap and knee slaves, vapours, and minute-jacks!
> Of man and beast the infinite malady
> Crust you quite o'er! . . .
> Burn, house! sink, Athens! Henceforth hated be
> Of Timon man and all humanity!
>
> [*Timon of Athens*, 3.6.94–105]

The *saeva indignatio* of Timon seems to become more a psychodramatic than an artistic expression, by the principle on which, when very angry, we tend to speak less skillfully than when only annoyed. But the attitude of disgust is that same attitude that achieves sublimely tragic reverberation in the great utterances of Lear:

> I pardon that man's life. What was thy cause?
> Adultery?
> Thou shalt not die. Die for adultery? No.
> The wren goes to't, and the small gilded fly
> Does lecher in my sight.
> Let copulation thrive; for Gloucester's bastard son
> Was kinder to his father than my daughters
> Got 'tween the lawful sheets. . . .
> Burning, scalding, stench, consumption. Fie, fie, fie!
> pah, pah! Give me an ounce of civet, good apothecary,

to sweeten my imagination. There's money for thee.
GLOUCESTER. O, let me kiss that hand!
LEAR. Let me wipe it first; it smells of mortality.

[*King Lear*, 4.6.109–33]

The mysterious rage of Leontes is another expression of this persisting view of the probability of baseness in human relationships. The dual potentiality of man, either to be like the animals or like the angels, was often insisted on by Shakespeare's philosophically minded predecessors in the Renaissance. As Pomponazzi, for instance, says, "Man is clearly not of simple but of multiple ... nature, and he is to be placed as a mean between mortal and immortal things. . . . And to man, who thus exists as a mean between the two, power is given to assume whichever nature he wishes" (*De immortalitate animae*, Cap. I.). Leontes's rage, following so suddenly on the benign scene appropriate to comedy, is a sort of reflection of the Renaissance emphasis on man's multiple possibility. To it, moreover, must be added darker thoughts, from Augustine and Calvin, about man's inherent corruption. All such thoughts receive their validation from experience: in Shakespeare's life, about which we can only speculate, or in our own, about which we can be certain.

The eruption of Leontes's suspicion represents a kind of absolute standard of the anticomic; and it is therefore the means by which the magnetic attraction of people to one another, the comic cohesiveness, is reversed. Things fall apart. Society disintegrates under the blasting reality of Leontes's rage. Polixenes the friend becomes Polixenes the fugitive. Camillo the loyal retainer becomes Camillo the traitor, rather than accept Leontes's command and remain as Camillo the murderer. Antigonus the trusted counselor becomes Antigonus the doomed wanderer. Mamillius the prince and heir becomes Mamillius the pining child. Hermione the faithful wife becomes Hermione the accused whore and Hermione the prisoner—finally, Hermione the seeming-dead. And all these things are wrought by Leontes's paranoid rage. As Paulina tells him in the cathartic moment of truth:

That thou betray'dst Polixenes, 'twas nothing;
That did but show thee, of a fool, inconstant,
And damnable ingrateful. Nor was't much
Thou wouldst have poison'd good Camillo's honour,
To have him kill a king—poor trespasses,

More monstrous standing by; whereof I reckon
The casting forth to crows thy baby daughter
To be or none or little, though a devil
Would have shed water out of fire ere done't;
Nor is't directly laid to thee, the death
Of the young Prince, whose honourable thoughts—
Thoughts high for one so tender—cleft the heart
That could conceive a gross and foolish sire
Blemish'd his gracious dam. This is not, no,
Laid to thy answer; but the last—O lords,
When I have said, cry "Woe!"—the Queen, the Queen,
The sweet'st, dear'st creature's dead; and vengeance for't
Not dropp'd down yet. . . .
                    But, O thou tyrant!
Do not repent these things, for they are heavier
Than all thy woes can stir; therefore betake thee
To nothing but despair. A thousand knees
Ten thousand years together, naked, fasting,
Upon a barren mountain, and still winter
In storm perpetual, could not move the gods
To look that way thou wert.

                                        [3.2.182–211]

The cleansing release afforded by Paulina's denunciation is some measure of the amount of desolation caused by Leontes's maddened thoughts. Such a lengthy and bitter excoriation is necessary to discharge the outrage that Leontes's actions have provoked; and it prepares the way for the possibilities of comic reclamation. Having delivered herself of her counterrage, Paulina subsides into an attitude more inviting to the prospect of ultimate reconciliations:

                    Alas! I have show'd too much
The rashness of a woman! He is touch'd
To th' noble heart. What's gone and what's past help
Should be past grief. Do not receive affliction
At my petition. . . . Now, good my liege,
Sir, royal sir, forgive a foolish woman.

                                        [3.2.217–24]

The volcanic flow of Leontes's rage having erupted and subsided by the second scene of the third act, the action of the play moves in place (to the seacoast of Bohemia) and in time (sixteen years) to allow further cooling to occur. The last symbol of the molten world is the grotesque exit of Antigonus, the babe Perdita now safely deposited on the shore:

> A savage clamour!
> Well may I get aboard! This is the chase;
> I am gone for ever. [*Exit, pursued by a bear.*]
>
> [3.3.57–59]

The bear, which appears as suddenly and ferociously as the rage of Leontes, clears the coast for a new entrance—one equally unlikely in a sea's environment—that of a shepherd. And at that moment the balm of pastoral begins to be applied to the burning wounds inflicted by the action so far. As the clown reports the sinking of the ship at sea, and the death of Antigonus on land ("how the poor souls roar'd, and the sea mock'd them; and how the poor gentleman roared, and the bear mock'd him" [3.3.96–98]), the shepherd replies with words that justify the play's division into two worlds of space and time:

> Now bless thyself; thou met'st with things dying, I with things new-born. Here's a sight for thee; look thee, a bearing-cloth for a squire's child!
>
> [3.3.109–12]

The first two scenes of the fourth act establish the passage of sixteen years, and connect the new present with the past by means of the conversation between Polixenes and Camillo. At the beginning of the third scene, Autolycus appears, singing the carefree words that we recognize as the symbol of transformation to the ideal realm of pastoral:

> When daffodils begin to peer,
>   With heigh! the doxy over the dale,
> Why, then comes in the sweet o' the year;
>   For the red blood reigns in the winter's pale.
>
> [4.3.1–4]

The figure of Autolycus, the pastoral thief, serves in some ways the same function as Jaques in *As You Like It*. Like Jaques, Autolycus indicates a slight falling off from the golden ideal. Such an indication is a reminder, however harmless, of the searing possibilities opened up by Leontes. The division of the two worlds of space and time, though it must be sharp, cannot be absolute; continuity of theme and interest must be preserved. The child Mamillius lost in the first world finds a counterpart in the babe Perdita saved for the second; the rage of Leontes finds a counterpart in the activity, harmless though it be, of Autolycus. Unlike Jaques, however, Autolycus is not a cerebral critic of the pastoral world, but a kind of life-force, which reinforces the theme of "things new-born" at the same time that it prevents us from wholly forgetting the troubles that accompany remembrance of the past. Though benign, he is nonetheless a thief, which is not socially acceptable; so his role confirms the hint of malaise found in the conception of winter, rather than spring, as the pastoral matrix. But he sings, and proves, that "red blood reigns in the winter's pale." Traversi speaks well on this matter:

Autolycus, indeed, has a part of his own to play in the complete conception. His comic function is that of one who is regarded as a little apart from the main structure, whose behaviour is in some sense irreducible to the social values of the play, calculated to throw upon the symbolic symmetry itself a touch of relativity, a sense of the incalculable individuality of the processes of life. . . . The key to Autolycus, and to his peculiar position in the action, can, indeed, be defined in the phrase from his own song that "the red blood reigns in the winter's pale." The reference to winter implies at once a contrast and a point of reference. It connects the episode now before us with the play's title, and establishes a relationship between the birth of spring in the heart of winter and the affirmation of the warm, living "blood" of youth against the jealousy and care-laden envy of age, an affirmation shortly to be confirmed in the contrast between the young lovers and their elders. In Autolycus himself, of course, this outpouring of spontaneous life moves on the margin of social forms. It has indeed a predatory aspect comically expressed in his first action, the picking of the Clown's pocket; but this itself is, to some degree, a devaluation of his victim's new-found riches and the social pretensions which these have aroused in him (*Shakespeare: The Last Phase* [New York, n.d.], pp. 138–39).

It should be noted, furthermore, that the picking of the Clown's pocket mockingly prefigures the "sheep-shearing" scene that follows.

That scene represents one of the most concentrated expressions of pastoral ever achieved by Shakespeare. Its essence lies in the extended imagery of the giving of flowers; for by giving flowers here, healing blossoms are strewn over the entire desert seared by Leontes:

PERDITA.   You're welcome, sir.
Give me those flow'rs there, Dorcas. Reverend sirs,
For you there's rosemary and rue; these keep
Seeming and savour all the winter long.
Grace and remembrance be to you both!
And welcome to our shearing.

[4.4.72–77]

The tropes of welcoming, of giving, of grace, all float in upon these words; and the perfumed scent and beautiful sight of flowers are heaped, almost overpoweringly, over the vast desolate anxiety established by the play's beginning:

POLIXENES.   Shepherdess—
A fair one are you—well you fit our ages
With flow'rs of winter.
PERDITA.   Sir, the year growing ancient,
Not yet on summer's death nor on the birth
Of trembling winter, the fairest flow'rs o' th' season
Are our carnations and streak'd gillyvors,
Which some call nature's bastards. Of that kind
Our rustic garden's barren; and I care not
To get slips of them.
POLIXENES.   Wherefore, gentle maiden,
Do you neglect them? . . .
Then make your garden rich in gillyvors
And do not call them bastards.

[4.4.77–99]

The torment of Leontes's earlier ravings about his supposed "bastard" child is transformed into the loveliness of flowers and the acceptance of kings. And Perdita provides more fragrance and color:

                              Here's flow'rs for you;
Hot lavender, mints, savory, marjoram;
The marigold, that goes to bed wi' th' sun
And with him rises weeping; these are flow'rs
Of middle summer, and I think they are given
To men of middle age. Y'are very welcome.

[4.4.103–8]

And from the cornucopia of symbolic well-being, in seemingly inexhaustible abundance, issue flowers that blanket and perfume all things:

> Now, my fair'st friend,
> I would I had some flow'rs o' th' spring that might
> Become your time of day—and yours, and yours,
> That wear upon your virgin branches yet
> Your maidenheads growing. O Proserpina,
> For the flowers now that, frighted, thou let'st fall
> From Dis's waggon!—daffodils,
> That come before the swallow dares, and take
> The winds of March with beauty; violets, dim
> But sweeter than the lids of Juno's eyes
> Or Cytherea's breath; pale primroses,
> That die unmarried ere they can behold
> Bright Phoebus in his strength—a malady
> Most incident to maids; bold oxlips, and
> The crown-imperial; lilies of all kinds,
> The flow'r-de-luce being one. O, these I lack,
> To make you garlands of, and my sweet friend,
> To strew him o'er and o'er!
>
> [4.4.112–29]

That Shakespeare here achieves a kind of absolute in the invocation of symbolic bliss is attested by Milton's reworking of "O Proserpina, / For the flowers now that, frighted, thou let'st fall / From Dis's waggon" into his description of the Garden of Eden itself:

> Not that fair field
> Of *Enna*, where *Proserpin* gath'ring flow'rs
> Herself a fairer Flow'r by gloomy *Dis*
> Was gather'd
> . . . might with this Paradise
> Of *Eden* strive. . . .
>
> [*Paradise Lost*, 4.268–75]

Milton's lines also equate the splendor of Eden with the quintessence of pastoral, for his reworking of Shakespeare's Proserpina-and-Dis passage immediately follows a specifically Ovidian and Virgilian description of Eden as the golden world:

> Thus was this place,
> A happy rural seat of various view:
> Groves whose rich Trees wept odorous Gums and Balm, . . .
> Flow'rs of all hue, and without Thorn the Rose: . . .
> The Birds thir quire apply; airs, vernal airs,
> Breathing the smell of field and grove, attune
> The trembling leaves, while Universal *Pan*
> Knit with the *Graces* and the *Hours* in dance
> Led on th' Eternal Spring. Not that fair field
> of *Enna*. . . .
>
> [*Paradise Lost*, 4.246–69]

The introduction of *"Pan"* and "Eternal Spring" identifies Milton's Eden as more than analogously or accidentally the golden world.

Milton thus renders homage to Shakespeare's pastoral vision as evoked by the flower passages in the fourth act of *The Winter's Tale*. Elsewhere he pays his respects in another way. The "pale primroses, / That die unmarried" provide the code by which Shakespeare's catalog of flowers becomes interchangeable with the catalog set forth in *Lycidas*:

> Bring the rathe Primrose that forsaken dies,
> The tufted Crow-toe, and pale Jessamine,
> The white Pink, and the Pansy freakt with jet,
> The glowing Violet,
> The Musk-rose, and the well attir'd Woodbine,
> With Cowslips wan that hang the pensive head,
> And every flower that sad embroidery wears. . . .
>
> [*Lycidas*, 142–48]

The homage appears even more explicit in light of the fact that Milton, in the first draft of his poem, used the word "unwedded" rather than the word "forsaken."

Milton's instinct for the essence of the pastoral feeling here joins with his understanding of its central use: to soften the harshness of actuality, especially to soften the fact of death. The delicately mourning flowers in *Lycidas* are specifically requested "To strew the Laureate Hearse where *Lycid* lies." The same function is obliquely suggested in *The Winter's Tale*. When Perdita concludes the passage with the words "To strew him o'er and o'er!" Florizel says:

What, like a corse?
PERDITA. No; like a bank for love to lie and play on;
Not like a corse; or if—not to be buried,
But quick, and in mine arms. Come, take your flowers.
Methinks I play as I have seen them do
In Whitsun pastorals.

[4.4.129–34]

Flowers used not to mitigate death but to affirm life and love endorse
the change from the devastation wrought by Leontes's rage to the
restoration of a happy society by means of "things new-born." That
Leontes's rage in this play, as opposed to the hegemony of rage in
Timon of Athens, will be merely an interlude between the pastoral
bliss of Leontes's and Polixenes's childhood and the pastoral bliss
established by the fourth act, is in any case suggested in the shepherd's
very first words when he appears as the harbinger of the pastoral mood:

I would there were no age between ten and three and twenty,
or that youth would sleep out the rest; for there is nothing in
the between but getting wenches with child, wronging the
ancientry, stealing, fighting—

[3.3.59–62]

The "in the between" implies that the woeful events of the play are
merely an interval. But the *Lear* situation is in fact here reversed: the
wrongs are not done by children to elders, but, as noted above, by
elders to children and the ideal of childhood. Leontes makes life impossible for Mamillius, rejects Perdita, repudiates his childhood friendship. This motif, of jealous eld encroaching upon young life, thrusts
itself so powerfully into the play that not all its traces are erased even
by the perfumed therapy of fourth-act pastoral. Polixenes, disguised at
the sheepshearing, reveals himself in order to threaten his son Florizel:

[*Discovering himself*] Mark your divorce, young sir.
Whom son I dare not call; thou art too base
To be acknowledg'd—thou a sceptre's heir,
That thus affects a sheep-hook!

[4.4.409–12]

And he threatens also the youthful beauty of Perdita:

And thou, fresh piece
Of excellent witchcraft, who of force must know

The royal fool thou cop'st with—
SHEPHERD.   O, my heart!
POLIXENES. I'll have thy beauty scratch'd with
   briers and made
More homely than thy state. For thee, fond boy,
If I may ever know thou dost but sigh
That thou no more shalt see this knack—as never
I mean thou shalt—we'll bar thee from succession;
Not hold thee of our blood, no, not our kin. . . .
                           And you, enchantment,
Worthy enough a herdsman—yea, him too
That makes himself, but for our honour therein,
Unworthy thee—if ever henceforth thou
These rural latches to his entrance open,
Or hoop his body more with thy embraces,
I will devise a death as cruel for thee
As thou art tender to't.

[4.4.414–33]

Although it echoes the authoritarian and kin-dissolving assaults of
Leontes, Polixenes's wrath is filtered through the magic fact of pastoral, as is shown by his acknowledgments of Perdita's charm and even
by his threats to have her beauty "scratch'd with briers." It is, however,
the persistence of this threat of age against youth, muted by flowered
loveliness though it is, that authenticates the equivocal role of Autolycus. Indeed, he explicitly recognizes himself as somehow prefiguring,
keeping open as it were, the same disharmonies as those arising from
authoritarian age:

> So that in this time of lethargy I pick'd and cut most of their
> festival purses; and had not the old man come in with a whoo-
> bub against his daughter and the King's son and scar'd my
> choughs from the chaff, I had not left a purse alive in the whole
> army.

[4.4.604–9]

   With such strains of disharmony still running through it, the world
established by the pastoral healing of the fourth act is just a better human society, with all the variegations of daily life, rather than a paradise. Even so, as Bertrand Evans says:

From the point of view of the management of awarenesses, the most complex and most effective scene in *The Winter's Tale* is IV.iv—the sheep-shearing. Bedecked with rural trappings, alive with shepherds and shepherdesses, seeming-shepherds and seeming-shepherdesses, bright with costumery, spectacular to the eye, resonant with music, song, and the babble of voices, a feast for eye and ear—this is a pastoral scene like no other. The sparkling lyrics of Autolycus—'inkles, caddises, cambrics, lawns. Why, he sings 'em over as they were gods or goddesses' —the general holiday spirit, the dance of the twelve Satyrs: all this would be abundance if there were nothing more (*Shakespeare's Comedies* [Oxford, 1960], p. 300).

And all the inhabitants of the pastoral environment contribute towards the joyous society achieved in the fifth act. Even the shepherd and the clown join in. They decide to take to Polixenes the "fardel" that proves Perdita's ancestry ("Show those things you found about her, those secret things" [4.4.684–85]). Cozening them out of the fardel, along with their money, Autolycus then decides himself to complete their reconciling mission ("To him will I present them. There may be matter in it" [4.4.825–26]).

In a larger movement, at the end of the fourth act and throughout the fifth act, the tide of separation that had borne so many figures away from the destroyed happiness of Sicilia reverses itself, and with gathering wonder the play begins to draw together into a renewed and purged community the scattered members of the earlier group. Florizel and Perdita, determined to save their love, decide to flee from Polixenes's rule:

> FLORIZEL. Not for Bohemia, nor the pomp that may
> Be thereat glean'd, for all the sun sees or
> The close earth wombs, or the profound seas hides
> In unknown fathoms, will I break my oath
> To this my fair belov'd. . . .
>   I am put to sea
> With her who here I cannot hold on shore.
>
>   [4.4.480–91]

The resonant dignity of his language seems all-encompassing in its affirmation of trust, loyalty, and coming together; in its rejection of the divisiveness of authoritarian rage. Camillo converts the random idea of flight into the specific idea of reunion:

> . . . make for Sicilia,
> And there present yourself and your fair princess—
> . . . Methinks I see
> Leontes opening his free arms and weeping
> His welcome forth; asks thee there "Son, forgiveness!"
> As 'twere i' th' father's person; . . .
>
> [4.4.535–42]

And Camillo, speaking aside, indicates still further agency in the great bringing together:

> What I do next shall be to tell the King
> Of this escape, and whither they are bound;
>
> [4.4.652–53]

So once more the figures of the play take ship over "the profound seas" of space, time, and separation. The repeated voyagings link this play more closely to *Pericles* than to any other of Shakespeare's comedies. Although a certain fantasticalness—as in the oracle (3.2.130–33) or in the matter of Hermione's supposed statue coming to life—seems to link *The Winter's Tale* to the forced solutions of *Cymbeline*, the resemblance to *Pericles* is much closer. For not only do the motifs of danger and restless voyaging suggest those of *Pericles*, but the tones of the two plays are almost identical in the affirmations of joy with which they both conclude. Both involve multiple reconciliations, after separation and supposed death, of father with daughter and of husband with wife. Both, after their existential wanderings, recognize their mutual happiness in language of startling intensity—an intensity that we associate more with tragic exhilaration than with comic benignity:

> PERICLES. O Helicanus, strike me, honour'd sir;
> Give me a gash, put me to present pain,
> Lest this great sea of joys rushing upon me
> O'erbear the shores of my mortality,
> And drown me with their sweetness. O, come hither,
> Thou that beget'st him that did thee beget;
> Thou that wast born at sea, buried at Tharsus,
> And found at sea again!
> . . . I embrace you.

Give me my robes. I am wild in my beholding.
O heavens bless my girl! . . .

[*Pericles*, 5.1.189–222]

And Pericles's reunion with his child Marina is followed by his reunion with his wife Thaisa:

THAISA.   Now I know you better.
When we with tears parted Pentapolis,
The King my father gave you such a ring.
                [*Shows a ring.*]
PERICLES. This, this! No more, you gods! your present kindness
Makes my past miseries sports. You shall do well
That on the touching of her lips I may
Melt and no more be seen.

[*Pericles*, 5.3.37–43]

The conclusion of *The Winter's Tale*, doubling its happiness, like *Pericles*, into separate reconciliations of father with daughter, and then of husband with wife, shares the same exalted tone of wonder and renewed joy. The associated tyranny of winter and age is broken by the arrival of youth and spring: "Welcome hither, / As is the spring to th' earth," says Leontes in greeting Florizel and Perdita (5.1.151–52). No longer the persecutor of the young, but their advocate instead, Leontes agrees to speak for the lovers to Polixenes; and Polixenes, already cognizant of Perdita's true birth, dissipates his own authoritarian rage in a matching acceptance of the youthful pair. Unlike *Pericles*, the play reports these happy events—and the reunion of the two kings—rather than presents them dramatically, with the result that in addition to the joy of those directly involved, society at large participates in their gratification. The language of the anonymous gentlemen reporting the reunions is saturated with joy and wonder: "A notable passion of wonder appeared in them . . ." (5.2.15–16); "Did you see the meeting of the two kings?" "No." "Then have you lost a sight which was to be seen, cannot be spoken of. There might you have beheld one joy crown another . . . their joy waded in tears. . . . Our king, being ready to leap out of himself for joy of his found daughter . . . then asks Bohemia forgiveness; then embraces his son-in-law. . . . Now he thanks the old shepherd. . . . I never heard of such another encounter, which lames report to follow it and undoes description to do it" (5.2.39–56). Although the gentleman insists that the sight "was to be seen, cannot be spoken of," Shakespeare's way of speaking of it could scarcely be surpassed by seeing it.

> FIRST GENTLEMAN. Are they returned to the court?
> THIRD GENTLEMAN. No. The Princess hearing of her mother's statue, which is in the keeping of Paulina— . . . thither with all greediness of affection are they gone, and there they intend to sup.
> SECOND GENTEMAN. Shall we thither and with our company piece the rejoicing?
> FIRST GENTLEMAN. Who would be thence that has the benefit of access? Every wink of an eye some new grace will be born.
>
> [5.2.90–107]

And this tone, not merely of benignity, but of astonished delight, is taken up by other minor figures. All separations are ended, all sunderings redeemed into brotherhood:

> CLOWN. . . . for the King's son took me by the hand, and call'd me brother; and then the two kings call'd my father brother; and then the Prince, my brother, and the Princess, my sister, call'd my father father. And so we wept. . . .
>
> [5.3.134–38]

In golden reverberation the shepherd says, "we must be gentle, now we are gentlemen" (5.2.146).

The mystical joy, the dramatic juxtaposition of motifs of separation and reunion, the coming together of father and daughter, suggest, in both *Pericles* and *The Winter's Tale*, the end of *King Lear*. But where *Lear* is true to the tragic fact of death, though the language nevertheless holds out the possibility of heavenly reunion, both comedies retreat into their genre's typical artificiality and typical reluctance to face the reality of death. They thereby achieve a unique position in Shakespeare's art, for they combine tragic intensity with comic well-being. The combination in each case is achieved at a certain cost, that of probability, but the cost is debited to comedy's special account with the artificial.

Both that artificiality and its attendant tone of tragically intense joy are displayed in the statue scene that concludes *The Winter's Tale*. Boldly accepting, despite its wild implausibility, the idea that a person might be able to pass as a statue, the play then builds upon this initial artificiality, with no further recourse to improbability. All other improbabilities are not only accounted for, but actually transformed into the probable:

> LEONTES.   But yet, Paulina,
> Hermione was not so much wrinkled, nothing
> So aged as this seems.
> POLIXENES.   O, not by much!
> PAULINA. So much the more our carver's excellence,
> Which lets go by some sixteen years and makes her
> As she liv'd now.
>
> [5.3.27–32]

And the realism of the situation is further emphasized:

> LEONTES. Would you not deem it breath'd, and that those veins
> Did verily bear blood?
> POLIXENES.   Masterly done!
> The very life seems warm upon her lip.
> LEONTES. The fixure of her eye has motion in't,
> As we are mock'd with art.
> PAULINA.   I'll draw the curtain.
> My lord's almost so far transported that
> He'll think anon it lives.
>
> [5.3.64–70]

This teasing realism in which life is made to seem like stone, and stone to suggest life, indicates the true function of the statue scene. One of the deepest of all mysteries is that of the difference between thought and thing, between mind and matter. Much of human desire is and always has been a longing to animate the inanimate. We need discuss neither anthropological formulations such as Tylor's animism, nor the speculations of philosophers: Strato's hylozoism, Leibniz's monadology, or, with reference to the separation of thought and thing, Sartre's *pour soi* and *en soi*, or Coleridge's persisting question, "what is the difference or distinction between THING AND THOUGHT?" We need not invoke such matters because the realization of the difference between thought and thing, and the desire to animate the inanimate, are part of the fabric of all men's awareness. The longing to reconcile the two realms, and the knowledge of their utter difference, reach their greatest urgency at that almost universally suffered moment when a human being, living, stands beside the loved statue that is a corpse and experiences the abyss of separation between the living and the inanimate. Furthermore, a recurring strain of experience and statement in our culture recognizes that cruelty, or human uncaringness, somehow removes life from the realm of the animate and gives it to that of the inanimate. The use of force, as Simone Weil has argued, makes a person into a thing; certain criminal acts, as Coleridge saw, seem to forfeit their perpetrator's humanity and turn him into a thing. And common metaphorical usage equates a cruel heart with a heart of stone. "I am asham'd," says Leontes: "Does not the stone rebuke me / For being more stone than it?" (5.3.37–38). Moreover, the state of being stone is also used as a metaphorical recognition of human deficiency in feeling, as in Lear's anguished outcry: "Howl, howl, howl, howl! O, you are men of stones!"

Conversely, the change of stone to humanness represents a profound fulfillment of human hopes. If blood did come from a stone, then all the world would be different. Some of the deepest dreams of magic have to do with the animation of statues. Augustine, in his *De civitate Dei*, attacks Hermes Trismegistus, as Frances Yates says, "for praising the Egyptians for the magic by which they drew . . . spirits or demons into the statues of their gods, thus animating the statues, or making them into gods" (*Giordano Bruno and the Hermetic Tradition* [Chicago, 1964], p. 10). So Paulina is at pains to say that the statue's "actions shall be as holy as / You hear my spell is lawful" (5.3.104–5), and she insists on the distinction between her power of animation and that of black magic:

> If you can behold it,
> I'll make the statue move indeed, descend,
> And take you by the hand, but then you'll think—
> Which I protest against—I am assisted
> By wicked powers.

[5.3.87–91]

But setting aside the question of "unlawful business" (5.3.96) as does Paulina, it is clear that the animation of an inanimate body represents one of the pinnacles of human hopes. "Do you see this?" asks Lear as he looks on the dead Cordelia, "Look on her, look, her lips, / Look there, look there!" But his thought that he sees life on dead lips is, in the harsh world of tragedy, a final illusion of madness; and Lear joins Cordelia by dying himself rather than by her coming back to life.

The Winter's Tale, however, rests secure within the magic boundaries of comedy. Leontes's illusion of life upon dead lips is there miraculously transformed into reality:

> LEONTES.   Let no man mock me,
> For I will kiss her.
> PAULINA.   Good my lord, forbear.
> The ruddiness upon her lips is wet;
> You'll mar it if you kiss it; stain your own
> With oily painting.
>
> [5.3.79–83]

But Leontes's proposal marks the conclusion of the statue's stoniness and the regaining of humanity:

> PAULINA.   Music, awake her: strike.
> 'Tis time; descend; be stone no more; approach;
> Strike all that look upon with marvel. Come;
> I'll fill your grave up. Stir; nay, come away.
> Bequeath to death your numbness, for from him
> Dear life redeems you.
>
> [5.3.98–103]

And as the stone of the statue, like the stone of Leontes's heart, comes again to life and mutual happiness, the play exults not only in the achievement of new society, but in the symbolic conquest of death. In religious supplication and wonder Leontes's words repudiate his initial wrong; to the restored Hermione and the fraternal Polixenes he says:

> What! look upon my brother. Both your pardons,
> That e'er I put between your holy looks
> My ill suspicion.
>
> [5.3.147–49]

Even Paulina, the widow of the devoured Antigonus, is restored to the blessedness of marriage by being matched with Camillo, the formerly rejected counselor. And her benediction, ringing with the special strain of intense gladness finally achieved in this play, signalizes the holy reclamation of all its survivors into the state of joy: "Go together, / You precious winners all; your exultation / Partake to every one" (5.3.130–32). Where all are winners, all go together, and all partake of exultation, there is found that social happiness that constitutes the aim and dearest hope of comic action.

VI. So Rare a Wondered Father

The Tempest and the Vision of Paradise

Standing first in Heminge and Condell's arrangement of the plays, and last chronologically among Shakespeare's major achievements, *The Tempest* in still other ways constitutes the alpha and omega of Shakespeare's comedy. For here the two great realities of Shakespeare's comic vision—the movement toward social concord on the one hand, and on the other the recognition of disharmony and disruption (identifiable as early as *The Two Gentlemen of Verona*, and grown almost cancerously into the bitterness of the middle comedies)—come face to face in a final confrontation. *The Tempest* reaffirms the festive happiness of *A Midsummer-Night's Dream*, and at the same time completes and overcomes the motif of Jacobean "cohaerence gone" that strained against Shakespeare's comic dream in *Measure for Measure* and *Troilus and Cressida*, in *Cymbeline* and *Pericles*. Accepting in full the social asymmetry of the bitter comedies, the mighty pastoral of *The Tempest* serenely reasserts the enchantment of brotherhood and social harmony.

The completeness of pastoral's victory is here unique. For the jars it muffles and the shocks it concludes are not the "human follies" of comic sport, but rather the crimes of religion's testament: brother against brother, the intent of rape, the intent of murder, the reality of lies, disloyalty, and plots both large and small. Never before in Shakespeare's comedy has the paradisal vision been so profoundly challenged. And never before has the pastoral affirmation so completely dominated the materials of the play; for the corresponding bliss of *A Midsummer-Night's Dream* is attained without opposition from the harsher aspects of existence. In *The Tempest* disharmonies, for all their prevalence, have no purchase; the goodness that flows from Prospero, in his island haven, represents not only absolute benignity but absolute power as well. All the motifs of betrayal that persistently tormented

Shakespeare's view of reality are here, but the pastoral vision reduces treachery to something like the willful naughtiness of children. The principle of evil represented by Caliban is formidable: ingratitude for kindness, the attempted rape of his benefactor's daughter, and gruesomely planned murder (not only is his name an anagram for "cannibal," but as G. Wilson Knight well says, "all Shakespeare's intuition of the untamed beast in man" is "crystallized" in his character [*The Shakespearian Tempest* (London, 1968), p. 258]). But so impotent is that evil under the omniscient gaze and awful power of Prospero that Caliban's motives enlist sympathy rather than arouse horror. Just as in *Paradise Regained* our foreknowledge gives the evil efforts of Satan, Belial, and the other devils, doomed as they are to failure, a sense of Sisyphean pathos, so Caliban's schemes seem, by their hopelessness, ridiculous and somewhat sad. For even evil needs a structure of hope; and that hope must here be abandoned.

So, too, for all other intents of evil in the play, overmatched as they are by Prospero's mysterious good. The Machiavellian aspiration, which dominated so much of the Elizabethan and Jacobean dramatic imagination, and which, in Shakespeare's Octavius, Claudius, Macbeth, and Bolingbroke, became an absolute standard of the perverted hope that forfeits all values of mutual human regard—the Machiavellian aspiration is here as incapable of evil fruition as is the transcendent evil of Caliban. Just as Claudius kills his brother, or as Macbeth kills his king, so Sebastian and Antonio plot to kill brother and king. They plot in the manner of Richard of Gloucester, of, indeed, the whole long dramatic tradition of the power-greedy and amoral Machiavellian plotters:

> ANTONIO.   Will you grant with me
> That Ferdinand is drown'd?
> SEBASTIAN.   He's gone.
> ANTONIO.   Then tell me,
> Who's the next heir of Naples?
>
> [2.1.234–36]

And then:

> ANTONIO.   Say this were death
> That now hath seiz'd them; why, they were no worse
> Than now they are. There be that can rule Naples
> As well as he that sleeps; lords that can prate

> As amply and unnecessarily
> As this Gonzalo: I myself could make
> A chough of as deep chat. O, that you bore
> The mind that I do! What a sleep were this
> For your advancement! Do you understand me?
> SEBASTIAN. Methinks I do.
>
> [2.1.251–60]

And Sebastian accepts with alacrity the Machiavel's main chance, unlike the equivocating Pompey of *Antony and Cleopatra*, who retreats before Menas's proposal ("These three world-sharers, these competitors, / Are in thy vessel. Let me cut the cable; / And, when we are put off, fall to their throats. / All there is thine."). In play after play, not only in Shakespeare, but in his contemporaries as well—Marlowe, Marston, Jonson, Webster—such murderous intent is depicted as fulfilled by the actual fact of murder, and the subsequent action wrestles with the consequences of the deed. Every preliminary for such a deed is observed in *The Tempest*:

> SEBASTIAN. But, for your conscience—
> ANTONIO. Ay, sir, where lies that? . . .
>   twenty consciences,
> That stand 'twixt me and Milan, candied be they
> And melt, ere they molest! Here lies your brother,
> No better than the earth he lies upon,
> If he were that which now he's like—that's dead;
> Whom I with this obedient steel, three inches of it,
> Can lay to bed for ever; whiles you, doing thus,
> To the perpetual wink for aye might put
> This ancient morsel, this Sir Prudence, who
> Should not upbraid our course. . . .
> SEBASTIAN.   Thy case, dear friend,
> Shall be my precedent; as thou got'st Milan,
> I'll come by Naples. Draw thy sword. One stroke
> Shall free thee from the tribute which thou payest;
> And I the King shall love thee.
>
> [2.2.266–85]

We might almost be reading Webster or Tourneur, or Shakespeare at his most bloodily tragic, so explicit and lengthy is the Machiavellian preparation as here presented. And all for nothing. The deepest plots and most ruthless readiness advance evil's cause not an iota. The intervention of Prospero's agent, Ariel, leaves the conspirators almost ludicrously explaining the fact of their drawn swords to their suddenly awakened victims:

> GONZALO.   What's the matter?
> SEBASTIAN. Whiles we stood here securing your repose,
> Even now, we heard a hollow burst of bellowing
> Like bulls, or rather lions. . . .
> ALONSO.   Heard you this, Gonzalo?
> GONZALO. Upon mine honour, sir, I heard a humming,
> And that a strange one too, which did awake me;
> I shak'd you, sir, and cried; as mine eyes open'd,
> I saw their weapons drawn—
>
> [2.2.300–311]

Evil, indeed, is in this enchanted place not only stripped of its effectiveness, but stripped even of its Luciferan dignity. Sebastian and Antonio, swords drawn, are converted in the twinkling of an eye from fell assassins to sheepish explainers. And the same thing happens to Caliban. The "abhorred slave, / Which any print of goodness will not take" (1.2.351–52), the "lying slave, / Whom stripes may move, not kindness!" (1.2.344–45), who, treated "with human care," sought in return "to violate / The honour of my child" (1.2.346–48)—this creature, in grotesque reflection and doubling of Sebastian and Antonio's death plot, plans with the clown and the butler the death of Prospero:

> Why, as I told thee, 'tis a custom with him
> I' th' afternoon to sleep; there thou mayst brain him,
> Having first seiz'd his books; or with a log,
> Batter his skull, or paunch him with a stake,
> Or cut his wezand with thy knife. Remember
> First to possess his books; for without them
> He's but a sot, as I am, nor hath not
> One spirit to command; they do all hate him
> As rootedly as I.
>
> [3.2.83–91]

In the hideous explicitness of Caliban's proposal the intent of evil does justice to all the random brutality of actual experience. But this horror in the subplot is disarmed as magically as its aristocratic Machiavellian counterpart; Prospero treats the intent of unspeakable brutishness ("I'll yield him thee asleep, / Where thou mayst knock a nail into his head" [3.2.57–58]) as a threat hardly worth noticing: in the midst of the wedding masque he suddenly remembers:

> I had forgot that foul conspiracy
> Of the beast Caliban and his confederates
> Against my life; the minute of their plot
> Is almost come.
>
> [4.1.139–42]

And although Caliban is

> A devil, a born devil, on whose nature
> Nurture can never stick; on whom my pains,
> Humanely taken, all, all lost, quite lost;
>
> [4.1.188–90]

Prospero's treatment of him and his confederates is not counteraction of equal brutishness, but the almost ludicrous punishment of pinchings, dunkings, crampings and other trivial harassments, which "plague them all / Even to roaring" (4.1.192–93). Thus, despite his unlimited evil, Caliban, thwarted by Prospero's power, becomes, in the words of Trinculo, in this drama a "most ridiculous monster" (2.2.155).

The childish impotence of evil emphasizes the almost divine power of Prospero's good. And it is accordingly in this play that Shakespeare seems to come closest to open identification of the comic ideal and the hope of religion, of pastoral realm and Christian heaven. While it is true that some theological authority frowned on any attempt at the representation of divine things, it is also true that a tradition of such representation did exist. Sidney praises David's Psalms as "a heavenly poesy, wherein almost he showeth himself a passionate lover of that unspeakable and everlasting beauty to be seen by the eyes of the mind, only cleared by faith," and hails his "notable *prosopopeias*, when he maketh you, as it were, see God coming in his majesty." It may well be that Shakespeare in this play avails himself of that mode that Bacon, in his *De augmentis scientiarum*, calls "Parabolical" poetry, which "is of a higher character than the others, and appears to be something sacred and venerable; . . . It is of double use . . . for it serves for an infoldment; and it likewise serves for an illustration . . . for such things

. . . the dignity whereof requires that they should be seen as it were through a veil; that is, when the secrets and mysteries of religion . . . and philosophy are involved in fables or parables." And Henry Reynolds, in a platonizing treatise called *Mythomystes*, published about 1633, urges that the name "poet" is a "high and sacred title," that one should look "farther" into "those their golden fictions" for a "higher sence," something "diuiner in them infoulded & hid from the vulgar." The tradition that divine things must be 'infoulded & hid from the vulgar" was an ancient one: "Holy things," said Plotinus, "may not be uncovered to the stranger, to any that has not himself attained to see" (*Enneads*, 6.9.11).

Furthermore Christianity, as well as the Platonist tradition, emphasizes that sacred matters are both presented and veiled by means of parabolical statement:

> And when he had said these things, he cried, He that hath ears to hear, let him hear. And his disciples asked him, saying, What might this parable be? And he said, Unto you it is given to know the mysteries of the kingdom of God: but to others in parables; that seeing they might not see, and hearing they might not understand.
>
> [Luke 8.8–10]

So Milton speaks of Spenser's *Faerie Queene* as a poetic statement "where more is meant than meets the ear." In his pastoral *Comus*, the Spirit talks of "the Gardens fair / Of *Hesperus*, and his daughters three / That sing about the Golden tree. . . . there eternal Summer dwells." And there Adonis is said to be "Waxing well of his deep wound"—a statement prefixed by the exhortation, "List mortals, if your ears be true." Milton seems by this exhortation symbolically to link the recovery of Adonis with the resurrection of Christ, just as the pastoral "eternal Summer" suggests the Christian heaven.

Parabolical utterances, rather than direct statements, are required because, as Paul says, we must see divine things "through a glass darkly." Inasmuch as the parabolical conceals as well as communicates, its existence must somehow be signaled. Such signals are constituted by an obliquely insistent request for special attention: Milton's "List mortals, if your ears be true," or Jesus' "He that hath ears to hear, let him hear." And words like those appear prominently in Prospero's lengthy discussion with Miranda in the first act: "The very minute bids thee ope thine ear" (1.2.37); "Dost thou hear?" (1.2.106); "Hear a little further" (1.2.135).

The play reinforces such indications in other ways. The language possesses a mysterious resonance and elevation. Prospero does not ask, "What do you remember?" he asks instead "What seest thou else / In the dark backward and abysm of time?" (1.2.49–50). He does not say, "Look there"; he says, rather, "The fringed curtains of thine eye advance" (1.2.408). Even the most sorrowful thoughts somehow seem, because of the mystery of the language, to be wonderful. As Ferdinand says:

> Sitting on a bank,
> Weeping again the King my father's wreck,
> This music crept by me upon the waters,
> Allaying both their fury and my passion
> With its sweet air. . . .

And the music, which is Ariel's song, makes the idea of death beautiful, wonderful, but not fearful:

> Full fathom five thy father lies;
>   Of his bones are coral made;
> Those are pearls that were his eyes:
>   Nothing of him that doth fade
> But doth suffer a sea-change
> Into something rich and strange.

> [1.2.389–401]

Something of that same wonder permeates Alsonso's counterstatement about the supposed death of Ferdinand:

> Therefore my son i' th' ooze is bedded; and
> I'll seek him deeper than e'er plummet sounded.
> And with him there lie mudded.

> [3.3.100–102]

Darkly wonderful unexpectedness continually springs from the language of the play, especially in the first interview between Prospero and Miranda, and so too do flickerings of ancient meanings. The reassurance uttered in a specific incident has a deeper and more universal comfort:

                                      Be collected;
              No more amazement. Tell your piteous heart
              There's no harm done.

                                                      [1.2.13–15]

In haunting and symbolically indistinct words, old catastrophes and
unknown fallings off are mentioned: "What foul play had we, that we
came thence?" asks Miranda in a question that all struggling humanity
could use for its own. And Prospero's answer keeps the same tone: "By
foul play, as thou say'st, were we heav'd thence; / But blessedly holp
hither" (1.2.60–63).

   As old mysteries of sin and redemption seem to whisper behind the
topics discussed by Prospero and Miranda, so also do more reverberating implications surround the figure of Prospero himself. In a matrix
where the past becomes the "dark backward and abysm of time,"
Prospero's own antecedents seem to suggest something more than the
deposition of a Duke. The ambiguity of the language everywhere hints
at deeper things. Ariel tells the newcomers that "man doth not in-
habit" the island (3.3.57). Miranda is told by Prospero that she does
not know "Of whence I am"; that she does not know "that I am more
better / Than Prospero" (1.2.19–20). Sebastian and Antonio, conversely, are "worse than devils" (3.3.36). "Had I not / Four, or five,
women once, that tended me?" asks Miranda. "Thou hadst, and more,
Miranda," replies Prospero ambiguously (1.2.46–48); and he tells her
that "a cherubin / Thou wast that did preserve me" (1.2.152–53). Indeed, when Prospero says that "Thy father was the Duke of Milan, and
/ A prince of power" (1.2.54–55), Miranda, strangely, asks: "Sir, are
not you my father?" (1.2.55).

   Moreover Prospero, by his ability to control the elements, even to
restore lives that seem lost, is invested with the power of a god. His
power, in fact, is more than that of a god: "His art is of such pow'r,"
says Caliban, "It would control my dam's god, Setebos, / And make
a vassal of him" (1.2.372–73). And the aged magician possesses also
the physical presence of a divine being: not the form of a pagan deity,
but that of the infinitely wise God whom Christians worship. The reverend age associated anthropomorphically with God mantles Prospero's shoulders also, as do the divine attributes of justice, wrath,
gentleness, and forgiveness. When Anselm of Canterbury argued for
the existence of God from the idea of perfection that he found in his

own mind, the monk Gaunilo made rebuttal by arguing that the idea of a perfect island did not make such an island exist. But in Shakespeare's art the perfect island does exist, and God, linked with that island in the theological arguments of the schoolmen, exists there also, although parabolically shadowed forth. As Ferdinand says of Prospero, "So rare a wond'red father and a wise / Makes this place Paradise" (4.1.123–24).

Prospero, indeed, bears the same relationship to his island haven as does Francesco Sansovino's Mythra, who, in a book reprinted at intervals throughout Shakespeare's lifetime, is represented as God ruling over an island Utopia. After a "descrittione dell' Isola d'Utopia," Sansovino notes that some inhabitants of the island worship the sun, the moon, or the moving stars. "The greater part, however, I mean the wisest, do not worship any of these things, but believe that there is a secret and eternal divinity above any human capacity, which with its virtue and grandeur stretches over this world, and this God they call father." On the island of Utopia, moreover, the inhabitants "hold in the temples no image of the gods, in order that each man can freely image God (*liberamente imaginarsi Dio*) in what form he pleases" (*Del Governo et amministratione di diversi regni, et republiche, cosí antiche, come moderne* [Vinegia, 1607], f. 183ᵛ, 198, 200).

On Shakespeare's own island, the parabolical suggestions of "Paradise" and "wond'red father" accord as fully with the pastoral tradition as they do with Christianity. Drayton notes of pastorals that "*the most High, and most Noble matters of the World may be shaddowed in them, and for certaine sometimes are*" (*Works*, ed. Hebel, 2:518). Furthermore, both Ovid and Virgil, with those historical effects the pastoral ideal is so profoundly entwined, were in the Renaissance repeatedly interpreted as allegories and foreshadowings of Christian mystery (see, e.g., Don Cameron Allen, *Mysteriously Meant: The Rediscovery of Pagan Symbolism and Allegorical Interpretation in the Renaissance* [Baltimore, 1970], pp. 135–99). And Plato, in a major prototype of the pastoral golden world, speaks of an Age of Kronos in which God himself was shepherd. Like Prospero ruling his enchanted island, and like the Christian God ruling over Eden, Plato's shepherd-God governs a paradisal realm:

> When God was shepherd there were no political constitutions and no taking of wives and begetting of children. . . . People

instead had fruits without stint from trees and bushes; these needed no cultivation but sprang up of themselves out of the ground without man's toil. For the most part men disported themselves in the open, needing neither clothing nor couch; for the seasons were blended evenly so as to work them no hurt, and the grass which sprang up out of the earth in abundance made a soft bed for them.

[*Statesman*, 271E–272A]

Even the supernatural agency of Ariel, similar but inferior to the authority of Prospero, is pastorally foreshadowed in the Age of Kronos: "Over every herd of living creatures was set a heavenly daemon to be its shepherd. . . . So it befell that savagery was nowhere to be found nor preying of creature on creature, nor did war rage nor any strife whatsoever. There were numberless consequences of this divine ordering of the world" (271D–E).

If Prospero, in brief, is naturalistically the deposed Duke of Milan, he suggests parabolically, along all lines of reference, the Ancient of Days: "His head and his hairs were white like wool, as white as snow; and his eyes were as a flame of fire. . . . And he laid his right hand upon me, saying unto me, Fear not; I am the first and the last: I am he that liveth, and was dead; and, behold, I am alive for evermore, Amen; and have the keys of hell and of death" (Rev. 1:14–18).

It is here that W. C. Curry, in his elucidation of Prospero as a theurgic magician in a non-Christian, Neoplatonic mold, seems to go astray. The diffusion of magical motifs in the early seventeenth century, as indeed today, placed those motifs in the public domain, as it were, without any necessary commitment to Neoplatonic magic on Shakespeare's part (we surely do not seek a learned magic in, say, *The Witch of Edmonton*). Furthermore, Neoplatonism itself, from Ficino to Cudworth, was customarily syncretized with Christianity. It accordingly does not follow, as Curry would have it, that "in the *Tempest*, with its Neo-Platonic concepts serving as an artistic pattern" Shakespeare "no longer employs Christian myth as the integrating principle . . . here he creates an altogether different world . . . which is integrated by a purely pagan philosophy" (*Shakespeare's Philosophical Patterns*, 2d ed. [Baton Rouge, 1959], p. 198). On the contrary, pagan motifs, from Plato to the Sibylline oracles, were eagerly syncretized to Christianity during the Renaissance, and their presence, even if established, cannot be used as an argument against Christian interpretation (for a concurring opinion see D. G. James, *The Dream of Prospero* [Oxford, 1967], p. 61). Curry seems closer to the mark in his statement that "Prospero is evidently a theurgist of high rank. But we cannot determine precisely the degree of his attainments" (p. 188). It is the very indeterminateness that suggests the parabolical, the seeing through a glass darkly. And what is there glimpsed is neither merely a theurgic magician nor merely a Duke of Milan; rather, in "a notable *prosopopeias*" or use of personification, we "see God coming in his majesty." This seemed strikingly clear to me the first time I read the play, and before I encountered any commentary at all; I have since been pleased to find that others have argued as much, not only among modern commentators, but among those of the past as well (for two nineteenth-century apprehensions, in 1859 and 1876, that Prospero is a representation of divinity, see A. D. Nuttall, *Two Concepts of Allegory: A Study of Shakespeare's* The Tempest *and the Logic of Allegorical Expression* [London, 1967], pp. 7, 9.) "The devil speaks in him," whispers Sebastian. Prospero's reply is one word: "No" (5.1.129).

The immensity of this mysterious father-figure's power is the first of his attributes we encounter. At the beginning of the second scene of the first act, Miranda says: "If by your art, my dearest father, you have / Put the wild waters in this roar, allay them" (1.2.1–2). Shakespeare's dramatic tact is here unerring; he does not simply verbalize the hypothesis of Prospero's power, rather the tempest that begins the play takes us into the reality of that power and then leads us, daunted, to an encounter with the author of the storm.

That author is also the savior from its terrors. It is generally agreed that Shakespeare's imagined tempest had its immediate source in the "most dreadfull Tempest" actually experienced by a ship under the command of Sir George Summers in July, 1609:

a dreadfull storme and hideous began to blow from out the North-east, which swelling, and roaring as it were by fits, some houres with more violence than others, at length did beate all light from heaven; which like an hell of darkenesse turned blacke upon us. . . . For foure and twenty houres the storme in a restlesse tumult, had blown so exceedingly, as we could not apprehend in our imaginations any possibility of greater violence, yet did wee still finde it, not onely more terrible, but more constant, fury added to fury, and one storme urging a second more outragious than the former. . . . Prayers might well be in the heart and lips, but drowned in the outcries of the Officers: nothing heard that could give comfort, nothing seene that might incourage hope.*

With reference to Prospero's relationship to his own storm, it is interesting to note that William Strachey, the reporter of these events, recognizes God as the author of affliction: "It pleased God to bring a greater affliction yet upon us; for in the beginning of the storme we had received likewise a mighty leake." And the deliverance from the storm is also, in this source, ascribed to God: "the almighty God wrought for us, and sent us miraculously delivered from the calamities of the Sea."**

Now the fact of storm (as G. Wilson Knight has extensively documented) constitutes one of Shakespeare's major dramatic preoccupations, one that extends throughout his career. Storms occur from *The Comedy of Errors* all the way to *The Tempest*. We need only think of the storm that rages off the coast of Illyria, or the one that occurs off the coast of Bohemia; of the storm that surrounds Macbeth's castle, or the one that harrows Othello's passage to Cyprus. As a persisting symbol of the harshness of reality, and also as a convenience for the dramatist who can utilize the fortuitous separations and reunions incident to storms, the repeated use of tempestuous weather is a fitting adjunct to Shakespeare's dramatic art, both comic and tragic. But the achievement represented by the great storm scene that gives *The Tempest* its name can be matched only by the howling chaos deluging *King Lear*. The storms in both plays are similar in their evoked intensity, and similar also in their centrality to their dramatic situations. In other respects, however, they differ significantly. The storm in *Lear* occurs on land, while that of *The Tempest* takes place at sea. The implications of the former are that all reality is inundated by forces alien to humanity, while the implications of the latter are those of a passage from alien turmoil to a peaceful haven: in *The Tempest* we hear, in mysterious words, "the last of our sea-sorrow" (1.2.170). The storm in *King Lear* indicates a kind of monism of dramatic situation, a no-exit predicament; that in *The Tempest,* a dualism of earth and heaven. And the differing emphases reinforce the respective differences of tragedy and comedy. The storm in *King Lear* serves to underscore, in a macrocosm-microcosm correspondence, the tempestuous emotions in King Lear's heart. But the storm in *The Tempest* has quite the op-

* *Purchas his Pilgrimes* (Glasgow, 1905–7), 19:6–7.
** Ibid., pp. 8, 32.

posite effect, for it serves to accentuate the unearthly tranquillity of Prospero's rule.

The storm in *The Tempest*, though comparable in intensity to that in *King Lear*, is really more closely related to the "sea-sorrow" in *The Winter's Tale* and *Pericles*, which are *The Tempest*'s immediate predecessors. As the "last" of such sea-sorrow, *The Tempest* takes all the divisions and uncertainties represented by voyaging on the treacherous waters, and brings them to safe and paradisal reunion on holy ground.

Indeed, the fact that the storm here begins the play, rather than occurs as part of the internal action, accentuates the "sea-sorrow" experienced in the other two plays and closes the action off from any repetition of that sorrow. For the opening storm is like a curtain that divides the world of the island from all the world preceding, a veil that leaves all existential anxiety and striving on the other side.

The symbol of "sea-sorrow"—voyagings and storms and shipwrecks —is the symbol taken up by the existential thinkers of the twentieth century as a description of the human predicament. In Karl Jaspers it is called "Scheitern" (shipwreck or foundering) and is identified as a final truth about all human life. Likewise, Ortega y Gasset, in calling for an end to reverential biographies of an Olympian Goethe, says: "Give us a Goethe who is shipwrecked in his own existence, who is lost in it and never knows from one minute to the next what will become of him." And such a biography, claims Ortega, is the only one that could achieve human plausibility, because

Life is, in itself and forever, shipwreck. To be shipwrecked is not to drown. The poor human being, feeling himself sinking into the abyss, moves his arms to keep afloat. This movement of the arms which is his reaction against his own destruction, is culture—a swimming stroke. . . . Consciousness of shipwreck, being the truth of life, constitutes salvation. Hence I no longer believe in any ideas except the ideas of shipwrecked men.*

The dramatic ideas of *The Winter's Tale*, *Pericles*, and in culmination, *The Tempest*, are those "ideas of shipwrecked men" which alone seem valid in the light of existential experience.

In *The Tempest*, the existential shipwreck gives way to a new security. But here too Shakespeare remains true to human needs as

* "In Search of Goethe from Within," in *The Dehumanization of Art: and Other Essays on Art, Culture, and Literature*, trans. Helene Weyl (Princeton, 1968), pp. 145, 136–37.

elucidated by philosophers of the human situation. Indeed, a title by Otto Bollnow—*Neue Geborgenheit: Das Problem einer Überwindung des Existentialismus* (*New Security: The Problem of an Overthrow of Existentialism*)—reveals how inseparably connected is the idea of haven and security with the existential idea of sea-sorrow. Every "Existenz," as Jaspers repeatedly emphasizes in the most central idea of all his philosophy, is orientated toward "Transzendenz." The enchanted island on the other side of the storm is the transcendence toward which shipwrecked existence reaches. And Paul, in the words of Calvin, "points out that faith, without holding to a consideration of the state of things present, or looking about at the things visible in this world . . . rises above the whole world and casts its anchor in heaven" (*Commentaries*, trans. J. Haroutunian and L. P. Smith [Philadelphia, 1958], p. 240).

So the pastoral ideal reveals itself as something far more necessary than a merely historical tradition in literature. As an analogue of the Christian heaven that exists as the goal of struggling mortals, of Jaspers's "transcendence" that flickers unattainably before all existence, it represents the deepest authentication of the meaning of human hope.

The necessity for that haven which is heaven is dramatically indicated in *The Tempest* by the fury of the awesome storm. Few more convincing testaments to Shakespeare's dramatic genius exist than the one provided by this first scene. For here he does not begin to build a plot, or describe character, or even, surprisingly, set the mood that will prevail in the play. Instead, without explanation, he simply represents the shattering fact of "Scheitern": the fact of human existence tossed on the deeps, with no knowledge of what is to come, with the most tenuous hold on life itself. The divisions and distinctions that obtain in daily life are here expressly declared to be illusions. When Gonzalo, the man of eminence whom society respects, exhorts the boatswain to "be patient," the boatswain's reply demolishes puny human distinctions in the face of reality's storm: "When the sea is. Hence! What cares these roarers for the name of king? To cabin! silence! Trouble us not!" (1.1.15–17). And when Gonzalo persists in his attempt to uphold the illusions of human significance by saying that the boatswain should "remember whom thou hast aboard" (1.1.18), the second reply is even more devastating than the first:

> You are a counsellor; if you can command these elements to
> silence, and work the peace of the present, we will not hand a
> rope more. Use your authority; if you cannot, give thanks you
> have liv'd so long, and make yourself ready in your cabin for the
> mischance of the hour, if it so hap.—
>
> [1.1.19–26]

Gonzalo's inability to alter the situation, despite his "authority" so mockingly acknowledged, accentuates the divine power of Prospero. For Gonzalo, in terms of humanity, is much like Prospero: he too is aged, he too has lived and suffered, he too is benign. But he is simply a man, and his Polonius-like absurdity, as a "counsellor" with no solution to the problems of reality, emphasizes his powerlessness, which in its turn throws into dramatic relief the unchallengeable potency of Prospero.

The fury of the storm testifies to the universality of humankind's situation, a predicament fully realized only when the veil of illusion is pierced: "All lost! to prayers, to prayers! all lost!" (1.1.49); "Mercy on us! / We split, we split! Farewell, my wife and children! / Farewell, brother! We split, we split, we split!" (1.1.57–59). "All lost": that statement, when life is seen steadily and whole, represents the ultimate judgment that all men must utter. "To prayers": when the philosopher of existence, Friedrich Jacobi, lay on his death bed, his final exhortation was to pray, because, he explained, that is all we mortals can do.

And the transcendent haven so desperately sought by storm-tossed humanity is hungrily summoned up by Gonzalo in the speech that concludes the opening scene: "Now would I give a thousand furlongs of sea for an acre of barren ground, long heath, brown furze, any thing" (1.1.62–64). Then, miraculously, beyond all Gonzalo's hope, the play presents the island. No "acre of barren ground," it is instead an enchanted delight played upon by sweet music, and it parabolically suggests an unexpressed remainder to Ferdinand's statement that "This is no mortal business, nor no sound / That the earth owes" (1.2.406–7).

If Ferdinand finds that things here are other than mortal, his father finds them other than natural. "These are not natural events," asserts Alonso. The other than mortal confirms the island as theological heaven; the other than natural, as poetic golden world. For "Nature," as Sir Philip Sidney says, "never set forth the earth in so rich tapistry as diverse poets have done—neither with so pleasant rivers, fruitful trees, sweet-smelling flowers, nor whatsoever else may make the too much loved earth more lovely. Her world is brazen, the poets only deliver a golden."

The difference between the golden island world and the brazen world of Naples and Milan is one of Platonic opposites. The Machiavellians of the real world, who pride themselves upon seeing things as they are, reveal themselves, in lengthy self-humiliation, as seeing nothing of reality. On the other hand, Gonzalo, mocked as a foolish unrealist, is in the island haven the speaker of certain truth. "I not doubt / He came alive to land," says Gonzalo about Ferdinand (2.1.115–16). "No, no, he's gone," replies Alonso sadly, acknowledging the reality that prevails in the probabilities of our brazen experience (2.1.116). But here Gonzalo's optimism is miraculously justified. Miraculously right also are his mysterious words of comfort—words that in another reality would be foolish: "be merry; you have cause, / So have we all, of joy; for our escape / Is much beyond our loss. Our hint of woe / Is common" (2.1.1–4). And the rightness of his vision, juxtaposed against the blindness of his too-human companions, is emphasized at length. Alonso's dejected answer to Gonzalo's counsel of joy is a curt "Prithee, peace." And to Alonso's dejection Sebastian and Antonio append cynical mockery:

> SEBASTIAN. He receives comfort like cold porridge.
> ANTONIO. The visitor will not give him o'er so.
> SEBASTIAN. Look, he's winding up the watch of his wit;
> by and by it will strike.
> GONZALO. Sir—
> SEBASTIAN. One—Tell.
>
> [2.1.10–15]

But Sebastian and Antonio are so preoccupied in mocking the man they consider a sententious old fool, that they do not realize that Gonzalo (and Adrian, who is also mocked) are speaking simple truth. "Fie, what a spendthrift he is of his tongue!" sneers Antonio of Gonzalo (2.1.23). And when Adrian cautiously begins, "Though this island seem to be desert—" the two Machiavellian realists again interject mocking banter. But Adrian continues, is joined by Gonzalo, and their descriptions of what they see are strongly contrasted with the egotistically blind mockery of Antonio and Sebastian:

ADRIAN. It must needs be of subtle, tender, and
delicate temperance.
ANTONIO. Temperance was a delicate wench.
SEBASTIAN. Ay, and a subtle; as he most learnedly
deliver'd.
ADRIAN. The air breathes upon us here most sweetly.
SEBASTIAN. As if it had lungs, and rotten ones.
ANTONIO. Or, as 'twere perfum'd by a fen.
GONZALO. Here is everything advantageous to life.
ANTONIO. True; save means to live.
SEBASTIAN. Of that there's none, or little.
GONZALO. How lush and lusty the grass looks! how green!
ANTONIO. The ground indeed is tawny.

[2.1.41–51]

The counterpoint of blindness with sight, of merry fatuity with serious
understanding, continues as Gonzalo embarks upon his great Utopian
vision, which epitomizes the coincidence of social hope and the pastoral ideal:

GONZALO. Had I the plantation of this isle, my lord—
ANTONIO. He'd sow't with nettle-seed.
SEBASTIAN.   Or docks, or mallows. . . .
GONZALO. I' th' commonwealth I would by contraries
Execute all things. . . .
I would with such perfection govern, sir,
T' excel the golden age.
SEBASTIAN.   Save his Majesty!
ANTONIO. Long live Gonzalo!

[2.1.137–63]

The discrepancy between Gonzalo's paradisal vision, which is now the
actual sight of reality, and the unheeding cynicism of his fellows, which
is now the mark of stupidity, is made still greater by Alonso's comment
on the great Utopian projection:

Prithee, no more; thou dost talk nothing to me.
GONZALO. I do well believe your Highness; and did it to minister
occasion to these gentlemen, who are of such sensible and nimble lungs that they always use to laugh at nothing.

[2.1.164–68]

Gonzalo, indeed, realizes as soon as he sets foot upon the island that the miraculous is now the real: "but for the miracle, / I mean our preservation, few in millions / Can speak like us" (2.1.6–8). His acceptance of the miraculous event reveals him as an easy inhabitant of the realm of hope, while Alonso, dejected and "out of hope" (3.3.11)— "I will put off my hope" (3.3.7)—and Sebastian and Antonio, vainly pursuing their irrelevant Machiavellian plot, cannot accept, and have no happy part in, the new reality. When Prospero's spirits enter with solemn and strange music, bringing in a banquet, Alonso's initial refusal to eat the food is contrasted with the childlike acceptance revealed by Gonzalo's answer:

> Faith, sir, you need not fear. When we were boys,
> Who would believe that there were mountaineers,
> Dewlapp'd like bulls, whose throats had hanging at 'em
> Wallets of flesh?

[3.3.43–46]

Gonzalo accordingly is not numbered among the evil men identified by Ariel's harpy interruption of the feast:

> You are three men of sin, whom Destiny,
> That hath to instrument this lower world
> And what is in't, the never-surfeited sea
> Hath caus'd to belch up you; and on this island
> Where man doth not inhabit—you 'mongst men
> Being most unfit to live.

[3.3.53–58]

Noteworthy in Ariel's pronouncement is the convergence of religious and comic themes. The actions of the three are identified by the theological concept of "sin," and at the same time by the social concept of "'mongst men / Being most unfit to live."

Since the sinful despair of Alonso is reproved by the miraculous survival of his son, and since all the plots and evil plans of Sebastian, Antonio, Caliban, and even Stefano come to nought before the power of Prospero, despair and evil are thereby shown to have no place in the enchanted haven. But if the most negative potentialities of humankind can achieve no actuality against the nullifying power of Prospero, positive potentialities come to perfect fruition. Side by side with the theme of evil, the play develops the archetypal comic theme of the progression to marriage. As, in *The Winter's Tale*, Perdita and Florizel bring new life and harmony to replace the disruptions of their elders, so here does Ferdinand bring a new intent of love to replace the power-struggles of his father and uncle. It would be difficult to improve on the beautiful statement of D. G. James: "There are, and always will be, the Antonios and Sebastians, frivolous, without reverence, treating the prompting of their moral natures as irrational, delusory, or meaningless. . . . But of Ferdinand and Miranda we shall say, if I may risk allegorizing them, that they represent the hope by which we live and without which we could not bear the burden of our lives" (*The Dream of Prospero*, p. 171).

The process of courtship is controlled by Prospero. This variation of the comic movement toward marriage is justified in the play by, on the one hand, Prospero's benignity, omniscience, and omnipotence, which are maintained absolutely; and on the other, by the projection of Miranda as a paradisal figure untainted by human sin. In terms of our actual experience of life, she is as ideal as the island itself; and her innocence and purity serve to rebuke all the meannesses of humankind. "O, wonder!" exclaims Miranda, "How many goodly creatures are there here! / How beauteous mankind is! O brave new world / That has such people in't!" But Prospero's laconic answer, desert-dry, is: " 'Tis new to thee" (5.1.181–84). For the "goodly creatures" number among them the unholy trinity formed by the despairing and self-centered Alonso, the faithless and murderous Sebastian, and the treacherous and lying Antonio—the "three men of sin," the "worse than devils," the "unfit to live" among men. Miranda's salutation, uttered in openness of heart, shames all human actions that fall below mankind's heaven-orientated possibilities; and her unwitting criticism, spoken as it is in words of praise, bites almost as deeply as the most scathing denunciations of Timon or Lear.

To achieve so perfect a rebuke, however, the character of Miranda must be conceived as wholly unsullied by experience of humanity's baser nature. Hence her first view of man, that of Ferdinand, expresses the same wonder as does her attitude in the fifth act: "I might call him / A thing divine; for nothing natural / I ever saw so noble" (1.2.417–19). In view of the need to preserve this exalted idealism unmarred, so that Miranda remain "perfect and peerless . . . created / Of every creature's best" (3.1.47–48), Prospero's management of the courtship makes psychological sense. Indeed, not only does he note that "this swift business / I must uneasy make, lest too light winning / Make the prize light" (1.2.450–52), which gives both a dramatic and psychological basis for the extension of the courtship and the temporary harshness toward Ferdinand; but he is also much concerned that the act of love preserve its full dignity by being channeled untainted into marriage:

> If thou dost break her virgin-knot before
> All sanctimonious ceremonies may
> With full and holy rite be minist'red,
> No sweet aspersion shall the heavens let fall
> To make this contract grow; . . .
>
> [4.1.15–19]

The courtship, in this context, is not merely celebrated by the lovely masque of Ceres and Juno, but is actually part of that celebration itself. Ferdinand accepts his role as "patient log-man" (3.1.67), because he —and the audience—understands that

> some kinds of baseness
> Are nobly undergone, and most poor matters
> Point to rich ends.
>
> [3.1.2–4]

His patience, and the obedience of Miranda, are possible because of the security of their sense of love, and their faith in their future's happiness. To Prospero's warnings about the need for preserving Miranda's virginity, Ferdinand replies: "As I hope / For quiet days, fair issue, and long life, / With such love as 'tis now, the murkiest den, / The most opportune place . . . shall never melt / Mine honour into lust" (4.1.23–28). For, as he says, "I / Beyond all limit of what else i' th' world, / Do love, prize, honour you" (3.1.71–73). So Prospero can tell him that "All thy vexations / Were but trials of thy love" (4.1.5–6); and the omniscient father secretly pronounces an early benediction on the lovers' hopes:

> Fair encounter
> Of two most rare affections! Heavens rain grace
> On that which breeds between 'em!
>
> [3.1.74–76]

The postponement of the sexual union of Ferdinand and Miranda, in short, is represented not as a denial of happiness, but as a game and rite of joy: a deliberate savoring and treasuring of the meaning and prospect of happiness. The courtship, like the masque that crowns it, proceeds with the deliberate dignity that only freedom from anxiety, harassment, and trouble can afford. It thus becomes a testament to the goodness of the island, and a counterpoise to the seething plots of evil that are hatching in its shadows. Even in the happiness of *A Midsummer-Night's Dream*, the lovers are represented as opposed to the authority of fatherhood. But here only evil is furtive and disharmonious: no antagonism mars the relationship of Prospero and Miranda, no selfish greediness or degrading haste distorts the courtship of Ferdinand and Miranda. In the brazen world of tragic reality, a Desdemona must hurt her father in order to please her lover, an Ophelia must hurt her lover in order to please her father; and Freud has spoken of these psychic facts as deep and fundamental wounds in human nature. In the Platonic opposites of the enchanted other realm of Prospero's island, however, even these age-old festerings are healed.

The masque confirms the deliberate and ceremonial dignity of these "two most rare affections," and also perfumes the island with Arcadian evocations. The idea of contract is emphasized:

> Come, temperate nymphs, and help to celebrate
> A contract of true love; be not too late.
>
> [4.1.132–33]

In the world of tragedy, Gertrude's selfish actions violate the meaning of contract: she commits "such a deed / As from the body of contraction plucks / The very soul, and sweet religion makes / A rhapsody of words" (*Hamlet*, 3.4.45–48). But comedy's aspiration, assisted here by religious parabolism, stresses the contractual dignity and lastingness of human society as symbolized by marriage. And the nymphs, along with the ancient goddesses, Iris, Ceres, and Juno, turn the play toward the classical matrix of the pastoral vision. The language of their pastoral evocation recovers once more the honeysuckle diction, gone so long from Shakespeare's art, that graces *A Midsummer-Night's Dream*:

> IRIS. Ceres, most bounteous lady, thy rich leas
> Of wheat, rye, barley, vetches, oats, and pease;
> Thy turfy mountains, where live nibbling sheep,

And flat meads thatch'd with stover, them to keep . . .
                          the Queen o' th' sky,
Whose wat'ry arch and messenger am I,
Bids thee leave these; and with her sovereign grace,
Here on this grass-plot, in this very place,
To come and sport. . . .
CERES. Hail, many-coloured messenger, that ne'er
Dost disobey the wife of Jupiter;
Who, with thy saffron wings, upon my flow'rs
Diffusest honey drops, refreshing show'rs,
                          . . . why hath thy Queen
Summon'd me hither to this short-grass'd green?
IRIS. A contract of true love to celebrate. . . .

                                        [4.1.60–84]

The images tumble out in pastoral profusion. In a consummate movement of dancing measures, comedy's coming together in marriage and
pastoral's vision of an ideal environment merge with one another and
are expressly hailed:

JUNO.   Honour, riches, marriage-blessing,
        Long continuance, and increasing,
        Hourly joys be still upon you!
        Juno sings her blessings on you.
CERES. Earth's increase, foison plenty,
        Barns and garners never empty,
        Vines with clust'ring bunches growing,
        Plants with goodly burden bowing;
        Spring come to you at the farthest,
        In the very end of harvest!
        Scarcity and want shall shun you
        Ceres' blessing so is on you.

                                        [4.1.106–17]

The abundance poured forth from such a cornucopia of comic and
pastoral benignity elicits from Ferdinand, as it must from all audiences
everywhere, the judgment that "This is a most majestic vision, and /
Harmonious charmingly" (4.1.118–19).

   But the majestic moment cannot last. Prospero remembers "that
foul conspiracy / Of the beast Caliban and his confederates," and the

"vision" fades and disappears like the masque, leading directly to Prospero's greatest speech:

> FERDINAND. This is strange; your father's in some passion
> That works him strongly. . . .
> PROSPERO. You do look, my son, in a mov'd sort,
> As if you were dismay'd; be cheerful, sir.
> Our revels now are ended. These our actors,
> As I foretold you, were all spirits, and
> Are melted into air, into thin air;
> And, like the baseless fabric of this vision,
> The cloud-capp'd towers, the gorgeous palaces,
> The solemn temples, the great globe itself,
> Yea, all which it inherit, shall dissolve,
> And, like this insubstantial pageant faded,
> Leave not a rack behind. We are such stuff
> As dreams are made on; and our little life
> Is rounded with a sleep. Sir, I am vex'd;
> Bear with my weakness; my old brain is troubled;
> Be not disturb'd with my infirmity.

[4.1.143–60]

This *coincidentia oppositorum* of human grandeur and human insignificance compresses the deepest paradox of man's existence into a burning focus of poetry. Coleridge once said that Shakespeare could achieve by dropping a handkerchief what Schiller could only approximate by burning up a whole town; to this we might add that in the words, "We are such stuff / As dreams are made on; and our little life / Is rounded with a sleep," Shakespeare evokes the wonder, pathos, and mystery that Bossuet's orations and sermons require waves and organ tones of Baroque prose to communicate.

Prospero's great speech is full of opposed and blended meanings, which penetrate through the situation of the play into larger prospects beyond. Prospero, who seems dismayed, lightens his own dismay by a reflecting care for that of Ferdinand: "You do look, my son, in a mov'd sort, / As if you were dismay'd." And his next utterance, "be cheerful, sir," standing as a kind of absolute command and assurance, seems to counsel cheer not merely in the face of present dismay, but in the face of all experience of existence. It seems, indeed, to echo the mysterious words of Jesus: "be of good cheer; I have overcome the world" (John

16:33). The statement, "Our revels now are ended," speaks not only for the disappearance of the masque, but as has often been suggested, seems almost to be Shakespeare's own farewell to his career as a playwright, and even to his career on earth; and if the word "travails" be substituted for the word "revels"—a substitution that the evil portion of the play's action, as well as Prospero's past troubles, might seem to countenance—the meanings remain strangely unchanged: for in this play, and climactically in this passage, travails dissolve into revels, and revels into peace. The words, "this insubstantial pageant faded," fuse in marvelous economy three realms: that of the spirit-masque within the play, that of the actual life of the theatre in which the man Shakespeare moved, and that of all human life everywhere. The diction of the whole speech diminishes and at the same moment elevates human aspirations: "the baseless fabric of this vision" is a statement of literal nihilism, but the words are of soaring affirmation. Words that indicate insubstantiality undermine but at the same time caress, the illusion of substantiality: "spirits," "melted," "air," "thin air," "baseless fabric," "vision," "dissolve," "insubstantial," "faded," "dreams," "sleep"— these are the units that combine to form the dreamy, airy mixture of exaltation and regret that characterizes the passage. By modifying the substantial "towers" with the insubstantial but elevated "cloud-capp'd," the substantial is simultaneously made grander and dissipated.

And the concluding words, "Bear with my weakness; my old brain is troubled," strangely contradict the established fact of Prospero's superhuman power. But they also render him, in his human frailty and age, somehow even more dignified and worthy of reverence than before. He descends from the isolated throne of power and rejoins, in the final meaning of comedy, the struggling family of humankind.

By doing so, he partakes of the dignity and pathos of that other old man, King Lear; the words, even, are almost the same. Purged alike of arrogance and madness, Lear says, "You must bear with me. / Pray you now, forget and forgive; I am old and foolish" (*King Lear*, 4.7.84–85). Divested alike of power and isolation—the two conditions of divinity—Prospero, in saying "Bear with my weakness; my old brain is troubled," almost duplicates Lear's words and so for a pregnant moment abrogates the polar oppositions of comedy and tragedy.

Indeed, Shakespeare's crowning achievement in comedy, *The Tempest*, constantly recalls *King Lear*, his crowning achievement in tragedy. The relationships until now have seemed to be mostly those of contrast: the storm in *The Tempest* contrasts, as noted above, with the storm in *Lear*. Lear is pathetically powerless, while Prospero is omnipotent. Lear rejects Cordelia and scorns her marriage; Prospero's love for Miranda is never disturbed, and her marriage is not only approved but arranged by him. Lear stumbles about on a godless heath, while Prospero thrives on a lush island crowded with supernatural beings. But the similarities are what make the contrasts hold true: both plays have as their central figure an aged man; both plays emphasize the relationship of that aged man to a loved daughter; both plays explore the idea of human wrongs, especially familial wrongs perpetrated against reverend age.

Yet the figures of Lear and Prospero, coinciding in the moment of their recognition of age and weakness—of the need for mankind to bear with one another's infirmities—then begin to diverge. Drawn by the requirements of tragedy, Lear maintains his transcendent meanings in the face of death; and death it is that claims both Cordelia and Lear, as well as Goneril, Regan, Edmund, and Gloucester. The requirements of comedy, however, are different: Prospero does not die, although, having divested himself of divinity, his aged humanity is marked by the emphasis that "Every third thought shall be my grave" (5.1.311). Furthermore, *The Tempest's* new awareness is translated into a rebirth of social concord. Such concord is brought about by Prospero's forgiving the evil.

Throughout his comic work, Shakespeare has relied on the theological act of forgiveness to reclaim certain deviations too severe, or even criminal, to be laughingly dismissed as follies. Indeed, the theme is so pervasive that R. G. Hunter, in his *Shakespeare and the Comedy of Forgiveness*, has treated it as constituting a valid subgenre of Shakespeare's endeavor. As early as *The Two Gentlemen of Verona*, the near-criminal figure of Proteus is reclaimed by the device of forgiveness. And in both *The Merchant of Venice* and *Measure for Measure* the theological rationale of forgiveness and mercy is explicitly adduced. Portia utilizes the paradoxes of St. Paul:

> The quality of mercy is not strain'd;
> It droppeth as the gentle rain from heaven. . . .
> 'Tis mightiest in the mightiest; it becomes
> The throned monarch better than his crown. . . .
> But mercy is above this sceptred sway; . . .

It is an attribute to God himself;
And earthly power doth then show likest God's
When mercy seasons justice. Therefore, Jew,
Though justice be thy plea, consider this—
That in the course of justice none of us
Should see salvation; we do pray for mercy,
And that same prayer doth teach us all to render
The deeds of mercy.

> [*The Merchant of Venice*, 4.1.179-97]

And Isabella argues almost as does Anselm in his *Cur Deus homo*:

Why, all the souls that were were forfeit once;
And He that might the vantage best have took
Found out the remedy. How would you be
If He, which is the top of judgment, should
But judge you as you are? O, think on that;
And mercy then will breathe within your lips,
Like man new made.

> [*Measure for Measure*, 2.2.73-79]

Such reasoning underlies Prospero's action of forgiveness; no such theological rationale, however, is overtly invoked to justify it. Indeed, rather as Christ, the Son of God, is referred to constantly in the gospels as the Son of Man, Prospero finds his reasons not in the divine analogy he shadows forth but in his participation in mankind:

ARIEL. Your charm so strongly works 'em
That if you beheld them your affections
Would become tender.
PROSPERO. Dost thou think so, spirit?
ARIEL. Mine would, sir, were I human.
PROSPERO.   And mine shall.

It is perhaps the most exquisite of the many wonderful moments in the play. Prospero continues:

Hast thou, which art but air, a touch, a feeling
Of their afflictions, and shall not myself,
One of their kind, that relish all as sharply,
Passion as they, be kindlier mov'd than thou art?
Though with their high wrongs I am struck to th' quick,

> Yet with my nobler reason 'gainst my fury
> Do I take part; the rarer action is
> In virtue than in vengeance; they being penitent,
> The sole drift of my purpose doth extend
> Not a frown further. Go release them, Ariel;
> My charms I'll break, their senses I'll restore,
> And they shall be themselves.

$$[5.1.17-32]$$

In the all too human situations of Portia and Isabella, the rationale for forgiveness is argued upward: as man's attempt to imitate God's perfection. Prospero, conversely, already parabolically representative of the divine, argues downward, in terms of participation in humanity— of kindness arising from the sense of our kind—for that same mercy. And to confirm the argument, he follows the decision to forgive by, as it were, giving up his divine power and isolation:

> I have bedimm'd
> The noontide sun, call'd forth the mutinous winds,
> And 'twixt the green sea and the azur'd vault
> Set roaring war. To the dread rattling thunder
> Have I given fire, and rifted Jove's stout oak
> With his own bolt; the strong-bas'd promontory
> Have I made shake. . . . But this rough magic
> I here abjure; and, when I have requir'd
> Some heavenly music—when even now I do—
> To work mine end upon their senses that
> This airy charm is for, I'll break my staff,
> Bury it certain fathoms in the earth,
> And deeper than did ever plummet sound
> I'll drown my book.

$$[5.1.41-57]$$

Though the argument is different in its direction, the invocation of forgiveness fits the theological parabolism of *The Tempest* perfectly; indeed, mercy functions here more profoundly than it does in any other Shakespearean comedy. Its dramatic necessity is clear, for the "three men of sin," like the "demi-devil" Caliban, are "unfit" for human society. Prospero says to Antonio:

You, brother mine, that entertain'd ambition,
Expell'd remorse and nature. . . . I do forgive thee,
Unnatural though thou art.

[5.1.75–79]

This is the most difficult act of forgiveness for Prospero, because
Antonio, traitorous and murderous, is his own Claudius-like brother.
Hence Antonio remains silent throughout the final act, except for two
lines in response to the bedraggled entrance of Caliban and his confederates:

SEBASTIAN.   Ha, ha!
What things are these, my Lord Antonio?
Will money buy 'em?
ANTONIO.   Very like; one of them
Is a plain fish, and, no doubt, marketable.

But this brief and coarse exchange, so wonderfully in character for both
speakers, is an invitation to the rebuked brother to join the new society,
and also a sulky acceptance. To Sebastian Prospero says:

For you, most wicked sir, whom to call brother
Would even infect my mouth, I do forgive
Thy rankest fault—all of them. . . .

[5.1.130–32]

Less tainted than the others, Alonso complements the giving of grace
by the asking of pardon:

Thy dukedom I resign, and do entreat
Thou pardon me my wrongs.

[5.1.118–19]

The dramatic necessity for forgiveness is clear, and so too is the
positive affirmation of joy. Such an affirmation once before issued from
a forgiving Shakespearean ruler. To reclaim the despicable Bertram in
All's Well, his mother asks that he be forgiven:

'Tis past, my liege;
And I beseech your Majesty to make it
Natural rebellion, done i' th' blaze of youth;
When oil and fire, too strong for reason's force,

O'erbears it and burns on.

KING.   My honour'd lady,
I have forgiven and forgotten all;

[*All's Well*, 5.3.4–9]

And when Bertram himself then asks pardon, the King's answer conveys a sense of joy and restoration:

All is whole;
Not one word more of the consumed time.
Let's take the instant by the forward top;
For we are old. . . .

[*All's Well*, 5.3.37–40]

The same joyous hushing of a troubled past pervades the forgiveness tendered by Prospero:

ALONSO. But, O, how oddly will it sound that I
Must ask my child forgiveness!

PROSPERO.   There, sir, stop;
Let us not burden our remembrances with
A heaviness that's gone.

[5.1.197–200]

But the forgiveness of Prospero, though similar in tone to that of Bertram's king, is far more intricately connected with the whole meaning of its play than is the mercy offered in *All's Well*. For if forgiveness fits the dramatic requirements of the ultimate reconciliation in *The Tempest*, it also accords with the theological overtones of the play. Mercy, in Portia's words, is "an attribute to God himself." That Prospero, the anthropomorphic figure of the divine, should offer it, is simply to authenticate his role as defined from the beginning of the drama. And that role channels the conclusion of *The Tempest* to a unique coalescence of the aims of comic reconciliation on the one hand, and the mysteries of religion on the other. Indeed, on the rarefied comic level to which *The Tempest* attains, religion no longer stands above comedy, but is actually its other face. As O. B. Hardison contends, in *Christian Rite and Christian Drama in the Middle Ages*, the Christian Mass itself "is comic in structure," having "a joyful resolution," exhibiting, as does *The Tempest*, "a movement from *tristia* to *gaudium*" (p. 83).

The final scene of this exalted play is bathed, therefore, in the unmistakable and specific language of religion. "A most high miracle," says the formerly cynical Sebastian (5.1.177). "Holy Gonzalo, honourable man," says Prospero in his greeting to his old friend (5.1.62). "Look down, you gods," says Gonzalo, "And on this couple drop a blessed crown" (5.1.201–2). And Alonso blesses this blessing: "I say, Amen, Gonzalo!" (5.1.204). Then Alonso says, "Give me your hands. / Let grief and sorrow still embrace his heart / That doth not wish you joy!" (5.1.213–15). And Gonzalo in his turn speaks with sacred words: "Be it so. Amen!" (5.1.215).

So does this most holy of betrothals confirm the shared aims of comedy and religion. And so does the entirety of this most mysterious and elevated testament of Shakespeare's comic understanding, as it melts into the thin air of its conclusion, leave in our minds, as symbol of its unique gladness, the words of Gonzalo:

> Was Milan thrust from Milan, that his issue
> Should become Kings of Naples? O, rejoice
> Beyond a common joy, and set it down
> With gold on lasting pillars. . . .

> [5.1.205–8]

For, set down in the golden harmonies of Shakespeare's language, upon the lasting pillars of his dramaturgic representations, *The Tempest* rejoices in a majestic vision of the final oneness of all comic, pastoral, and religious meanings.

Appendix

A Babble of Green Fields:
Falstaff as Pastoral Outcast

It has been widely assumed, with only occasional voices of protest, that Shakespeare's purpose in the Prince Hal plays was to describe the growth of the ideal king. Thus Tillyard, for instance, says that "in the Prince Shakespeare at last completes the many attempts he had made to define the perfect ruler." * "The main theme . . . of Shakespeare's morality play," agrees Dover Wilson, "is the growing-up of a madcap prince into the ideal king, who was Henry V."**

This view, it seems to me, is quite mistaken. Not only is there no scintilla of evidence that Shakespeare had any such intention in mind, but such an interpretation is at variance with his general disgust for the exigencies of power as expressed in the *Henry VI* plays, in *Measure for Measure*, in his sonnets, in *Macbeth*, in *Hamlet*, in *King Lear*, in *Henry VIII*, and indeed pervasively in his moral vision. Even Tillyard concedes that to make Prince Hal an ideal of kingly virtue represents an "innovation" when compared to Shakespeare's other representations of historical kingship; but he attempts to justify this contradiction by a forced analysis that amounts almost to a claim of reading Shakespeare's mind.

I think we need not resort to such drastic measures. The plays themselves present the moral coordinates of Shakespeare's intent; and that intent, I shall argue, is to show that Hal, the ideal prince of Elizabethan popular imagination ("a maiestie was he," says Holinshed, "that both liued and died a paterne in princehood, a lode-starre in honour, and mirrour of magnificence"), was in fact, like a Kennedy of our own day,

---

* E. M. W. Tillyard, *Shakespeare's History Plays* (Harmondsworth, Middlesex, 1969), p. 296.
** J. Dover Wilson, *The Fortunes of Falstaff* (Cambridge and New York, 1945), p. 22.

tainted by the opportunism and unscrupulous Caesarism that go hand in hand with the pursuit of political power.

It is to this end, I shall further argue, that the character of Falstaff is developed to such an extraordinary degree; for in the rejection of Falstaff the future victor of Agincourt reveals the moral expense of his public appearance of virtue. The victor of Agincourt, in truth, was, underneath the appearances, actually the architect of the political, social, and moral ruin witnessed by the three *Henry VI* plays.

That Falstaff is the popular figure of the Vice and buffoon is apparent; to that extent he can be cast off with ease to accord with the triumphal popular progress of Hal from wayward youth to all-conquering king. That Falstaff also is depicted in subtle and various ways as more than a stock figure, as indeed a figure of pathos and humanity, makes it eventually no less clear that the King's mask of virtue conceals a wooden heart. The course of the plays, in one sense, is to anatomize Hal to see what cause in nature can lead a man to violate the sanctity of his own human commitments.

Falstaff's pathos and humanity are developed by language and situation that participate, flickeringly and obliquely, in the hope and humane reference of two important forms: the pastoral and the Platonic. Criticism's sense of his participation in the first of these is most strikingly apparent in the virtually unanimous acclaim accorded Theobald's emendation of the Folio phrase, "a Table of greene fields." When in *Henry the Fifth* the Hostess describes Falstaff's death, she says, in Theobald's emended version, that " 'a babbl'd of green fields" (*Henry V*, 2.3.17–18).

The statement so perfectly coincides with our sense of what Falstaff must be, that it has achieved a rare and enviable status—one kind of peak of an editor's ambition—in which nearly everyone agrees that even if Shakespeare did not write " 'a babbl'd of green fields," he should have written it.*

---

* Theobald's, of course, is not the only emendation possible. If one adopts the suggestion of S. F. Johnson and others that "talkt" is the likely original of the compositorial "table," and that a modernized spelling text should therefore read "and 'a talked of green fields" (*Shakespeare Quarterly* 10 [1959]: 450–51), the essential pastoralism of the moment is still preserved. It is not preserved, however, in readings that attempt to justify the Folio version as it stands, e.g., Ephim G. Fogel's interpretation by which the Folio phrase means that Falstaff's nose was "a veritable image or picture ('table') of green fields—green as grassy meadows" (*Shakespeare Quarterly* 9 [1958]: 485–92). No less farfetched is Leslie Hotson's conjecture that the Folio phrase means that Falstaff's nose was the image of Sir Richard Grenville's, who was often referred to as "Greenfield" (*TLS*, 6 April 1956, p. 212). On the

For Theobald's inspired emendation focuses the central meaning of Falstaff's character: that he is an outcast from a pastoral realm. In the Machiavellian world of Bolingbroke and Prince Hal he cuts a ludicrous figure: old, fat, irresponsible. But his true allegiance is to the land of "green fields" of which in his final moment he speaks, or more appropriately for a buffoon, and a battered buffoon at that, of which he babbles.

Like the Vice of the morality plays, a comic type that forms only one ingredient of Falstaff's gigantic comic being, Falstaff seems to draw his inexhaustibly antisocial energies from an order outside the reality in which he moves. He marches to a different drummer than the society around him. But it is not clear that he takes his meaning from the same region as does the Vice. The latter is the devil's emissary, a tame demon, while Falstaff, in the passage where his death is described, is specifically declared not to belong in the place ruled by the devil:

> BARDOLPH. Would I were with him, wheresome'er he is, either in heaven or in hell!
> HOSTESS. Nay, sure, he's not in hell: he's in Arthur's bosom, if ever man went to Arthur's bosom.
>
> [*Henry* V, 2.3.7–11]

The realm of Arthur is a version of pastoral, as can be seen, for instance, in Milton's early indecision about whether to treat Arthur, rather than the lost paradise, as the subject of his great epic. And the pastoral orientation of Falstaff is reinforced by the Hostess's curious report that she "saw him fumble with the sheets, and play with flowers . . ." (*Henry* V, 2.3.14–15).

If Falstaff, in departing this world, plays with flowers, babbles of green fields, and is declared to be in Arthur's bosom, other portions of the passage describing his death seem to indicate still other connections with the pastoral hope. For his manner of death, as Dover Wilson has pointed out (Editor's Note in *King Henry* V [Cambridge, 1947], p. 141), suggests that of the great moralist and idealist, Socrates.* Falstaff, remarkably, is reported as dying from the feet upward:

---

other hand, P. L. Heyworth's recent suggestion that the phrase refers to "the traditional English carol popularly known as the Bellman's Song," which contains the line "The fields were green as green could be," and that therefore "*Carold* as the original of F *Table* has much to be said for it" (*TLS*, 4 February 1972, p. 129), preserves and even emphasizes the pastoral reference.

* Earlier, John Robert Moore had suggested that "The fat knight who drank

> So 'a bade me lay more clothes on his feet; I put my hand into
> the bed and felt them, and they were as cold as any stone; then
> I felt to his knees, and so upward and upward, and all was as
> cold as any stone.

[*Henry V*, 2.3.23–26]

It is difficult not to find in this upward scale of dying a seemingly deliberate echo of the death that is, next to Christ's, the most renowned
in all our heritage:

> The man who had administered the poison laid his hands on
> Socrates and after a while examined his feet and legs, then
> pinched his foot hard and asked if he felt it. He said "No";
> then after that, his thighs; and passing upwards in this way he
> showed us that he was growing cold and rigid. And again he
> touched him and said that when it reached his heart, he would
> be gone. The chill had now reached the region about the groin,
> and, uncovering his face, which had been covered, he said—and
> these were his last words—"Crito, we owe a cock to Aesculapius.
> Pay it and do not neglect it." "That," said Crito, "shall be done;
> but see if you have anything else to say." To this question he
> made no reply, but after a little while he moved; the attendant
> uncovered him; his eyes were fixed.

[*Phaedo* 117E–118]

Now it is uncertain how much of Plato Shakespeare might have
read. At one time it was fashionable, largely because of the influence of
Farmer's *An Essay on the Learning of Shakespeare* (1767), to dismiss
out of hand the possibility that the English poet could have been
erudite. At present, however, because of the efforts of scholars such as
Heinrich Anders and T. W. Baldwin, not to speak of later work such
as that of Virgil Whitaker, it is generally recognized that his "small
Latine, and lesse *Greeke*" were by the standards that prevail in our
own day rather more formidable than Jonson's disparaging phrase
would suggest. Whether his Greek was good enough for him to have

---

sack died like the fat philosopher who drank hemlock" ("Shakespeare's *Henry V*,"
Explicator 1 [1943], item 61). Katherine Koller, on the other hand, rejects the
Platonic parody theory and suggests instead that Falstaff's death constitutes a
parody of holy dying in the *ars moriendi* tradition ("Falstaff and the Art of Dying,"
MLN 60 [1945], 383–86). In 1958 Roger Lloyd once again urged that Falstaff's
death echoes that of Socrates ("Socrates and Falstaff," *Time and Tide* 39 [1958],
219–20).

made significant use of the great edition of Plato published by Henri Estienne in 1578 is a question difficult to answer. Certainly, if he read any Greek at all, it is likely that he would have read at least the *Apology, Crito,* and *Phaedo,* for these are the works with which many students begin. No English version of the *Apology* was available at the time of the Prince Hal plays, so Shakespeare would have had to learn about Socrates' counterindictment of society either from reports in other books, or from his friends, or by reading Platonic dialogues or paraphrases in Greek, Latin, Italian, or French. John Aubrey, about 1680, says that Shakespeare "understood Latine pretty well," having once been a schoolmaster; in any case it is probable that his Latin was sufficient to have read translations of Plato, but there is no evidence that he did so (although Shorey contends that the first eighteen sonnets are based upon *The Symposium*).

Unless new information is discovered, therefore, it is impossible either to establish conclusively that Plato "influenced" Shakespeare, or to ascertain that Shakespeare's intent was to suggest a comparison between Falstaff and Socrates.* Nonetheless, it remains hermeneutically proper to make use of the "typological" similarity (I employ E. D. Hirsch's term) in determining our own response to Shakespeare's representations.

In such a context, the similarity of Falstaff and Socrates interlocks with a pervasive similarity that exists between the structure of pastoral

---

* The impossibility is not changed even by considering the fact of the enormous regard for Plato that obtained in the Renaissance. But such a fact is not without interest. In Sidney's influential *Defense of Poesy,* for instance, this kind of testimonial occurs: "But now indeed my burthen is great, that Plato his name is laid upon me, whom, I must confess, of all philosophers I have ever esteemed most worthy of reverence, and with good reason, since of all philosophers he is the most poetical." Indeed, reverence for Plato, and the sense that Plato conformed most closely to the interests of poetry, were not attitudes restricted to culivated noblemen like Sidney; for example, Shakespeare's fellow-dramatist, fellow-poet, and fellow-commoner, Chapman, in the preface to his translation of Homer, says that "as the contemplative life is most worthily and divinely preferred by Plato to the active . . . so much preferre I divine Poesie to all worldly wisedome." So despite the lack of conclusive evidence, it should not be assumed that Shakespeare was necessarily ignorant of or uninterested in Plato. The converse seems more likely; after all, to be a genius is not to be insensitive, unaware, and less intelligent than other intellectuals. As Coleridge urges, Shakespeare could have been "no automaton of genius; no passive vehicle of inspiration"—rather, he must have "studied patiently, meditated deeply, understood minutely." Again, H. M. Richmond insists on Shakespeare's "intellect" and argues that "subtle philosophical coherence" is the key to his dramatic genius: "Only the profoundest intellectual formulations could sustain such conscious dramatic versatility" (*Shakespeare's Political Plays* [New York, 1967], pp. vii–viii).

and that of Platonism. Indeed, as a recent commentator has argued at length, "Platonism" is the "informing philosophy of pastoral literature from its Greek origins to the Renaissance and after" (Richard Cody, *The Landscape of the Mind: Pastoralism and Platonic Theory in Tasso's* Aminta *and Shakespeare's Early Comedies* [Oxford, 1969], p. 18). Shakespeare's extensive pastoral preoccupation, according to this view of "the poetic identity of Platonism and pastoralism" (p. 13), could not have existed without a Platonic involvement, whether such involvement was conscious and historical, or merely typological; and the slight hints of pastoral in the role of Falstaff would accordingly both reinforce and be reinforced by any hints of Platonism in that role. (In a different but related context, Donald Friedman has argued that the "model of mental and spiritual activity Marvell must have studied under the tutelage of the Cambridge Platonists, and which had descended to them through the intertwined lineages of neoplatonism and Christianity, is the generative source of his poetry," and that this model "seems also to demand its expression within the pastoral mode" [*Marvell's Pastoral Art* (Berkeley, 1970), p. 32]).

In any event, it is remarkable that, in addition to the similarity of the death scenes of Falstaff and Socrates, the situation and character of Falstaff exhibit faint but notable echoes of the situation and character of Socrates, especially as presented in the *Apology* and the *Phaedo*. To consider the significance of these echoes is to arrive at a clearer understanding of the true role, and comic greatness, of Falstaff.

The similarities are numerous. Both figures, Falstaff and Socrates, bear hallmarks of physical grotesqueness. Falstaff is marked by his obesity; Socrates, by his Silenus features and his snub nose. Both figures are old: Falstaff, "blasted with antiquity" (*II Henry IV*, 1.2.173–74); Socrates, "more than seventy years of age" (*Apology* 17D). Both figures are arraigned as deviants from the established social order, and in each case the most important special charge is the corruption of youth: Falstaff is denounced as "that villainous abominable misleader of youth" (*I Henry IV*, 2.4.446–47), and Socrates—in Jowett's English—is identified as "this villainous misleader of youth" (*Apology* 23D: Σωκράτης τίς ἐστι μιαρώτατος καὶ διαφθείρει τοὺς νέους), as "a doer of evil" who "corrupts the youth" (*Apology* 24B: ἀδικεῖν τούς τε νέους διαφθείροντα). Both figures die as a result of censure by their social order.

In *II Henry IV*, moreover, the bringing into the foreground of the

Chief Justice parallels the dramatically antagonistic role of Meletus in the *Apology*. The disapproving Henry IV and the ultimately rejecting Prince Hal parallel the subsidiary grouping of the Socratic accusers, Anytus and Lycon. To this correspondence Shakespeare's language seems to call attention. The Chief Justice affirms that he is "well acquainted" with Falstaff's way of "wrenching the true cause the false way" (*II Henry IV*, 2.1.106–7), and these are words that echo the most general of the allegations concerning the social malfunction of Socrates, that he "made the worse appear the better cause" (*Apology* 18B: καὶ τὸν ἥττω λόγον κρείττω ποιῶν). "To make the worse appear the better cause": this special phraseology is emphasized in the *Apology* by a repetition at Stephanus 23D: καὶ τὸν ἥττω λόγον κρείττω ποιεῖν.

The most noticeable similarity—the one marked by Dover Wilson, whereby Falstaff's death mimics that of Socrates—suggests another possibility. The death of Falstaff serves no intrinsic function in *Henry V*. Falstaff has been unequivocally rejected by Hal at the close of *II Henry IV*; he need therefore no longer be regarded as an encumbrance to Hal's Machiavellian change in *Henry V* from roistering companion to stately focus of patriotic success and English national pride. Indeed, the structure of *Henry V* concedes as much, for Falstaff does not even appear in that play (and the pledge, in the Epilogue to II Henry IV, to "continue the story, with Sir John in it" surely did not bind Shakespeare's art). If we add to this rather curious fact the realization that it is rare for a comic figure, especially a central figure, to be represented as dying—inasmuch as the alleviation of death-anxiety is one of the chief aims of comedy as a genre—it may become apparent that an at least partly extrinsic explanation is necessary to account for the death scene in *Henry V*. Such an explanation seems to be that if Falstaff's death serves no function in the plot, it serves a function in the meaning of the character itself. Certainly the death does serve, whether intentionally or not, to anchor the parallelism between the comic knight and the Greek philosopher.

If Falstaff, the archetypal comic figure, seems by his death to move, to spill over, as it were, into the tragic realm, so, conversely, does Socrates, almost an archetype himself of the tragic attitude ("the true philosophers practice dying, and death is less terrible to them than to any other men"—*Phaedo* 67E), move near the comic in his "rather absurd" description of himself as a "gadfly" to the state (*Apology* 30E), in his continual reference to his own ignorance, and in Plato's repeated reminders of his grotesque appearance. More explicitly, Socrates is treated as a pure comic deviant by Aristophanes in *The Clouds* —as the *Apology* somewhat bitterly notes (19C).

Socrates, however, defines the limits of comedy's power. Like a comic figure, he deviates from the social norm; like a comic figure, he elicits laughter. But laughter does not reduce him to social compliance. Rather, drawing his power from a higher law than society's, he asserts his individuality with an insistence that belongs to tragedy. Society cannot deal with him by comic ridicule; society must kill him, and thereby concede his dignity as a critic and autonomous counterforce.

Socrates, in short, challenges the fundamental assumption of comedy: that society is the standard of good. Just such a challenge, though denied the dignity and the direct tragedy of Socrates, is presented by Falstaff. The fat knight is not only a deviant from society, and therefore ridiculous; he is also in strange ways a critic of society, and therefore ambiguously and flickeringly a tragic figure. His chief function is not to assert the rightness of a comic world, but to criticize the wrongs of a world of power and struggle.

For before all else, Falstaff is a character out of place. The three history plays that incorporate his comic being most profoundly are notably not comic environments. They are, instead, Machiavellian realms. Although Falstaff deviates from society (he defaults on his obligations as a soldier, he flaunts his unwillingness to assume the expected decorums of age, he treats idleness, drinking, gaming, irreverence, and confidence tricks as proper modes of behavior), society on its part deviates from itself. Society here, indeed, is illegitimate in its foundations, for its king is a usurper, with the blood of the rightful king upon his hands. It is a society devoted to plots, treacheries, and disruptive strife, rather than to the symbolic well-being of marriage. Indeed, the royal figures in *I Henry IV*, Prince Hal and King Henry, are represented in true Machiavellian fashion as unrelated to love, betrothal, or marriage. The Machiavellian, in fact, is precisely the man who wants to stand above and control society, not participate in and honor it. The only scene in the play that depicts a happy marriage, or even the affections of the sexes, is the scene between Hotspur and his wife; and that scene is one of parting.

The fission, then, between Falstaff the aged buffoon, deviating from the claims of constituted society, and Falstaff the disappointed idealist, outcast in a corrupt and alien world, generates his enormous comic power. Ever since Morgann's epoch-marking essay of 1777, the guiding principle in the interpretation of the character of Falstaff has been that of paradoxical dualism. As an amalgam of those two comic archetypes, the miles gloriosus and the Vice, Falstaff is that much larger than the former type alone, as exampled by Parolles, or than the Vice alone, as represented by Sir Toby Belch. But not only is Falstaff larger in his comic type than are other creations, he is also more complex; and his complexity exhibits the particular configuration of paradox. Falstaff, as Morgann perceived:

is a character made up by *Shakespeare* wholly of incongruities;—a man at once young and old, enterprizing and fat, a dupe and a wit, harmless and wicked, weak in principle and resolute by constitution, cowardly in appearance and brave in reality; a knave without malice, a lyar without deceit; and a knight, a gentleman, and a soldier, without either dignity, decency, or honour: This is a character, which, though it may be de-compounded, could not, I believe, have been formed, nor the ingredients of it duly mingled, upon any receipt whatever: It required the hand of *Shakespeare* himself to give to every particular part a relish of the whole, and of the whole to every particular part;—alike the same incongruous, identical *Falstaff*, whether to the grave Chief Justice he vainly talks of his youth . . . ; or cries to Mrs. *Doll*, "*I am old, I am old,*" though she is seated on his lap, and he is courting her for busses.*

Again, Bradley, consistently more sensitive on the subject of Falstaff than are modern critics, documents the rule of paradox by other examples:

He will make truth appear absurd by solemn statements, which he utters with perfect gravity and which he expects nobody to believe; and honour, by demonstrating that it cannot set a leg, and that neither the living nor the dead can possess it; and law, by evading all the attacks of its highest representative and almost forcing him to laugh at its own defeat; and patriotism, by filling his pockets with the bribes offered by competent soldiers who want to escape service, while he takes in their stead the halt and maimed and the gaol-birds; and duty, by showing how he labours in his vocation—of thieving; and courage, alike by mocking at his own capture of Colvile and gravely claiming to have killed Hotspur; and war, by offering the Prince his bottle of sack when he is asked for a sword; and religion, by amusing himself with remorse at odd times when he has nothing else to do; and the fear of death, by maintaining perfectly untouched, in the face of imminent peril and even while he *feels* the fear of death, the very same power of

* Maurice Morgann, "An Essay on the Dramatic Character of Sir John Falstaff," in *Eighteenth Century Essays on Shakespeare*, ed. D. Nichol Smith, 2d ed. (Oxford, 1963), pp. 266–67.

dissolving it in persiflage that he shows when he sits at ease in his inn. These are the wonderful achievements which he performs, not with the sourness of a cynic, but with the gaiety of a boy.*

In emphasizing "the gaiety of a boy" as the controlling tone of Falstaff's actions, Bradley points the way to a realization of Falstaff's true home, the pastoral world; for that realm, as has been continually stressed in these pages, constitutes a symbolic statement of and longing for the happiness of childhood. The connection is made even more clear by Franz Alexander's comment, in an article in *Psychoanalytic Quarterly* for 1933, that Falstaff "represents the deep infantile layers of the personality, the simple innocent wish to live and enjoy life." "The main reason why he makes us so happy," confirms Bradley, ". . . is that he himself is happy and entirely at his ease. 'Happy' is too weak a word; he is in bliss, and we share his glory" (p. 261).

As Morgann was the first to see, Falstaff cannot be understood as a "constitutional coward," and yet—and this fact we are enabled to express through our modern critical terms of paradox, tension, and ambiguity—he is at the same time almost by definition the character of the braggart warrior (even though Morgann argues that he is not intended for the character of a miles gloriosus [p. 238]). We insist on the paradox of cowardice and noncowardice even in preference to Bradley's good statement that "Falstaff is neither a liar nor a coward in the usual sense, like the typical cowardly boaster of comedy. He tells his lies either for their own humour, or on purpose to get himself into a difficulty. He rarely expects to be believed, perhaps never. He abandons a statement or contradicts it the moment it is made" (p. 264).

In this paradoxical tension of cowardice and noncowardice, Falstaff exhibits a stark contrast to the univocal Parolles, who is completely demolished by exposure:

> PAROLLES.   If my heart were great,
> 'Twould burst at this. Captain I'll be no more. . . .
>   Who knows himself a braggart,
> Let him fear this; for it will come to pass
> That every braggart shall be found an ass.
> Rust, sword; cool, blushes; and, Parolles, live
> Safest in shame.
>
> [*All's Well*, 4.3.307–15]

* A. C. Bradley, "The Rejection of Falstaff," *Oxford Lectures on Poetry* (London, 1926), p. 263.

But Falstaff, whose pretenses to valor are exposed with equal finality by the assault of the Prince and Poins at Gadshill, exhibits a peculiar—and characteristic—invulnerability to destruction by comic ridicule:

> PRINCE. Falstaff, you carried your guts away as nimbly, with as quick dexterity, and roar'd for mercy, and still run and roar'd, as ever I heard bull-calf. . . . What trick, what device, what starting-hole, canst thou now find out to hide thee from this open and apparent shame?
>
> FALSTAFF. By the Lord, I knew ye as well as he that made ye. Why, hear you, my masters. Was it for me to kill the heir-apparent? Should I turn upon the true prince? Why, thou knowest I am as valiant as Hercules; but beware instinct—the lion will not touch the true prince.
>
> [*I Henry IV*, 2.4.251–65]

In gravely claiming the title of "lion," Falstaff wickedly equates that unlikely status with that of "true prince" for Hal. As Morgann says, with reference to Falstaff's entrance to the inn, immediately following his flight at Gadshill:

Poins provokes him by a few simple words, containing a fine contrast of affected ease,— "*Welcome, Jack, where hast thou been?*" But when we hear him burst forth, "*A plague on all Cowards! Give me a cup of sack. Is there no 'virtue extant!'* "—We are at once in possession of the whole man, and are ready to hug him, guts, lyes, and all, as an inexhaustible fund of pleasantry and humour. *Cowardice,* I apprehend, is out of our thought; it does not, I think, mingle in our mirth (pp. 260–61).

In this insouciant insolence, this almost sublime imperturbability, Falstaff sets an ocean between himself and the completely confounded Parolles. As Morgann remarks,

There is in truth no such thing as totally demolishing *Falstaff*; he has so much of the invulnerable in his frame that no ridicule can destroy him; he is safe even in defeat, and seems to rise, like another *Antaeus*, with recruited vigour from every fall; in this, as in every other respect, unlike *Parolles* or *Bobadil*: They fall by the first shaft of ridicule, but *Falstaff* is a butt on which we may empty the whole quiver, whilst the substance of his character remains unimpaired. His ill habits, and the accidents of age and corpulence, are no part of his essential constitution; they come forward indeed on our eye, and solicit our notice, but they are second natures, not *first*; mere shadows, we pursue them in vain; *Falstaff* himself has a distinct and separate subsistence; he laughs at the chace . . . And hence it is that he is made to undergo not one detection only, but a series of detections; that he is not formed for one Play only, but was intended originally at least for two . . . (p. 279).

Thus the paradox: on the one hand "the most perfect Comic character," as Morgann says, "that perhaps ever was exhibited," a figure who declares that "the brain of . . . man is not able to invent anything that intends to laughter more than I invent or is invented on me" (*II Henry IV*, 1.2.7–10), a figure who is "not only witty in myself, but the cause that wit is in other men" (*II Henry IV*, 1.2.11–12); and on the other, this same figure revealing himself as proof against ridicule and impervious to the rebuking action of comic wit.

But in the paradox lies the key to an understanding of Falstaff's whole dramatic force. Morgann resolves the paradox by positing two natures for Falstaff, one apparent but false, and the other real although hidden:

. . . it may not perhaps be easy . . . to resolve how it comes about, that, whilst we look upon *Falstaff* as a character of the like nature with that of *Parolles* or *Bobadil*, we should preserve for him a great degree of respect and good-will, and yet feel the highest disdain and contempt of the others, tho' they are all involved in similar situations. The reader, I believe, would wonder extremely to find either *Parolles* or *Bobadil* possess himself in danger: What then can be the cause that we are not at all surprized at the gaiety and ease of *Falstaff* under the most trying circumstances; and that we never think of charging *Shakespeare* with departing, on this account, from the truth and coherence of character? Perhaps, after all, the *real* character of *Falstaff* may be different from his *apparent* one; and possibly this difference between reality and appearance, whilst it accounts for our liking and our censure, may be the true point of humour in the character, and the source of all our laughter and delight (pp. 210–11).

Morgann's oscillation between the intentionalistic and the affective modes of criticism encumbers but does not corrupt the brilliance of his understanding and the acuteness of his perception. His uncertainty in handling the phenomenon of paradox, however, is a more serious methodological defect and deprives him of the final understanding toward which his initial insight directs him. Specifically, modern critical theory enables us to see that rather than attempt to resolve the paradox of Falstaff, we may maintain it as a fundamental dramatic tension and merely attempt to elucidate it.

One need not, therefore, make a choice between Falstaff as cowardly and Falstaff as courageous ("*Courage*," says Morgann, "is a part of *Falstaff's Character*" and belongs to "his constitution" [p. 217]), but rather maintain the ambiguity of Falstaff as both coward ("I was now a coward on instinct" [*I Henry IV*, 2.4.266–67]) and courageous man: Falstaff flees from the battle at Shrewsbury, flees from the mock-assault of the Prince and Poins; in the face of another moment of danger, however, the sheriff's search for him on criminal charges, he calmly falls asleep. "Fast asleep behind the arras, and snorting like a horse" is Peto's description of his reaction at this moment of danger (*I Henry IV*, 2.4.510–11). And other examples of Falstaff's courage are pointed out by Morgann and Bradley. As Bradley says:

Shallow remembered him five-and-fifty years ago breaking Scogan's head at the court-gate. . . . Colvile, expressly described as a famous rebel, surrenders to him as soon as he hears his name. . . . What do these facts mean? Does Shakespeare put them all in with no purpose at all, or in defiance of his own intentions? It is not credible.

And when, in the second place, we look at Falstaff's actions, what do we find? He boldly confronted Colvile, he was quite ready to fight with him. . . . When he saw Henry and Hotspur fighting, Falstaff, instead of making off in a panic, stayed to take his chance if Hotspur should be the victor. He *led* his hundred and fifty ragamuffins where they were peppered, he did not *send* them. To draw upon Pistol and force him downstairs and wound him in the shoulder was no great feat, perhaps, but the stock coward would have shrunk from it (Bradley, pp. 266–67).

From a behavioral standpoint, therefore, Falstaff seems courageous on some evidence, but cowardly on other evidence. When he acts like a miles gloriosus, he becomes that figure and mobilizes its comic meaning, and then we see him from society's standpoint; but in another context his cowardice may be a simple refusal to submit to society's expectations.

Instead of a real and apparent Falstaff, accordingly, there is a single Falstaff seen from two perspectives. One is the Falstaff living irresponsibly in society, as a comic deviant and an object of ridicule; the other is the Falstaff out of place in that society, the citizen of another world, and therefore impervious to the criticism of the alien society in which he finds himself. "The bliss of freedom gained in humour is the essence of Falstaff," says Bradley,

> . . . he is the enemy of everything that would interfere with his ease, and therefore of anything serious, and especially of everything respectable and moral. . . . I say he is therefore their enemy; but I do him wrong; to say that he is their enemy implies that he regards them as serious and recognises their power, when in truth he refuses to recognise them at all. They are to him absurd . . . (p. 262).

The Socratic echoes in Falstaff's character therefore function dramatically to bulwark the sense that he represents another order. Falstaff is obviously the buffoon—an "extraordinary buffoon," in Morgann's phrase; he is also, though much less obviously, the gadfly to the state. His irresponsibility is, in one perspective, comic deviance; in the other perspective, the cynicism of the disappointed idealist. Censured by his social milieu, he vigorously answers back. "Well," says the Chief Justice, the moral voice of that milieu, "God send the Prince a better companion!" To which Falstaff retorts: "God send the companion a better prince!" (*II Henry IV*, 1.2.187–90). And in view of Hal's studied deception in matters of friendship, the second statement stings no less than the first. "You have misled the youthful Prince," accuses the Meletus-like Justice. "The young Prince hath misled me," retorts Falstaff with equal or greater truth (*II Henry IV*, 1.2.136–37). Falstaff is on the one hand a deviant who refuses to accept the binding social force of honor ("Honour is a mere scutcheon"—*I Henry IV*, 5.1.139); on the other, the frustrated idealist who, by implication, finds society itself giving mere lip service to honor. The social irresponsibility of his pocketing the money for a troop of soldiers and substituting a band of "pitiful rascals" is at the same time a countercriticism of society's irresponsibility in destroying human life in the cause of a murderous and usurping ruler:

> FALSTAFF. I have misused the King's press damnably. I have got, in exchange of a hundred and fifty soldiers, three hundred and odd pounds. . . . And such have I, to fill up the rooms of them as have bought out their services, that you would think that I had a hundred and fifty tattered Prodigals lately come from swine-keeping, from eating draff and husks. . . . No eye hath seen such scarecrows.
>
> [*I Henry IV*, 4.2.12–41]

But when the Prince, speaking for his father's society, reproachfully comments that "I never did see such pitiful rascals," Falstaff's reply is witheringly cynical:

> Tut, tut; good enough to toss; food for powder, food for powder; they'll fill a pit as well as better: tush, man, mortal men, mortal men.
>
> [*I Henry IV*, 4.2.62–65]

The cynicism, however, exists only in the perspective of constituted society and its stated goals; in the perspective of the ideal order it becomes a poignant and ironic assertion of the social futility and inhumanity of the war.

Again, when Falstaff proposes the socially deviant act of robbery, the Prince holds back: "Who?—I rob, I a thief? Not I, by my faith" (*I Henry IV*, 1.2.133). But Falstaff's answer, characteristically, is both comically ludicrous and idealistically scathing:

> There's neither honesty, manhood, nor good fellowship in thee, nor thou cam'st not of the blood royal, if thou darest not stand for ten shillings.
>
> [*I Henry IV*, 1.2.134–36]

In view of Hal's subsequent betrayal of Falstaff's friendship, it is indeed possible that there is neither "honesty, manhood, nor good fellowship" in the Prince, and there is substance in the mocking qualification that follows. As Bolingbroke stole the crown and thereby qualified himself for kingship, so his son, on his climb to such a dubious maturity, can show himself a fit successor by beginning with the theft of a mere ten shillings—for we must learn to walk before we run. The criticism is further emphasized by a second ironic linking of theft, kingship, and their relation to Prince Hal. "Shall the son of England," queries Falstaff, "prove a thief and take purses?" And then he muses: "a question to be ask'd" (*I Henry IV*, 2.4.401–2). To ask the question is to introduce, on a small scale, the question of Machiavel, in the prologue to *The Jew of Malta*: "What right had Caesar to the empery? / Might first made kings. . . ."

It is not, however, until the death scene in *Henry V* that Falstaff's absent environment is made present by the green fields of which he babbles. Playing with flowers, going to Arthur's bosom, Falstaff reveals himself as an outcast from his true home: the pastoral world of ideal social harmony. Until this moment the nature of that world has not been positively identified, though it has been implied. Falstaff's corpulence, which is his badge of deviance in the Machiavellian society of the present, implies a more graceful figure in a happier era ("When I was about thy years, Hal, I was not an eagle's talon in the waist. . . . A plague of sighing and grief! it blows a man up like a bladder" [*I Henry IV*, 2.4.320–24]). Likewise, his age, so blasted in the Machiavellian society of the present, implies a more youthful vitality in another environment. Shallow recalls that past: "Then was Jack Falstaff, now Sir John, a boy, and page to Thomas Mowbray, Duke of Norfolk. . . . I knew him a good backsword man" (*II Henry IV*, 3.2.23–25, 62–63). He continues to reminisce:

> O, Sir John, do you remember since we lay all night in the windmill in Saint George's field? . . . Ha, cousin Silence, that thou hadst seen that that this knight and I have seen! Ha, Sir John, said I well?
> FALSTAFF. We have heard the chimes at midnight, Master Shallow.
>
> [*II Henry IV*, 3.2.188–210]

Such memories, although they ostensibly recall youthful brawls and amorous adventures, still suggest alternatives to the shabby present and are replete with nostalgia for another time.

Moreover, amid the extravagances of Falstaff's language, haunting words, implying other times, other situations and other ideals, sometimes occur. For instance, he suddenly renders a judgment: "A bad world, I say. I would I were a weaver; I could sing psalms or anything" (*I Henry IV*, 2.4.125–26). A little ludicrous in its immediate context, the statement nonetheless raises a question as to the nature of society. Once the question is raised, the answer is apparent: war and perfidy and usurpation are the insignia of the world in which Falstaff moves, and the moral force in this society resides with the tragic nonconformist, Hotspur, not with the normative spokesman, King Henry. The moral legitimacy claimed by Henry's repeated promise to mount a crusade to the Holy Land is never verified, is in fact hypocritical. The promise is made at the very beginning of *I Henry IV*, in ringing tones of public virtue:

> Therefore, friends,
> As far as to the sepulchre of Christ—

Whose soldier now, under whose blessed cross
We are impressed and engag'd to fight—
Forthwith a power of English shall we levy,
Whose arms were moulded in their mothers' womb
To chase these pagans in those holy fields
Over whose acres walk'd those blessed feet
Which fourteen hundred years ago were nail'd
For our advantage on the bitter cross.
[*I Henry IV*, 1.1.18–27]

Both in cadence and stated intent the words are impressive. But they are merely words. For a prince, as Machiavelli counsels, should "seem to him that sees and heares him all pitty, all faith, all integrity, all humanity, all religion. . . . every man may come to see what thou seemest, few come to perceive and understand what thou art." Indeed, on his deathbed Henry himself concedes that the "purpose now / To lead out many to the Holy Land" was so that his "friends" might not look "Too near unto my state" (*II Henry IV*, 4.5.205–13). Even the external pomp of a foreign crusade is never realized; instead, harsh actuality diminishes that ideal to a series of internal power struggles that reach their climax in the appalling perfidy of Henry's lieutenant, Lancaster—"a transaction," in Morgann's opinion, ". . . so singularly perfidious, that I wish *Shakespeare*, for his own credit, had not suffered it to pass under his pen without marking it with the blackest strokes of Infamy" (p. 239). Lancaster's betrayal of his word to the rebels epitomizes the moral degeneracy of the whole society:

ARCHBISHOP. I take your princely word for these redresses.
LANCASTER. I give it you, and will maintain my word. . . .
[*II Henry IV*, 4.2.66–67]

But as soon as the Archbishop and his allies disband their army (Hastings assures Lancaster and Westmoreland that "our army is dispers'd"), King Henry's generals amaze even the conspirators by their cool treachery:

WESTMORELAND. Good tidings, my Lord Hastings; for the which
I do arrest thee, traitor, of high treason;
And you, Lord Archbishop, and you, Lord Mowbray,
Of capital treason I attach you both.
MOWBRAY. Is this proceeding just and honourable?

WESTMORELAND. Is your assembly so?
ARCHBISHOP. Will you thus break your faith?
LANCASTER.   I pawn'd thee none. . . .
                          [*II Henry IV*, 4.2.106–12]

Westmoreland's counterquestion, however, has some point. Nobody on either side is "just and honourable."

The significance of this degeneracy becomes more clear when the situation in *I Henry IV* is compared with that in *All's Well*. For it is not only in the figures of Falstaff and Parolles that the two plays are similar (the parallelism of the plays was pointed out as early as 1931, albeit unsatisfactorily, in W. W. Lawrence's *Shakepeare's Problem Comedies*). Both are pedagogic dramas, that is, both focus upon a young man's growing up to take his place as a leader of society—specifically, to take the place of a dead father. Both young men are for a time accompanied by a kind of miles gloriosus, who in each case seems to mislead the youth. Each young man, after a period of deviation from the standards of his elders, rejects the misleader and accepts the standards of his true father. But there the similarity ends. The world of *I Henry IV* is far more equivocal, from a moral standpoint, than that of *All's Well*, just as the character of Falstaff is more complex than that of Parolles. King Henry's tainted position as moral spokesman and representative of the social norm (he is opposed by Falstaff comically, Hotspur tragically, and the Archbishop of York theologically), is in striking contrast to the phalanx of morality and sobriety personified in *All's Well* by LaFeu, the Countess, and the King. Parolles there is unequivocally the deviant because of the unassailable nature of the social norms against which he rebels. But Falstaff's world, like Hamlet's, is out of joint. And in comic ambiguity, but also in unerring simplicity, Falstaff so identifies it: "A bad world, I say." In the context of a "bad world," Falstaff's age and obesity become not merely the marks of ludicrous deviation, but the scars of a life of disappointed faith in human fellowship—a disappointment brutally emphasized by Prince Hal's rejection, and hypostasized in Falstaff's ultimate tragic-and-comic utterance: "There lives not three good men unhang'd in England, and one of them is fat and grows old" (*I Henry IV*, 2.4.123–25).

It is noteworthy that when Falstaff reappears in *The Merry Wives of Windsor*, which is set in a comic environment analogous to that of

pastoral, he has lost none of his humor, and none of his laughable qualities, but his profundity is entirely absent. For that profundity depends
on his role as a kind of Socrates in an unjust society. In the society of
The Merry Wives, Falstaff is purely the comic deviant; he there has no
added dimension as the obliquely tragic emissary from the Socratic
world. The true home of Socrates is an ideal place that exists outside
the world of seeming reality:

> If someone could reach to the summit, or put on wings and fly
> aloft, when he put up his head he would see the world above,
> just as fishes see our world when they put up their heads out of
> the sea. And if his nature were able to bear the sight, he would
> recognize that that is the true heaven and the true light and the
> true earth. For this earth and its stones and all the regions in
> which we live are marred and corroded. . . . But the things above
> excel those of our world. . . .
>
> [*Phaedo*, 109E–110A]

No such representation of another reality would be compatible with
the comic necessities of Falstaff's character; the timeless other realm of
"green fields" is suggested only flickeringly, and mockingly, in utterances that seem to have a worldly or ludicrous import:

> FALSTAFF. You that are old consider not the capacities of us that
> are young. . . .
> CHIEF JUSTICE. Do you set down your name in the scroll of
> youth, that are written down old with all the characters of age?
> Have you not a moist eye, a dry hand, a yellow cheek, a white
> beard, a decreasing leg, an increasing belly? Is not your voice
> broken, your wind short, your chin double, your wit single, and
> every part about you blasted with antiquity? And will you yet
> call yourself young? Fie, fie, fie, Sir John!
> FALSTAFF. My lord, I was born about three of the clock in the
> afternoon, with a white head and something a round belly.
> For my voice—I have lost it with hallooing and singing of
> anthems.
>
> [*II Henry IV*, 1.2.162–79]

The answer seems at first to be wholly irrelevant to reality, to be merely
another expression of Falstaff's imperturbability in the face of criti-

cism. But it carries an amazing suggestiveness; behind the calm insolence an eternal order of things is glancingly implied, and there is even a sacramental commitment in the startling statement that he has lost his voice by the "singing of anthems." Furthermore, by insisting, despite his palpable age, on setting his name "in the scroll of youth," by calling himself "young," and by mysteriously remaining the same in adulthood as in infancy, Falstaff reveals himself as an inhabitant of the pastoral as well as of the comic realm, both of which seek to reconstitute childhood's happiness. In such a pastoral context, it seems only partly by chance that Falstaff sings fragments of an old Arthurian ballad: " 'When Arthur first in court' . . . 'And was a worthy king.' How now, Mistress Doll!" (*II Henry IV*, 2.4.33–35). All these indications point to what Bradley calls a "freedom of soul," which, though "in part illusory," was "attainable only by a mind which had received from Shakespeare's own the inexplicable touch of infinity which he bestowed on Hamlet and Macbeth and Cleopatra, but denied to Henry the Fifth" (p. 273).

And when Pistol brings the news of Henry the Fourth's death and Hal's accession to the crown ("And tidings do I bring, and lucky joys / And golden times, and happy news of price"—*II Henry IV*, 5.3.94–95), Falstaff's comment, though ludicrously avaricious and vengeful in terms of the comic relationships existing among him, Pistol, and the nether-society of taverns and prostitutes, is mysteriously sacramental from the perspective of the other realm: ". . . the laws of England are at my commandment. Blessed are they that have been my friends; and woe to my Lord Chief Justice!" (*II Henry IV*, 5.3.135–37). When he prepares to greet the new king, Falstaff's language wonderfully conveys the ambivalences of his role, for avarice is made to sound like true affection, and true affection is made to sound like avarice:

> FALSTAFF. I will leer upon him, as 'a comes by; and do but mark the countenance that he will give me. . . . O, if I had had time to have made new liveries, I would have bestowed the thousand pound I borrowed of you. But 'tis no matter; this poor doth show better; this doth infer the zeal I had to see him. . . . It shows my earnestness of affection—
> SHALLOW. It doth so.
> FALSTAFF. My devotion—
> SHALLOW. It doth, it doth, it doth.

FALSTAFF. As it were, to ride day and night; and not to deliberate, not to remember, not to have patience to shift me—
SHALLOW. It is best, certain.
FALSTAFF. But to stand stained with travel and sweating with desire to see him; thinking of nothing else, putting all affairs else in oblivion, as if there were nothing else to be done but to see him.

[*II Henry IV*, 5.5.6–27]

And then, like a stone hurled in the face, comes the brutal and unthinkable rejection:

FALSTAFF. God save thy Grace, King Hal; my royal Hal! . . . God save thee, my sweet boy! . . .
KING. I know thee not, old man. Fall to thy prayers.
How ill white hairs become a fool and jester!
I have long dreamt of such a kind of man,
So surfeit-swell'd, so old, and so profane;
But, being awak'd, I do despise my dream. . . .
Reply not to me with a fool-born jest;
Presume not that I am the thing I was,
For God doth know, so shall the world perceive,
That I have turn'd away my former self;
So will I those that keep me company.

[*II Henry IV*, 5.5.41–60]

Falstaff's answer calls upon all the resources of Shakespeare's dramatic understanding; neither protests, jollity, lengthy vaunts, nor even sadness issue from him. Stunned, he finds voice only for the trivia of daily existence: "Master Shallow, I owe you a thousand pound" (*II Henry IV*, 5.5.74). The statement, referring ostensibly to Falstaff's manipulation of Shallow for the loan, is heavy with suppressed emotion; for once before has the sum of a thousand pounds, and the moral conception of "owing," appeared in Falstaff's language, but then with a true focus of meaning:

PRINCE. Sirrah, do I owe you a thousand pound?
FALSTAFF. A thousand pound, Hal! A million. Thy love is worth a million: thou owest me thy love.

[*I Henry IV*, 3.3.135–38]

Once that love is betrayed, only the dead thought of "a thousand pound" remains. A moment later, shock is replaced by pathetic hope and inability to accept Hal's perfidy: "Do not you grieve at this; I shall be sent for in private to him. Look you, he must seem thus to the world" (*II Henry IV*, 5.5.77–80).

It is necessary to insist on the moral corruption of Hal's action, and to set aside those numerous and remarkably insensitive interpretations that see in the rejection a justifiable and even commendable turning from wild youth to responsible maturity. To cite an influential example from the preceding generation of scholars, Dover Wilson claims that "Shakespeare shows the rejection to be both right and necessary" (*The Fortunes of Falstaff*, p. 126). To cite another from among our contemporaries, A. R. Humphreys claims, in a notable variant of the "intentional fallacy," that Hal's course of action is made to "seem heartless in a way Shakespeare probably never intended"; for "the rejection speech is official rather than personal, a required public demonstration" (Introduction to the New Arden edition of *II Henry IV*, p. lix).

Required? By whom? To conform with what moral teaching? Now it may be that a youth should not consort with the likes of Falstaff; but if he does accept such a man, he also accepts the responsibilities of friendship. All human meaning depends upon such a fact. The whole agony of Hamlet testifies to the moral horror of precisely such breaches of human contract, express or implied. Kant, who thought longer and more deeply than most about such matters, concluded that the categorical imperative, the cornerstone of all morality whatever, could be formulated as the following command: "Act so that you treat humanity, whether in your own person or in that of another, always as an end and never merely as a means" (*Gesammelte Schriften*, Akademie Ausgabe, IV, 429). By turning away from Falstaff, Hal reveals that he has simply used his companion and now has no further use for him: that Falstaff has been treated "merely as a means."

Hal is despicable in his rejection of Falstaff. Furthermore, he is contemptible in his moralizing statement that "white hairs" ill become a fool and jester; for not only have Falstaff's hairs been white all through their friendship, but "white hairs," whether on a fool, jester, or king, ought to arouse sympathy, and the less becoming the behavior the more sympathy they should arouse. We feel that even a Wolsey is justified in objecting that another thankless English king should not have "given me over in my grey hairs." Indeed, there is, in Hal's rejection, something of the callousness of Goneril and Regan. And Falstaff, suddenly cast adrift in his old age, shares something of the tragic pathos of Lear, even to the fact of their both being remanded to prison.

To argue, as do some commentators, both here and in broader contexts, that the moralities of human interaction suggested by Shakespeare's presentations either should be seen as the result of stage conventions, or, conversely, are enslaved to perversely naïve popular conceptions supposedly dominant at the time, or, still again, can be explained as Shakespeare's inability satisfactorily to transmute his source materials, is, I contend, to reveal fundamental misunderstandings of the nature of his art and its relationship to life. It is subtly to patronize Elizabethan experience; to postulate, in reckless exaggeration, existential differences (as opposed to those of the surface) between our own humanity and that of Shakespeare's time, which, after all, was a mere five or six lifetimes ago. The attitudes crystallized most clearly in the work of Stoll, which have lain so heavily on Shakespeare studies, must be rejected once and for all—in his own books and whenever they appear in the work of his spiritual kindred and progeny. They discount Shakespeare's genius and reduce his humanity. The historical fact that "that traitorous heretic, Sir John Oldcastle" (to quote Cavendish) commenced a battle "against King Harry the Fifth" and then was executed does not control what Shakespeare chooses to do with his fictional Falstaff; Oldcastle's Lollard sympathies do not dictate Falstaff's sacramental phrases, nor does the historical falling out of Henry and Oldcastle dictate Falstaff's dismissal. Nor, in the *Famous Victories*, does Harry's promise to his father to "abandon and vtterly abolish" the "company for euer" of his "vilde and reprobate companions" predestine what Shakespeare actually must do with the relationship of Hal and Falstaff (in fact, in that play it is Ned and Tom, even more than Oldcastle, who receive the brunt of Henry the Fifth's rejection).

Instead of the source materials dictating the finished Shakespearean play, it is Shakespeare's imagination, both verbal and moral, that reshapes and gives significance to the source materials. The anecdotal episodes Shakespeare culls from the *Famous Victories*, recounted there with such uncritical factuality, are invested by his transforming art with the wonder of human meaning. In the earlier play, Harry naïvely tells Tom that "your former life greeues me, and makes me to abandon and abolish your company for euer," while he says to Ned that "Thou saiest I am changed; so I am, indeed." The change is there a fact as little accountable, and as little to be criticized, as the appearance of a genie from a bottle. In Shakespeare's art, however, the human meaning, the moral significance, of such a "change" is precisely the point called in question.

It is, indeed, a matter Shakespeare deals with elsewhere and often. Gertrude too "changes," immediately after her first husband's death, but her son, as we know, does not regard that change as a fact to be accepted with unreproachful equanimity. Cressida changes. Timon's friends change. Proteus changes. Cleopatra, expected to change, rises to tragic splendor by not changing. Our entire tradition, in short, celebrates constancy and loyalty; the "change" in the allegiance of a Judas or a Benedict Arnold is scorned in all times and places. Men should be able, as Coleridge says, "to contemplate the Past in the Present, and so to produce . . . that continuity in their self-consciousness, which Nature has made the law of their animal Life. . . . Men are ungrateful to others only when they have ceased to look back on their former selves with joy and tenderness. They exist in fragments." Least of all does our tradition countenance change in friendship, effected under the guise of more pressing obligations: "The unique and paramount friendship," writes Montaigne, "dissolves all other obligations."

The words of Montaigne show how unsatisfactory is any argument that new responsibilities, attendant upon a supposedly compelling Renaissance mystique of kingship, justify Hal's change. That many were affected by such a mystique is undeniable; that others found it less compelling is equally undeniable. After all, Charles I, the son of that James who promulgated the doctrine of the divine right of kings, was beheaded by his subjects. "And whats a Prince?" asks Chapman's Strozza—"A vertuous man is subiect to no Prince, / But to his soul and honour" (*The Gentleman Usher*, 5.4.56–60).

In any event, neither Shakespeare nor other writers were obliged to subscribe to commonplaces of the day; although they may have done so in some instances, no rule can be supplied for predicting those instances. The illogic of any argument to the contrary has been well set forth in Robert Ornstein's *The Moral Vision of Jacobean Tragedy*.

Actually, Elizabethan and Jacobean attitudes about kingship were ambivalent. One of Ford's characters says that "kings are earthly gods; . . . for their actions / They only are accountable to heaven"; yet in the same play we read: "Princes are but men / Distinguished in the fineness of their frailty" (*Perkin Warbeck*, 3.2.57–59, 4.5.63–64). In *The Maid's Tragedy*, Amintor, on the one hand, says:

> O, thou hast named a word that wipes away
> All thoughts revengeful! In that sacred name,
> "The king," there lies a terror. What frail man
> Dares lift his hand against it?

And he says again:

> . . . there is
> Divinity about you that strikes dead
> My rising passions; as you are my king,
> I fall before you, and present my sword
> To cut my own flesh, if it be your will.

But on the other hand Melantius, in the same play, says:

> Whilst he was good, I called him king,
> and served him . . .
> But since his hot pride drew him to
> disgrace me . . . I
> Have flung him off with my allegiance,
> And stand here, mine own justice, to revenge
> What I have suffered in him. . . .
> [2.1.308–11, 3.1.240–44, 5.2.38–49]

Even the mystique did not excuse a king from morality; Amintor, despite his awe before kingship, identifies his wrongdoer as "that devil-king" (4.1.261). If to Sir Thomas Elyot "the hearts of princes be in God's own hands," a prince was nonetheless obliged to rule "only for the weal of his people to him subject" (personal friendships need not encumber this obligation, and, as Falstaff says, an embarrassing friend could "be sent for in private"). And as there was Elyot to enunciate the official pieties of rulership, there was also Machiavelli to propound a more cynical view. We must not forget that Claudius, who speaks so eloquently of the "divinity" that "doth hedge a king," has not himself honored that conception. If "To be a king is half to be a god" (*I Tamburlaine*, 2.5.56), Richard II finds that to be a king is in no way to abrogate his condition as a human being. That, indeed, is the chief point of Shakespeare's play. Bacon, after urging morally that "it is a poor centre of a man's actions, *himself*," can, to be sure, add that "the referring of all to a man's self is more tolerable in a sovereign prince"; but it is also Bacon who commends "Machiavel" for writing "what men do and not what they ought to do."

Moreover, in the vision of a Golden Age that so entranced Renaissance minds, kingship is deprecated. "No sovereignty" is Gonzalo's ideal (*The Tempest*, 2.1.150). "Kings had never borne / Such boundless empire over other men," says Chapman in a related context, "Had all maintained the spirit and state of D'Ambois" (*Bussy D'Ambois*, 3.2.95–97).

In short, the attempt to exculpate Hal's change on the grounds of a mystique about kingship cannot be honored; his action finds its true rationale only in Machiavellian expediency.

What is despicable in human behavior for Kant was also despicable for Shakespeare, and should be no less despicable for us. It is all one tradition. Eleanor Prosser has recently found it necessary to write a long and carefully documented book to demonstrate what, except for the priestcraft of some scholars, should not have had to be demonstrated: that "the best way to approach *Hamlet* today is to forget all one has ever heard about Elizabethan codes and countercodes, about dramatic sources and theatrical conventions. . . . Our intuitions have always been valid" (*Hamlet and Revenge*, 2d ed. [Stanford, 1971], p. 256).

So also here. Hal's speech reveals him not only as callous, but shows him a liar as well. He says, in words of public virtue:

> For God doth know, so shall the world perceive
> That I have turn'd away my former self;

Reprehensible though such a statement is—even if true—it becomes still more reprehensible by its palpable dishonesty. For as early as the end of the second scene of the first act of *I Henry IV*, Hal soliloquizes, as befits a youthful Machiavel, in a way that shows he fully intends to use Falstaff simply as a means, and shows, furthermore, that his later action does not turn away his "former self," but merely confirms its abiding duplicity:

> I know you all, and will awhile uphold
> The unyok'd humor of your idleness;
> Yet herein will I imitate the sun,

Who doth permit the base contagious clouds
To smother up his beauty from the world,
That, when he please again to be himself,
Being wanted, he may be more wond'red at
By breaking through the foul and ugly mists
Of vapours that did seem to strangle him . . .
So, when this loose behaviour I throw off
And pay the debt I never promised . . .
My reformation, glitt'ring o'er my fault,
Shall show more goodly and attract more eyes. . . .
                    [*I Henry IV*, 1.2.188–207]

Such a steely intent shows that Hal deliberately betrays his friendship with Falstaff. "Hal's soliloquy," pleads Humphreys, broadening the intentional into the genetic fallacy, "is a morality-manifesto rather than heartless policy" (p. lix). Simply on its face, however, it is what Bacon calls "Simulation": "when a man industriously and expressly feigns and pretends to be that he is not"—which is "culpable." And it shows Hal to be the true son of his Machiavellian father. Indeed, in a subsequent interview, Henry the Fourth urges his son to a course of planned hypocrisy that is merely a variant of the one on which the precocious youth has already embarked:

KING. God pardon thee! Yet let me wonder, Harry,
At thy affections, which do hold a wing
Quite from the flight of all thy ancestors. . . .
Had I so lavish of my presence been, . . .
So stale and cheap to vulgar company,
Opinion, that did help me to the crown,
Had still kept loyal to possession
And left me in reputeless banishment. . . .
By being seldom seen, I could not stir
But, like a comet, I was wond'red at;
That men would tell their children "This is he";
Others would say, "Where, which is Bolingbroke?"
And then I stole all courtesy from heaven,
And dress'd myself in such humility
That I did pluck allegiance from men's hearts, . . .
The skipping King, he ambled up and down

With shallow jesters and rash bavin wits. . . .
And in that very line, Harry, standest thou; . . .

[*I Henry IV*, 3.2.29–85]

The passage constitutes one of Shakespeare's most explicit revelations of Machiavellian character. Of all Machiavels conceived by the playwright, "this vile politician, Bolingbroke," "this king of smiles" (*I Henry IV*, 1.3.241, 246), this man whose excuses even Holinshed terms "fraudulent," is matched only by Octavius for complete loyalty to the Machiavellian ethos; for Macbeth is harrowed by conscience, Claudius enslaved by love. Bolingbroke, however, untouched by either, surpasses even the monstrous Richard III in that he not only achieves but also maintains power.

To emphasize the Machiavellian, Shakespeare ignores the precedent of a conscience-stricken king afforded him by Samuel Daniel's *Civile Wars*, where the dying Bolingbroke realizes that his "climing care" has caused him to "passe those boundes, nature, and law ordained." The king there attempts to "make the charge of horror lesse," to "acquit that's past / . . . Of acted wrong, with giving up againe / The crowne to whom it seem'd to appertaine." Not so with Shakespeare's Bolingbroke. In the time-honored situation here of a father complaining of his son's behavior, there is, surprisingly but fittingly, not a word of moral reproach; rather the reproach is that the son will lose power by such behavior. Most fathers, both in fact and fiction, invoke, even where hypocritically, ideal standards of conduct. The Machiavel, however, is precisely the figure who believes in no standard except that of power. Here there is neither moralizing nor emotion, but simply the rational analysis of the course that leads to power. And in the honesty with himself that complements the Machiavel's hypocrisy with others, Henry calmly says he "stole" courtesy—not that he was courteous; that he "dress'd" himself in humility—not that he was humble; that he "pluck'd" allegiance—not that he deserved it.

But Bolingbroke need not have worried about his son. As Falstaff says in another context, "cold blood" is what Hal "did naturally inherit of his father" (*II Henry IV*, 4.3.112–13). Indeed, the point is made at length in the extended business of Hal's vigil beside his dying father's bed:

PRINCE. . . . I will sit and watch here by the King.
Why doth the crown lie there upon his pillow,

Being so troublesome a bedfellow? . . .
                    My gracious lord! my father!
This sleep is sound indeed; this is a sleep
That from this golden rigol hath divorc'd
So many English kings. Thy due from me
Is tears and heavy sorrows of the blood. . . .
My due from thee is this imperial crown. . . .
                              [*II Henry IV*, 4.5.20–41]

And then Hal puts on the crown, murmurs "Lo, where it sits," and leaves the room. The King immediately wakens and calls out; then asks for the Prince of Wales; then asks for the crown: "Where is the crown? Who took it from my pillow?" (4.5.58); and later, "But wherefore did he take away the crown?" (4.5.89). When Hal comes back with the protestation that "I never thought to hear you speak again," the King replies: "Thy wish was father, Harry, to that thought" (4.5.92–93). And although Hal then obtains his father's pardon, and father and son discourse at length on the entail of power within the family, the truth has been revealed: the son seeks the crown as avidly as did the father.

The question posed by the Prince Hal plays, therefore, as to what kind of man Hal will grow up to be, resolves into a simple answer: he will be a man just like his father. At the beginning there seem to be three alternatives. Hal can become a man of power, like his father; or he can become a man of individual if rebellious honor, like Hotspur; or he can become a deviant from society, like Falstaff. The three possibilities suggest the Machiavellian, the tragic, and the comic conceptions of reality; and Shakespeare explores the consequences of each conception. Hotspur, who "will ease my heart, / Albeit I make a hazard of my head" (*I Henry IV*, 1.3.127–28), pursues the ideals of loyalty, honor, and personal dignity, and, like Othello, who "was great of heart," dies rather than accept any diminution of his being. Falstaff finally finds no place in the world of King Henry, and so returns to Arthur's bosom. Prince Hal lives to rule over his father's world.

Indeed, the interrelation of Hal's choices is presented psychologically as well as philosophically. With deep instinctive understanding for the truth of human encounters, Shakespeare brings to life a pattern not clearly understood before Freud's careful elucidations of the dynamics of human personality. The father, King Henry, rejects his son, Harry, and awards his approval to another young man named Harry—Henry Hotspur. The point is made with merciless directness:

> KING. Yea, there thou mak'st me sad, and mak'st me sin
> In envy that my Lord Northumberland
> Should be the father to so blest a son—
> A son who is the theme of honour's tongue; . . .
>   O that it could be prov'd
> That some night-tripping fairy had exchang'd
> In cradle-clothes our children where they lay,
> And call'd mine Percy, his Plantagenet!
> Then would I have his Harry and he mine. . . .
>   [*I Henry IV*, 1.1.77–90]

Such a rejection hinders Prince Hal from identifying with his father. As Hotspur says,

> And that same sword-and-buckler Prince of Wales—
> But that I think his father loves him not
> And would be glad he met with some mischance—
> I would have him poison'd with a pot of ale.
>   [*I Henry IV*, 1.3.230–33]

Rejected by his father, Prince Hal finds a surrogate father, Falstaff. This truth is emphasized by the inspired scene in the Boar's-Head Tavern:

> PRINCE. Do thou stand for my father, and examine me upon the particulars of my life.
> FALSTAFF. Shall I? Content! This chair shall be my state, this dagger my sceptre, and this cushion my crown.
>   [*I Henry IV*, 2.4.365–68]

And then Falstaff, in the role of King Henry, begins:

> Harry, I do not only marvel where thou spendest thy time, but also how thou art accompanied. . . . And yet there is a virtuous man whom I have often noted in thy company, but I know not his name.
> PRINCE. What manner of man, and it like your Majesty?
> FALSTAFF. A goodly portly man, i' faith, and a corpulent; of a

cheerful look, a pleasing eye, and a most noble carriage. . . . And
now I remember me, his name is Falstaff. . . . there is virtue in
that Falstaff: him keep with, the rest banish.

[*I Henry IV*, 2.4.387–416]

With the ambivalence that continually underlies his words, Falstaff
on the one hand cuts a ludicrous figure in his representation of Hal's
father, and on the other speaks with resonating significances: "there is
virtue in that Falstaff: him keep with."

Equally pregnant with meaning (and scathing in the implications of
Falstaff's question, "Depose me?") is the psychodramatic turnabout
that follows; for Hal says:

> Dost thou speak like a king? Do thou stand for me, and I'll play
> my father.
> FALSTAFF. Depose me? . . .
> PRINCE. Well, here I am set.
> FALSTAFF. And here I stand. Judge, my masters.
> PRINCE. Now Harry, whence come you?
> FALSTAFF. My noble lord, from Eastcheap.

And, marvelously, it becomes apparent that Hal plays the role with a
much truer ear for King Henry's style than had Falstaff; and once in
that role he prefigures his future action in rejecting Falstaff:

> PRINCE. The complaints I hear of thee are grievous.
> FALSTAFF. 'Sblood, my lord, they are false. Nay, I'll tickle ye for
> a young prince, i' faith.
> PRINCE. Swearest thou, ungracious boy? Henceforth ne'er look
> on me. Thou art violently carried away from grace; there is a
> devil haunts thee in the likeness of an old fat man; a tun of man
> is thy companion. Why dost thou converse with that trunk of
> humours, that bolting-hutch of beastliness, that swoll'n parcel
> of dropsies, that huge bombard of sack, that stuff'd cloakbag of
> guts, that roasted Manningtree ox with the pudding in his belly,
> that reverend vice, that grey iniquity, that father ruffian, that
> vanity in years?

[*I Henry IV*, 2.4.418–41]

Yet, though Hal plays the parts of both King Henry and Prince Hal
with a better actor's ear than does Falstaff, it is Falstaff who speaks in

the reverberating tones through which Shakespeare expresses his concern for broader truths. "Whom means your Grace?" he asks after the Prince's diatribe:

> PRINCE. That villainous abominable misleader of youth, Falstaff, that old white-bearded Satan.
> FALSTAFF. My lord, the man I know. . . . That he is old—the more the pity—his white hairs do witness it; . . . If to be old and merry be a sin, then many an old host that I know is damn'd . . . but, for sweet Jack Falstaff, kind Jack Falstaff, true Jack Falstaff, valiant Jack Falstaff—and therefore more valiant, being, as he is, old Jack Falstaff—banish not him thy Harry's company.
>
> [*I Henry IV*, 2.4.445–62]

So Falstaff stands as surrogate father to Prince Hal, and by that fact is marked for sacrifice when Hal no longer needs him: that is, when the Prince is able to step into the King's shoes. Indeed, Hal signals the coming rejection of Falstaff by a canny substitution of the Chief Justice in the role of father-surrogate: "You shall be as a father to my youth" (*II Henry IV*, 5.2.118). By killing the other Harry—Harry Hotspur—Prince Hal symbolically regains his place in the King's Machiavellian succession, and the King himself at last dead, Hal, as King Henry V, carries out the action laughingly foreshadowed, under the guise of friendship, in the game at the Boar's-Head tavern. And the result is the death of Falstaff, who, invulnerable to the world's rebukes, is vulnerable only in the heart. "The King has kill'd his heart," says the Hostess simply (*Henry V*, 2.1.85–86). And Nym concurs:

> The King hath run bad humours on the knight; that's the even of it.
> PISTOL. Nym, thou hast spoke the right; His heart is fracted and corroborate.
>
> [*Henry V*, 2.1.118–21]

To that extent it can in truth be said that Hal achieves maturity and acts in a way that would gladden his father. But a cold-hearted maturity it is, and the arena of his power constitutes a questionable kingdom. Despite Shakespeare's evident love for the physical and spiritual entity of England (as expressed, say, in John of Gaunt's speech), the political state of England is here scarcely less corrupt than Coriolanus's Rome.

In its rancid *Realpolitik*, Bolingbroke's England illustrates Yeats's realization that "Shakespeare cared little for the State," and it justifies his further discernment that "the world was almost as empty" in Shakespeare's eyes "as it must be in the eyes of God."

To understand this fact is not to sentimentalize Falstaff (on the other hand, to say, as does Geoffrey Bullough, that "the turning-off of Falstaff shows that Shakespeare's—as well as Henry's—sense of values was firmly based" is incredibly to sentimentalize Hal, and to postulate a Shakespeare not only morally corrupt but silly as well). Although it may be objected that my argument has tended to make Falstaff the trilogy's hero and at the same time to deny its ostensible plot, and although it is true that emphasis on his pastoral-Platonic overtones, taken alone, leads in that direction, in actual fact such aspects of Falstaff's character are held in unresolved tension by unheroic vices; and these form an antithesis of pastoral benignity.

One can, of course, maintain with Robert Langbaum that "if Hotspur is the chivalric hero, Falstaff is the natural hero, the Hero of Existence. . . . He is a hero because of his hard core of character, his fierce loyalty to himself, because he is more alive than other people" (*The Poetry of Experience* [New York, 1963], p. 175). Yet Falstaff in certain ways flaunts immorality as unmistakably as does Henry the Fourth. He is thus a representative of viciousness as well as of joy, and by that ambivalence is prevented from occupying a true heroic center in the plays. As Morgann says, "To return then to the vices of *Falstaff*. —We have frequently referred to them under the name of ill habits; —but perhaps the reader is not fully aware how very vicious he indeed is;—he is a robber, a glutton, a cheat, a drunkard, and a lyar; lascivious, vain, insolent, profligate, and profane." And Dr. Johnson says that "Falstaff is a thief, and a glutton, a coward, and a boaster, always ready to cheat the weak, and prey upon the poor; to terrify the timorous and insult the defenceless." But Johnson cannot perceive the other dimension of Falstaff—nor, for that matter, can he understand the insights of Morgann's inspired criticism, for, when asked his opinion about Morgann's essay, he answered: "Why, Sir, we shall have the man come forth again; and as he has proved Falstaff to be no coward, he may prove Iago to be a very good character." And yet even Johnson must concede that Falstaff, "thus corrupt, thus despicable, makes himself necessary to the prince that despises him, by the most pleasing of all qualities, perpetual gaiety," and that "It must be observed" that

Falstaff "is stained with no enormous or sanguinary crimes, so that his licentiousness is not so offensive but that it may be borne for his mirth."

And if Johnson concedes Falstaff "perpetual gaiety," Dover Wilson, although enmeshed in what I regard as systematic misunderstandings of Falstaff, Hal, and Henry the Fourth, suddenly, in speaking of Falstaff's retreat to the rural company of Shallow and the bumpkins, testifies to the sense of Falstaff's pastoral dimension by the unexpected comment, "*Et in Arcadia ipse!*" (*The Fortunes of Falstaff*, p. 111). The phrase seems to be justified, no doubt beyond its author's intent, by a subliminal relationship. Falstaff, who, though temporally old, is psychologically a Gargantua-like child, finds in Gloucestershire the memory of an earlier time. This environment is activated by his child-like ethos to become the nostalgic "child-scape" that Heninger identifies as the object of all "pure pastoral" description.

At any rate, if Falstaff can be charged with no "enormous or sanguinary crimes," Bolingbroke and Hal can hardly claim as much. The crime of regicide (it is not repudiated by Hal) stains Bolingbroke's own hands, and the one constant in the realm he rules is betrayal. "God knows, my son," says Bolingbroke to Hal, "By what by-paths and indirect crook'd ways / I met this crown" (*II Henry IV*, 4.5.184–86). And "indirect crook'd ways" remain the norm of this society. Hotspur is betrayed from the first: by the King, by his allies, even by his own father. Neither Glendower nor Northumberland arrives to support him at the battle of Shrewsbury. Indeed, the Machiavellian Northumberland, excused as "grievous sick" before the battle (*I Henry IV*, 4.1.16), is after the battle reported by Rumour, the prolocutor for the second part of *Henry IV*, to lie "crafty-sick" (Induction, 37). Hotspur's widow makes the charge scathingly explicit:

> NORTHUMBERLAND. Alas, sweet wife, my honour is at pawn;
> And but my going nothing can redeem it.
> LADY PERCY. O yet, for God's sake, go not to these wars!
> The time was, father, that you broke your word,
> When you were more endear'd to it than now;
> When your own Percy, when my heart's dear Harry,
> Threw many a northward look to see his father
> Bring up his powers; but he did long in vain.
> Who then persuaded you to stay at home?

There were two honours lost, yours and your son's.
For yours, the God of heaven brighten it!
For his, it stuck upon him as the sun. . . .
          He was indeed the glass
Wherein the noble youth did dress themselves.

                  [*II Henry IV*, 2.3.7–22]

The action of Northumberland, as that of Lancaster and Westmoreland on the king's side (Lancaster swears by "the honour of my blood"), bears out Falstaff's cynical and ludicrously elaborated pronouncement that "Honour is a mere scutcheon," a view which, from the pastoral perspective, explains the fat knight's irresponsibility and flight at Shrewsbury as truly as, from the Machiavellian perspective, does cowardice. And Northumberland's answer to his daughter-in-law appeals, in another form, to the same rationale invoked by Hal in banishing Falstaff. "Fair daughter," says Northumberland, "you do draw my spirits from me / With new lamenting ancient oversights" (*II Henry IV*, 2.3.46–47). "Presume not that I am the thing I was," says Hal. Those worshiping power, Northumberland and Hal, attempt to justify their shifts and scramblings by forgetfulness of the moral commitments made in the past.

Thus the rejection of Falstaff, like the death it foreshadows, focuses the deepest truths about the cosmos of the prince Hal plays, about the character of Hal himself, and about the meaning of Falstaff's role. The banishment of the "reverend vice" confirms microcosmically what Bolingbroke's betrayal of King Richard ordained macrocosmically. The rejection reveals also that Falstaff has no true place in such a world. Old, fat, and foolish, he paradoxically belongs to a better order. As a pastoral outcast, battered by circumstance and ridicule, he alternately stumbles and rollicks through the world of power and strife. But underneath the buffoonery one aspect of his character remains true to the Socratic ideal. From the perspective of his veiled and glancing criticisms, the famous victories of Henry the Fifth seem less bright. And in a certain sense it is true, as Falstaff says, that "Banish plump Jack, and banish all the world" (*I Henry IV*, 2.4.462–63)—the world, that is, of flowers and green fields. For the golden world of pastoral hope is here, as in history, forfeited by the plots and struggles of the Machiavellian illusion.

Index

A

Agathon, 3
Alexander, Franz, 186
Allen, Don Cameron, 105, 154
Anders, Heinrich, 180
Anselm of Canterbury, 153, 171
Anytus, 183
Argenti, Agostino, 25
Aristophanes, 3, 12, 184
Aristotle, 16
Armstrong, Elizabeth, 104
Arnold, Benedict, 200
Arnold, Matthew, 33
Aubrey, John, 181
Augustine, St., 129, 143
Augustus Caesar, 44

B

Bacon, Sir Francis, 150, 201, 202, 203
Baldwin, T. W., 180
Barber, C. L., 78
Barclay, Alexander, 23, 24
Barish, Jonas, 67
Bartoli, Clementi, 23
Beaumont, Francis, 17, 126
Beccari, Ferrarese, 25
Benny, Jack, 6
Berger, Harry, 20
Bergson, Henri, 15, 18, 26, 56, 73
Bevington, David, 68
Bion, 33
Blake, William, 41, 45
Bloch, Ernst, 40, 43
Bollnow, Otto, 159
Bossuet, Jacques-Bénigne, 168
Bradbrook, Muriel, 69
Bradley, A. C., 185, 186, 189, 190, 196
Brook, Peter, 85
Bruno, Giordano, 69
Buber, Martin, 4
Bullough, Geoffrey, 209
Byron, George Gordon, Lord, 3, 5

C

Callimachus, 113
Calvin, John, 129, 159
Carlyle, Thomas, 5, 11, 39
Cassirer, Ernst, 88
Cavendish, George, 199

Cervantes, Miguel de, 12
Chalker, John, 44
Chambers, E. K., 29
Chaplin, Charlie, 16
Chapman, George, 181, 200, 202
Charles I, 200
Charlton, H. B., 78
Chaucer, Geoffrey, 12, 14
Childhood, 32, 45, 110, 125, 131–32, 136; an old infant play, 8, 56; in comedy and pastoral, 30; defined by play, 31; and Christianity, 37; child-like longing, 89; attacked in *The Winter's Tale*, 123–24; and Falstaff's character, 186, 195, 196, 210
Cody, Richard, 182
Coleridge, Samuel Taylor, 4, 40, 123, 142, 143, 168, 181
Comedy, 70, 78, 118, 144, 146, 166; opposite and complement of tragedy, 3, 141, 157, 169, 183; celebrates herd instinct, 4; refers to society for origin and meaning, 4, 10, 11, 12, 15, 18–19; and marriage, 5, 10, 13, 14, 15, 27, 79–80, 117–18, 144, 164, 166, 167; looks to perpetuity of group, 5; deals in types, 5; characterized by artificiality, 5–6, 10, 26, 50, 51, 74, 78, 141; more often achieved than tragedy, 7; plots playful, 7–8; employs symmetrically repetitive series, 8–9, 50, 52–56, 73, 117; tends toward happy repose, 10, 11, 146; posits deviation from norm, 11–13, 15, 75, 103, 112, 184; uses theme of affections of sexes, 13–15, 17, 26–27, 60; rejects romantic love, 14, 57–59, 112, 114–18; uses theme of abuse of money, 15, 73; cures only minor ills, 16; avoids death, 16–18, 99, 141, 170, 183; bitter in Shakespeare, 19–20, 101, 121, 127, 146; affinities with pastoral, 25–27, 30, 167; strives for euphoria of childhood, 30; affirms play element, 30–32; and paradise, 36–37, 150; as serious as tragedy, 47; uses linguistic parody, 73–76, 86–87; and religion, 174, 175
Community. *See* Society

Text set in Electra Linotype

Composition, printing by
Heritage Printers, Inc., Charlotte, North Carolina

Binding by
Kingsport Press, Kingsport, Tennessee

Sixty-pound Olde Style wove paper by
S. D. Warren Company, Boston, Massachusetts

Designed and published by
The University of North Carolina Press
Chapel Hill, North Carolina